JOSEPH H

Dr Joseph Hone is a writer and academic based at Newcastle University, where he researches and teaches the literature of the long eighteenth century. He was educated at Oxford and has held fellowships at Cambridge, Harvard, Yale, and the Institute of English Studies in London. His first book, *Literature and Party Politics at the Accession of Queen Anne* (2017) was shortlisted for the University English Book Prize.

ALSO BY JOSEPH HONE

Literature and Party Politics at the Accession of Queen Anne
Alexander Pope in the Making

JOSEPH HONE

The Paper Chase

The Printer, the Spymaster, and the
Hunt for the Rebel Pamphleteers

VINTAGE

1 3 5 7 9 10 8 6 4 2

Vintage is part of the Penguin Random House group of companies
whose addresses can be found at global.penguinrandomhouse.com

Copyright © Joseph Hone 2020

Joseph Hone has asserted his right to be identified as the
author of this Work in accordance with the Copyright,
Designs and Patents Act 1988

First published in Vintage in 2022

First published in hardback by Chatto & Windus in 2020

penguin.co.uk/vintage

A CIP catalogue record for this book is
available from the British Library

ISBN 9781529111408

Photographs of the Memorial reproduced
by permission of the author

Map of London © Bill Donohoe

Printed and bound in Great Britain by Clays Ltd, Elcograf S.p.A.

The authorised representative in the EEA is Penguin Random House
Ireland, Morrison Chambers, 32 Nassau Street, Dublin D02 YH68

Penguin Random House is committed to a sustainable future
for our business, our readers and our planet. This book is made
from Forest Stewardship Council® certified paper.

To my parents

Contents

LONDON in 1705

1 Devil Tavern
2 Nando's Coffeehouse
3 Mitre Tavern
4 Edwards's printing house
5 Fleet Prison

6 Mackworth's house
7 Stationers' Hall
8 Hicks Hall
9 Braddyll's printing house
10 Royal Exchange

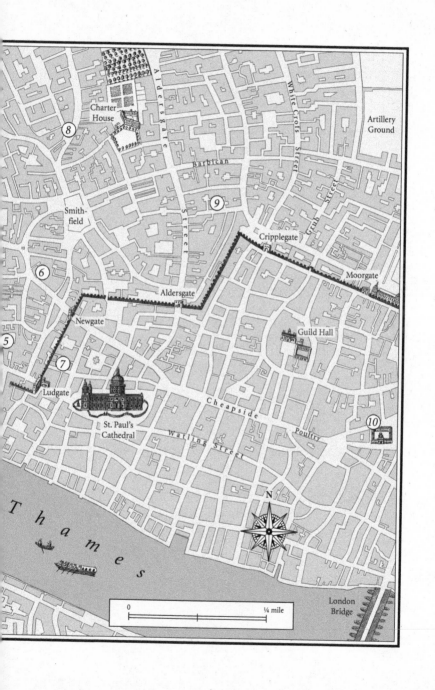

Charter
House

Aldersgate Street

White Crofs Street

Artillery
Ground

⑧

Barbican

Grub Street

Smith-
field

⑨

Cripplegate

Moorgate

⑥

Aldersgate

Newgate

Guild Hall

⑤

⑦

Ludgate

Cheapside

⑩

St. Paul's
Cathedral

Watling Street

Poultry

N

T h a m e s

0   ¼ mile

London
Bridge

Author's Note

The story told in this book occurred in an age before uniform standards of spelling, grammar, and typography had been established. While original orthography does help preserve some of the texture of the age, archaic spelling can also be disorienting for readers unaccustomed to the distinctive patterns of early modern writing. I have adopted a compromise. In the service of clarity, I have standardised quotations from primary sources. Most idiosyncrasies of spelling and some unusual formatting features are preserved, but I regularise the alphabet, some confusing punctuation, and most quirks of typography, such as the capitalisation of nouns and italicisation of names, which was routine in this period but can be distracting to the modern eye. Italics for emphasis or which have some effect on meaning have been preserved. Contracted and dashed words and names have silently been expanded, superscripted letters silently lowered, and ampersands routinely standardised to 'and'. The old method of denoting pounds by an 'l' has been replaced by the modern symbol '£'. Underlined text in handwritten letters has been italicised, as have the titles of books. In the spirit of authenticity, all reported speech is quoted verbatim from contemporary documents. Unless otherwise stated, all dates are given in the 'old-style' Julian calendar used in England until 1752, but with the new year beginning on 1 January and not 25 March.

Prologue
The Woman in the Vizard Mask

The summer of 1705 had been blisteringly hot. Farmland all across England's southern pastures was slowly succumbing to drought. At Greenwich, on the southern banks of the Thames, the ageing polymath John Evelyn noted in his diary that 'all the country was burnt up'. By the middle of June it had not rained in London for over a month. There was no wind. He could not remember having experienced such 'exceedingly dry and hot' weather for 'many years'. The city streets reeked from the drying ooze of human waste and sweat.

A woman walked down Fetter Lane, in the busy legal district of Holborn. Through the dust and crowds she cut a striking figure. Observers described her as a shapely woman, 'something taller' than average and 'pretty burley', with an oval-shaped face, fair hair, and piercing black eyes. Swathed in a black robe, she was not dressed for the weather; yet her clothes nonetheless marked her out as 'a very genteele woman'. Her stride was deliberate. She knew exactly where she was going, having walked this way before. Weaving through the throng of law students and merchants and booksellers who gathered on the street, she took a sharp left, abandoning the wide expanse of the main road for the 'close abodes' of Nevil's Alley.

It was like entering a different city. The dome of Christopher Wren's new cathedral at St Paul's loomed only half a mile to the east, still clad in scaffolding and ladders; but the woman could not have seen it. This warren of small alleys and courtyards had narrowly escaped the fire which had consumed much of the city some forty years earlier.

The buildings here were hundreds of years old, jutting out into the street in a ramshackle mishmash of gnarled wood and plaster. The shade was welcome. Before long, though, her eyes adjusted and the grime of the place became visible. The woman had learned from her previous visits not to let this bother her. She marched over to an innocuous-looking building, pulled a 'vizard mask' of black velvet out of her bag, covered her face, and knocked on the door.

A robust Welshman answered, his hands blackened with ink. His name was David Edwards, a skilled printer with more than twenty years' experience in the trade. On her previous two visits the woman had found only his wife, Mary, and promised to return another day. In turn, Mary had warned her husband to expect a suspicious-looking customer. Edwards dealt with plenty of shady types in his business and was a keen reader of people. Although the woman's face was covered, he was struck by her voice, the melody of which he claimed to recall a full year later. The woman's request was quite simple. She came with 'copy to be printed', producing when asked a hefty manuscript from her bag: not large sheets of paper, rather a thick wedge of small pages. Edwards glanced over the packet. Each page was folded down the middle, the left side densely packed with a neat italic script, and the right with occasional marginal jottings. With the exception of a few crossings out here and there, it was a tidy example of penmanship and would pose no difficulties. In large writing at the top of page one was a title: 'The Memorial of The Church of England Humbly offer'd to the Consideration of all True Lovers of our Church and Constitution'.

While Edwards sat reading the first five or six pages of the manuscript, his visitor explained that this essay had been approved by some powerful men and 'was for the advantage of the church'. Later, under very different circumstances, he claimed to have been shocked by what he read. Certainly the book would sell; but in the present climate it was simply too dangerous for him to print such a vicious polemic. Eyes were everywhere. Turning back to the woman, and noticing that she had not removed her mask, he 'scrupled the doing of it and told her he had had a great deal of trouble already'. He mentioned George Sawbridge, over at the sign of the three fleur-de-lis in Little Britain.

Why didn't she take it to him? he asked, shuffling the woman towards the door. Sawbridge was Edwards's go-to business partner when dealing with controversial texts. He would put his name on the covers of books that Edwards manufactured, keeping the printer out of the limelight.

'By no means', she replied, sidestepping the printer and taking a seat: 'he had been spoke of for it, but not approved.' If Edwards wanted to sell the book, he would have to do all the work himself. Eventually, 'after some persuasion' and 'many arguments', he agreed to take on the job. The woman assured him that 'there was no harm in it' and that this could even 'be the making of him'. She would not reveal the identity of the author or authors of the manuscript when he asked, but alluded cryptically to men in high places who would 'stand by' him if necessary. Edwards would never meet them or know their names, she explained, but nor would he be entirely without allies. The printer would not forget this promise.

Having agreed in principle to print the book, Edwards now moved on to the terms of the deal. To have maximum impact the pamphlet would need to be printed and ready for sale within the fortnight. This would be pushing Edwards and his young press team to the limit; but with some extra labour they could manage it. In exchange for the rights to print the book, the masked woman demanded two hundred and fifty copies of the finished product. Edwards was free to keep any and all profits from the remainder of the print run and from any further editions of the text. The terms being settled, the woman passed over one half of 'an indented paper as a token for the delivery'. This sheet had been cut in two along a jagged line. Edwards was only to hand over the books when a courier arrived bearing the corresponding half of the paper. Until then, the masked woman urged, Edwards was to keep this job secret. Nobody beyond his inner circle could know. With those words still ringing in Edwards's ears, she stood, turned, and disappeared into the street.

Within days of printing *The Memorial of the Church of England*, Edwards was on the run, chased by government agents acting on the orders of the most important spymaster in the land. His wife, Mary, had already been taken into custody. 'I wou'd have burnt the book before I had concern'd my self with it', the printer later explained in a letter to his pursuers, 'had I understood their drift.' And yet why should Edwards regret not condemning a manuscript to the flames? Why should he need to flee his home and leave his business in tatters? After all, was this not the burgeoning age of enlightenment and liberty? Of ruthless satirists such as Jonathan Swift and of great thinkers such as John Locke and Isaac Newton?

Received wisdom tells us that by the start of the eighteenth century English letters had been 'emancipated, and emancipated for ever, from the control of the government'. After the government licensing of books, newspapers, and pamphlets officially came to an end in 1695, the free press heralded in an era of open-mindedness, tolerance, and progress in the fields of politics, science, and philosophy. It was the birth of the modern age, we are told. The abolition of censorship has, in the words of the grandiose nineteenth-century historian and politician Thomas Babington Macaulay, 'done more for liberty and for civilisation than the Great Charter or the Bill of Rights'.

It is tempting to assume, like Macaulay, that social and political 'progress' followed a neat upward curve from darkness to enlightenment, helped by the emergence of a free press. Tempting but wrong. For modern ideals of free speech, pluralism, and toleration did not spring suddenly into being. Nor did traditional attitudes towards treason and sedition disappear overnight. By the time David Edwards was forced to abscond, England had been riven by more than a century of political and religious tribalism. Catholics and anabaptists, puritans and Presbyterians, royalists and radicals, deists and traditionalists all jostled for power and influence. In 1649 the nation had witnessed the execution of Charles I, an event which turned the world upside down. When his son and heir, Charles II, took the throne in 1660, he inherited a nation torn apart by the horrors of civil war.

The question facing Englishmen in the latter part of the seventeenth century was whether the principal threat to society now came from the Catholics, whose loyalties would always be split between their king and their pontiff, or from the Protestant dissenters, who refused to accept the orthodox teachings of the Church of England. This was an era in which church and state were intricately interwoven. Few believed that it was possible to dissent in matters of religion without also dissenting in matters of politics. In the popular imagination, Catholics would plot and scheme to overthrow their monarchs and enslave the nation to Rome. But equally the Protestant sects were believed to hold radical 'levelling' principles, overturning the hierarchical structures on which English society was founded, making all men as one.

These disparate factions converged into parties. All sides agreed that the kingless rule of Oliver Cromwell had been wicked and corrupt and that Catholicism was beyond the pale. Yet still the ideological conflicts of the civil wars raged on. Dissenters and broadminded conformists gathered under the Whig banner to fight what they viewed as renewed tyranny and absolutism. Never a homogeneous group, their cause was the promotion of liberty in all its forms, as the ancient birthright of Englishmen. On the other side of the debate stood the Tories – conformists and churchmen all – for whom the path to civil war and anarchy was paved with religious dissent. Monarchy remained sacred in Tory doctrine and the king was owed blind, passive obedience by his subjects. Fanned by the growth of mass printed media, the flames of partisan conflict rose higher. By the time Queen Anne acceded to the throne in 1702, it was an accepted fact that 'fire and water are less contrary than Whig and Tory'. These two conflicting visions split the nation in two. Scorn, hatred, fear: those were the emotions that dominated the world of Newton and Locke. Enlightenment England could be a very dark place indeed.

In this war of ideas, underground printers were the foot soldiers. Ever since the outbreak of civil war, printed pamphlets had been the principal vessel for public debate. Even after the end of official prepublication censorship in 1695, state authorities stayed keen to stifle the production of seditious books. Underground printers remained one step ahead of the censors only by using cloak-and-dagger techniques to keep their movements secret. Authors remained anonymous and printers, in an effort to protect their own identities, refused to put their names on books.

Reading became an elaborate game in this world of anonymous pamphlets, of rowdy coffeehouses and taverns, of secretive factions and plots. Using their wits, the most sagacious men and women could perceive the identity of an author from matters of style alone. But for ministers of state, discovering the person or persons responsible for any one particular book could require the use of spies and informants and the interception of letters. It could require bribery, intimidation, and extortion. For the men and women of the book trade, the stakes could hardly be higher. If caught printing seditious or treasonable libels, they faced imprisonment, fines, brutal physical punishment, even execution.

The case of *The Memorial of the Church of England* unravelled slowly and unsteadily. What initially appeared to be a single vicious screed transpired to belong to a much broader effort to undermine the government. The *Memorial* claimed to expose corruption, greed, and perversion in the corridors of power, a 'hectick fever' lurking in the bowels of church and state. It was written in such an astonishing manner that, within days of its release, the print run had been seized by the authorities and would soon thereafter be condemned to the flames. The public outcry over the pamphlet's content triggered a nationwide manhunt for the author. But the energies released by this book would prove still more difficult to contain.

The man charged with investigating the case was no mere constable or local functionary. Robert Harley was among the most subtle, artful, and talented politicians ever to have lived. For Harley, the anonymity of *The Memorial of the Church of England* was not so much a prudent legal measure as it was a challenge. Under his eye, a confusing and contradictory array of evidence would slowly come to be moulded into something approaching a coherent narrative of events and motives, of actions and reactions. Where was the printer? What of the author? Who were they working for and what was their purpose? Following the paper trails and interrogating the *Memorial* as he would the witness to a crime, Harley began to coax out the book's secrets. It would take all of his considerable skills to untangle this knot.

At each stage of the investigation, Harley took notes, rich in anecdotal detail and pathos. Our insight into the case and its characters owes everything to the survival of Harley's papers and the verbatim accounts they contain. Thanks to these documents, the story of the *Memorial* is not merely one of pen and paper and ink, of a manuscript scratched out by candlelight or of printed pages issued from the press on Nevil's Alley. It is a story of living, breathing people: of the printer David Edwards and his tenacious wife Mary, of the drunken satirists William Pittis and Ned Ward, of the slimy industrialist Sir Humphrey Mackworth, of the goggle-eyed crookback lawyer Henry Poley, of a mysterious tall gentleman wearing pale clothes and a stately, pale wig. It is the story of James Drake and Henry Sacheverell and Daniel Defoe, of young porters carrying letters across London, of government ministers fighting for their careers, of pitiless thugs raiding printshops and destroying equipment. As it was handed from person to person, the *Memorial* brought many into its orbit. Not all would make it out alive.

For years to come, the fates and fortunes of David and Mary Edwards would be interwoven with those of Harley in strange and unexpected ways. When the woman in the vizard mask knocked on their door on that hot summer afternoon, the printer and his wife found themselves thrust into the centre of a dangerous game. Before the end, this couple, chased from their home by government agents, would themselves become the chasers. They could not have predicted the events that would follow, nor where the swirling currents of political intrigue would carry them. Nonetheless, knowingly or not, they had been preparing for this game their entire lives.

The
Memorial
of the Church of England

Humbly offer'd to ye Consideration of all True Lo[vers]
of our Church and Constitution.

Those, yt look no deeper

yn ye Surface of things, are apt
to conclude without hesitation
yt ye Church of E——nd is in a
very flourishing condition. Its
Dignities and Preferments make
a very goodly shew and ye Patronage of ye Q——n seems to promise a continuance of pros=
perity. But for all this fine
Complexion and fair Weather,
there is a Hectick fever lurking
in ye very Bowels of it, wch if
not timely cured, will infect
all ye Humours, and at length
destroy ye very being of it.

The Nation has a long
time ——— tounded wth Secta———

Condition of
ye Church not
to be Judg'd by
ye external
Appearance

PART ONE

A Time of Scribble

CHAPTER ONE

Land Pirates

London. 2 July 1683. It was Monday morning and members of the Stationers' Company were gathering for their regular session at Stationers' Hall. The hall itself was a tall, imposing structure, all high windows and clean neoclassical lines set into a courtyard just off Paternoster Row, near St Paul's churchyard. Members of the Company now gathered in the courtroom, nestled into private gardens between the main building and the city walls. Rules demanded that the doors be bolted against intruders. It was important that the dealings of the court should remain a secret. The Company maintained a lucrative monopoly over the English book trade: it was impossible to become a printer or publisher without first becoming a 'freeman' of the Company by serving a seven-year apprenticeship with one of its members. For more than a century the Company had restricted the 'art or mistery of impressing or printing any book' to its own number, thereby protecting the book trade from unruly outsiders. Any member caught leaking the 'lawful secrets, conferences or consultations' negotiated in the court session could be fined or dismissed.

Outside the courtroom, in a small adjoining antechamber, four boys lined up with their soon-to-be masters. The book trade was a great social leveller. These boys were the sons of butchers and gentlemen, clothworkers and yeomen. But henceforth, if they worked hard, their careers would be in the printing business. One by one, at the end of a lengthy court session that ranged over personal grievances, stock payments, and the election of new Company officials, each of the boys stepped forward, paid his fee to the wardens, and swore obedience to his new master, who in turn promised to care for the boy for the duration of his apprenticeship and educate him in the art of printing. Young David Edwards was the last to approach the court and give his vow. The Company secretary recorded his payment and the duration of his apprenticeship in the ledger. And with that, at the wardens' signal, Edwards and his new master Thomas Braddyll stepped out of the courtroom into the summer dust.

The other boys had not come far: one had travelled from the Cotswolds, another from Sussex, and the third was local to Kingston-upon-Thames, just a morning's ride from the city. Edwards, on the other hand, was a long way from home. Some two weeks earlier he had set out from his family household in the sleepy hamlet of Bodfari, tucked into the north-eastern corner of Wales, a few miles outside Denbigh. Visiting Bodfari in the seventeenth century, one would find a cluster of four or five houses around the tower of St Stephen's church. The altar and font had been replaced before the outbreak of civil war, in 1635, although the imposing bell tower – 'rather too stately for the church', according to Dr Johnson – was much older. The second-largest structure in the village, now a pub, was built up against the churchyard. Across the road, 'surrounded by masonry, with steps to go down into it', was the holy well of Ffynnon Ddeier, where the villagers worshipped on Ascension Day. Ancient Celtic traditions remained alive and well in this corner of rural Wales. Here, as an infant, Edwards would have been 'dipt up to his neck at three of the corners of the well' while a live cockerel was offered to the saints to prevent him crying in the night. In his notes on the parish, the antiquarian Edward Lhuyd recorded the continuance as late as 1699 of this bizarre local rite.

About Edwards's early life in Wales little is known. Although the baptism of his father, Thomas Edwards, is recorded in 1640 in the parish register, the next thirty years of records are missing. Given that seventeen was the usual age at which boys started their apprenticeships, Edwards was very likely born in 1666. Thomas Edwards was a minor local yeoman, so he probably could not have afforded to send David to a good school across the border in Cheshire. Whatever education he received was probably pieced together from visiting tutors and possibly from a period of more formal schooling in Denbigh.

He was a bookish child. Despite its remote location, Bodfari had ample connections to London printing. Five miles to the west lived Robert Salusbury of Galltfaenan Hall, a local gentleman whose two sons, Thomas and John, were now finishing their apprenticeships with members of the Stationers' Company: Thomas with Nevill Simons and John with Thomas Cockerill. John regularly sent books back to his father, who shared them with his neighbours and cousins at Lleweni Hall, a mere half-hour stroll from Bodfari. Edwards may well have heard tales of these local boys made good. By his seventeenth birthday he had decided to pursue a career in the book trade. And that meant moving to London.

By the time Edwards arrived in London there were around two hundred bookshops scattered across the city. These ranged in respectability from the neatly kept shops lining St Paul's churchyard, where one could find Samuel Pepys flicking through recently published plays and poems by John Dryden or Aphra Behn, to rickety stalls and warehouses where topical pamphlets were stacked in 'columns of scandal [that] reach'd the ceiling'. Up Cornhill the suppliers of newspapers rubbed shoulders with foreign merchants at the Royal Exchange. Jonathan Swift grimly imagined future readers searching everywhere for his works, only to find them among the vast selection of second-hand and remaindered titles sold on Duck Lane, in the district of Little Britain.

North of the city walls, beneath the trees of Moorfields and all along the railings of Bethlem hospital, were 'stalls of second-hand booksellers, where antiquaries rummaged for black-letter tracts' and 'slips of ballads fluttered in the breeze'. Among the men and women hunting for bargains one might spot the poet-physician Samuel Garth or the scientist Robert Hooke, who, a decade later, was appalled to discover nearly a hundred of his old friend Robert Boyle's 'chymicall bookes' lying exposed 'on the railes'. Hawkers touted their wares on the street and sold the latest pamphlets and newspapers to interested passers-by. Even the illiterate became acquainted with printed matter, when lighting pipes, lining pie dishes, or using the privy.

Despite this general familiarity with print, few beyond the capital had any idea about how books were made. Edwards himself had no knowledge of the intricacies of printing before he moved to London.

After one ingenious printer called Peter de Peene invented a miniature press, 'no bigger than a common hour glass', he was encouraged by friends 'to put this press into a box, with some ink and letters, and go about the countries to shew the art of printing to the country people'. For most Londoners, too, the internal workings of a printing house remained something of a mystery. When Edwards first arrived at Braddyll's workshop in Bull's Head Court off Jewin Street, just a stone's throw from the notorious epicentre of Grub Street, he discovered a nondescript building with one curious detail: the windows were filled not with glass, but with translucent waxed paper. They let in light but stopped pedestrians from snooping. This was to be his new home, where he would work, sleep, eat, drink, and study under the watchful eye of his master for the next seven years.

The first impression on entering Braddyll's house would have been one of purposeful activity. Up against the windows on the ground floor were vast slanted cases of type separated into different sizes: capitals in the upper case, and standard roman and italic in the lower case. Compositors stood upright at the cases, silently plucking out individual letters and arranging them into words and lines on their composing sticks. Once full, the sticks were carefully emptied into a wooden frame called a galley and, once the galley was filled with an entire page of text, secured with string. Having completed enough galleys to cover one side of a sheet, the compositor would fix them together and pass the resulting 'forme' on to the pressmen.

It was skilful work, demanding nimble fingertips, good eyesight, a deft sense of touch, and an obsession for detail. Letters needed to be the correct way up. Lines had to be consistent. Justifying text was an especially tricky job whereby the compositor would iron out tiny inconsistencies with slivers of blank type. Moreover, as Braddyll's fellow printer Joseph Moxon observed in his detailed account of London book production in 1683, it was essential that compositors 'should know where the author has been deficient' so they could 'discern and amend' errors in the copy. The appearance of the page and accuracy of the text relied to a great extent on the skill and judgement of the compositor.

By the shaded northern wall of the next room, so that the pressmen 'when at their hard labour in summer time, may be the less incommoded with the heat of the sun', was the press itself. This hulking mass of wood and iron was the domain of two men whose work was as fast and physical as the compositors' was careful and precise. The room smelt of ink and damp paper. Through the doorway Edwards could see one man using a pair of leather balls to beat an even layer of ink across a completed forme – neither too thin nor too thick – while his colleague laid a sheet out into a frame and folded it down over the inked forme. This was then rolled into the press by the second workman, who pulled the lever to bring down the 'platen', rolled the frame out again, removed the paper, and put it to one side. Meanwhile, the first pressman set about re-inking the forme for the next impression. Each stage had to be executed with precision. Only by 'a pull of the same strength upon the same forme, with the same beating', explained Moxon, could the printer be sure of producing a consistent impression.

When Edwards arrived it was high summer. Still there was a fire burning in the corner of the room. It was absolutely crucial that the printing house should remain free of damp. Freshly printed sheets of paper were strung up in rows along the ceiling. These could not be folded or collated until they had dried out. After being scrubbed of ink, blocks of type would be laid out to dry before the flames. As the nights grew colder, it was not uncommon for the violence of winter to freeze paper and type solid. If there was any moisture in the wood of the press, it could swell and distort the timber, causing the whole machine to seize up. And the cold affected the workmen as well as their tools. Waxed-paper windows did little to protect against the weather. Some years earlier, a scholarly author called Peter Heylyn complained that his book had been a victim of 'extreme cold weather' which had 'benummed the fingers of the compositors, and dulled the eyes of the correctors'.

Cold weather was not the only thing that dulled their eyes. In the back room of the printing house were several kegs of beer, which was much safer drinking than the filthy city water. Drunkenness was all too common in the printing house, prompting some authors to object, as did Isaac Newton in 1709, that their printers were 'mere sot[s]'. When Benjamin Franklin came over from Philadelphia to serve as a pressman and compositor, first with Samuel Palmer and then for John Watts at Wild Court, he observed that all the other printers 'were great guzzlers of beer' whereas he drank only water. 'My companion', Franklin reported disapprovingly, 'drank every day a pint before breakfast, a pint at breakfast with his bread and cheese, a pint between breakfast and dinner, a pint in the afternoon about six o'clock, and another when he had done his day's work.' Each worker was required to pay a weekly drinks levy, known as the *bienvenu*. An alehouse boy would deliver the beer to Braddyll's workshop at the weekend. Despite his refusal to share in the drinking, Franklin was still forced by his colleagues to cough up. The customs of the house were not optional.

Some of these practices may have baffled Edwards at first. By 'custom of time out of mind', Moxon reported, each printing house was known by its workers as 'chapel' and was subject to a set of 'chapel rules'. Although there is no record of the specific regulations enforced by Braddyll, Moxon offers some examples of rules 'usually and generally accepted' among London printers: swearing, fighting, abusive language, excessive drunkenness, leaving a burning candle unattended, and handling other workers' tools were all off limits. These commandments were printed and pinned to the wall of the press room to remind the workforce of the code to which they had subscribed. The document would be signed by all the regular and journeymen printers, who promised to comply with the rules. An example contemporaneous with Edwards's apprenticeship records specific rules for apprentices, mainly regarding junior tasks and house-keeping. 'The youngest prentice of this room, every Wednesday and Saturday, that he neglects the sweeping, and carrying the dirt out of this said room, forfeits two pence.' More serious offences such as brawling or 'playing at any game in the printing house' demanded a fine of sixpence. Money raised through fines went to drink.

On his arrival at Bull's Head Court after the ceremony at Stationers' Hall, Edwards would have been forced to undergo an elaborate initi-ation ceremony to become a 'Cuz, or Deacon' of the printing house.

Having approached the most senior workman while clutching a wooden sword, 'the boy kneels, and the father of the chapel, after exhorting him to be observant of his business, and not to betray the secrets of the workmen, squeezes a spunge of strong beer over his head', at which point the workmen 'walk round him, singing the Cuz's anthem', a nonsensical sing-song word game chanting through all the vowels and consonants in order: 'Ba-ba; Be-be; Bi-bi; Ba-be-bi; Bo-bo; Ba-be-bi-bo; Bu-bu; Ba-be-bi-bo-bu', and so on. Afterwards, Braddyll would have been expected to put on a lavish supper for his workmen. It was not the only feast Edwards would enjoy. Each year, when the dark evenings of autumn approached, the journeymen would replace the paper windows and begin working by candlelight. To mark the occasion, tradition demanded, in Moxon's telling, 'the master printer gives them a way-goose; that is, he makes them a good feast, and not only entertains them at his own house, but besides, gives them money to spend at the alehouse or tavern at night'.

Almost nothing is known about Braddyll's character. Was he generous to young Edwards or a niggardly master? Was he lean or plump, dark or fair, cowardly or bold? Like most in his profession, he exists half-obscured by the centuries. But evidence suggests he had a radical streak. In 1680 Nathaniel Ponder, the nonconformist publisher of John Bunyan's hugely successful *Pilgrim's Progress*, accused Braddyll of printing a surreptitious edition of the book in 'a base old letter, almost worn out, hardly to be read', and denounced him and his workmen as a bunch of 'land pirates'. Others were less hostile. The Whig bookseller John Dunton fondly described him as 'a first-rate printer' who was 'religiously true to his word, and faithful to the booksellers that employ him'. 'I dealt with him for many years, and have not only found him just, but as well accomplished for all the parts of his business as any other printer I can name.' He also recalled at least one occasion on which, when pressed by government agents, Braddyll denied all knowledge of a large run of seditious books that Dunton had 'burned in an oven' to avoid discovery.

When Edwards joined the workshop in 1683, Braddyll was still recovering from his latest brush with the law. Over the past few years there had been numerous run-ins with the authorities: in November 1680 he had been censured for printing radical pamphlets for the bookseller Richard Janeway; in the summer of 1681, he was reported to the Stationers' Company for breaching the regulations concerning 'a presse in a hole' – which is to say, an unregistered clandestine press; and in that December he had refused entry to a crew of government henchmen, who were 'reflected on and abused' by his workmen. This more recent incident was the most traumatic.

During the spring of 1683 Braddyll had been arrested for printing three sheets of a pamphlet which included a lengthy tirade against the reigning powers at court. He had been offered the job by a long-standing associate, a Baptist publisher called Francis Smith. The fact that Smith was cautiously splitting the job between several printers ought to have rung alarm bells. While in jail, Braddyll was visited by a notorious agent of the king's, a man called Roger L'Estrange. As the chief government censor and 'bloodhound of the press', L'Estrange took Braddyll's indiscretion extremely seriously. Facing a drawn-out spell in prison and the terrifying prospect of interrogation, the printer quickly offered L'Estrange information in exchange for his freedom. He knew the men responsible for the pamphlet, he told L'Estrange. He had met with them in a tavern on the other side of town. Their names were Thomas Dare, Samuel Harris, Aaron Smith, Samuel Starkey, Edward Whitaker, and Robert Ferguson. Most of the men belonged to the Green Ribbon Club, a secretive faction which met at the King's Head tavern on Chancery Lane where its members plotted against the government of Charles II. L'Estrange could not think of a more extreme group of seditious republicans.

Braddyll's association with Ferguson and his cronies places him near the centre of revolutionary politics in the 1680s. A few years earlier, Ferguson had become a prominent advisor to the Earl of Shaftesbury, who led calls to exclude the king's Catholic brother and heir, James, Duke of York, from the line of succession, on account of his religion. They feared James would return the nation to Rome, and that the hard-won religious liberties of Protestants would be sacrificed to the Pope, who many dissenters believed was the Antichrist himself. Instead, Shaftesbury proposed that King Charles's bastard son, the

Protestant Duke of Monmouth, should become the next in line to the throne.

During a period that has since become known as the 'Exclusion Crisis', Shaftesbury and his followers, the Whigs, repeatedly attempted to secure Monmouth's succession in law. After a last-ditch effort in the spring of 1681, when the king convened parliament at Oxford, Shaftesbury and the other Whig leaders began plotting more violent insurrection against the government. Ferguson took charge after Shaftesbury's untimely death in January 1683, and orchestrated a wild scheme to assassinate the king and his brother as they returned to London from the Newmarket races, on a narrow lane near the Rye House at Hoddesdon in Hertfordshire.

Unfortunately for the conspirators, a major fire at Newmarket forced the royal party to leave the races several days earlier than planned, and they missed their opportunity. On 12 June, just three weeks before Edwards took his oath at Stationers' Hall, the plot was betrayed from within. The authorities moved fast to swoop up the conspirators. Ferguson escaped to Scotland, where he found passage to the Netherlands and eventually joined Monmouth. Yet the prominent republican agitators Algernon Sidney and William, Lord Russell, were among those captured. On 21 July, Russell was dragged to the scaffold at Lincoln's Inn Fields. His executioner Jack Ketch bungled the job hideously. Only the high-born were beheaded in this era – commoners suffered the more gruesome fate of being hanged, drawn, and quartered – so Ketch was no expert axeman. According to the executioner's own testimony, Russell 'somewhat heav'd his body' as he struck the first blow, and the axe landed firmly in his shoulder. It took another two attempts to sever Russell's head.

A key figure in the arrests was Sir Philip Lloyd, who had been running the investigation into the Rye House conspirators. At Sidney's trial, the manuscript of his secret republican masterwork, *Discourses Concerning Government*, was brandished by prosecutors as a 'witness' to his crimes. It was Lloyd who had seized this damning manuscript from Sidney's chest of private papers and presented it to the court. It was also Lloyd who, three days after the raid on Sidney's house, stormed Braddyll's workshop searching for a mysterious 'hamper' of

papers which one of his spies claimed had been sent by the conspirators. The spy was wrong. Information soon surfaced that the hamper
had in truth been dispatched to a different printer, John Darby, another
sympathiser with the radicals whom L'Estrange believed to be 'as
dangerous and desperate an anabaptist as lives'.

Edwards started his apprenticeship less than a fortnight after this
raid on Braddyll's workshop. The household was still recovering from
the shock and, over the coming years, Braddyll kept his head below
the parapet. His name does not appear on any books throughout 1683
and only once in both 1684 and 1685. Whatever Braddyll and his junior
employees may have printed in those years, they kept their role secret.
The young apprentice Edwards was trained in this furtive atmosphere.
The friends Braddyll mentioned to L'Estrange were equally cautious.
Aaron Smith was arrested with the other conspirators on 4 July; but
Starkey and Thomas Dare had already fled to Amsterdam where they
were met by their fellow Green Ribbon man John Locke. Dare's house
became the principal den of radicalism in Amsterdam. Ferguson was
a regular visitor and Locke himself lodged there for a while. These
exiled activists were eventually spurred into action after Charles II
died peacefully on 6 February 1685, leaving his brother to succeed him
as James II. Guided by Ferguson and his supporters, Monmouth laid
plans for an invasion to the south of England, while his ally the Duke
of Argyll attacked from Scotland. On 11 June, Monmouth landed at
Lyme Regis carrying a declaration of his intent to claim the throne,
drawn up by Ferguson.

Monmouth's rebellion did not end well. Although he assembled a
substantial ragtag force as he marched across the West Country, he
was foiled within the month at Sedgemoor by James II's superior army.
On 15 July, he became, like his late friend Lord Russell, another victim
of Jack Ketch. A puritan minister called Roger Morrice was present
at the execution and conveyed the horror of the scene in his diary:
'Catch [i.e. Ketch] strock five blowes, after the first blow Monmouth
turned his head a little and looked up, and after the second or third
blow spoak a word or two, when Catch seemed to intermitt or lay
down the axe.' The backlash against Monmouth's allies was significant.
More than 1,400 rebels were captured after the battle of Sedgemoor

and now sat awaiting trial. Judge Jeffreys was dispatched to preside over the 'bloody assizes' at Winchester and Taunton, where he convicted more than a thousand rebels of treason. Many prisoners were transported to the West Indies, where disease or hard labour would claim their lives. But hundreds were sentenced to be hanged, drawn, and quartered. Their butchered remains were displayed in local markets and town squares, a dire reminder of the fate that attended rebellion.

It is impossible to know whether Braddyll was in any way involved with these tumultuous events, although his known associates place him just a heartbeat away from the action. Braddyll was an experienced member of the literary underground. He assisted the radicals by printing seditious books and, according to Dunton, by hiding or disposing of copies before they could be seized by government agents. If Edwards desired an education in the grubby trades of clandestine printing and betrayal, which so often went hand in hand, he could not have wished for a better master.

Although the duties of his apprenticeship kept Edwards busy from day to day, he must have been swept up by events in the city. Apprentices did not live cloistered away from public affairs. Under the terms of his contract to Braddyll, Edwards would have worked and studied from dawn till dusk, for which he received bed, board, clothing, and his education. But as a young man he would have been allowed an hour for dinner and could escape to the taverns in the evenings, to play dice and cards and dominoes, gossip about political affairs, and sing ballads and drinking songs late into the night.

It was a febrile atmosphere. Political commitments and allegiances were forged over mugs of ale and, once laid down, were difficult to escape. Back in 1681 several thousand Tory apprentices had presented a loyal address to Charles II, protesting against 'the disloyal proceedings of ill-minded men' among the Whigs and dissenters, whom they believed were plotting against their rightful king. John Dunton, though still in the final year of his apprenticeship, led a counter-attack. Incensed by 'the vanity of [the Tory apprentices] boasting themselves the onely loyal young men of this city', Dunton collected more than 20,000

signatures to present to the Lord Mayor of London, petitioning for a
new parliament to be called. 'If the Tory apprentices did all they could
to ruin their country', Dunton later recalled, then it was 'the duty of
the Whig apprentices to do all they could to save it', even 'to the last
drop of our blood'.

Of course, that was not the end of the story. On 13 July, the Tory
apprentices presented another address to the king, signed by 12,000
of their company, repeating their original declaration of loyalty.
Accusations of foul play went back and forth: the Whigs alleged their
opponents were being duped by a cabal that met each night at the
Crown tavern in Ivy Lane; meanwhile Tories accused the Whigs of
falsely inflating their address by bribing an unnamed 'printer's boy'
to gather random signatures: 'he produced abundance, and is now
ready to attest that the greater part of them were names of his own
invention'.

Not all apprentices were satisfied by the formal to and fro of peti-
tions and addresses. While some were content to protest peacefully,
others wanted to take direct action. Apprentices on both sides of the
political and religious divide were among the most active rioters of
their time. During the unrest surrounding the final days of the inter-
regnum, Samuel Pepys witnessed one such apprentice 'gett a football
(it being a hard frost) and drive it among the souldiers on purpose
… many souldiers were hurt with stones, and one I see was very
neere having his braines knockt out'. Throughout the early 1680s
crowds of young Whig supporters marched through the streets of
London braying anti-Catholic anthems, rallying around burning effigies of the Pope. In the spring of 1680 a separate group of Tory
apprentices secretly planned to commemorate the king's birthday by
torching representations of Oliver Cromwell in the same manner 'as
the phanaticks had done the Pope', before attacking nearby dissenting
chapels.

The early years of Edwards's apprenticeship were quiet in comparison, disturbed only by some short-lived demonstrations protesting
the execution of Monmouth and his allies in 1685. In the summer of
1688, however, the streets erupted once more. The arrest and public
trial of seven bishops who defied James II's orders for the toleration

of Catholics triggered uproar in the capital. Their acquittal on 30 June was greeted with 'wild huzzas and acclamations' and burnings of the Pope's effigy in the evening. Less than a fortnight later, on 10 July, the queen, Mary of Modena, gave birth to a prince. The baptism of this new heir, James Francis Edward, into the Catholic faith triggered a second wave of anti-Catholic frenzy, and prompted desperate rumours that the child was, in fact, an imposter smuggled into the palace by nuns from the convent next door. How could the queen have been pregnant, asked one feverish pamphleteer, when 'in other women, after four months being gone, there will be seen a visible swelling and increase of the breast, together with a fair appearance of milk: but all these symptoms were also wanting in the queen, nor did ever any lady which was proper to be a witness ever see a drop of milk in her breasts which were still the same to the eyes of all that view'd them, without any alteration of bulk or proportion?' This conspiracy theory proved surprisingly difficult to debunk. For the mob, it was evidence of a deep-seated plot to enslave the British people to Rome.

Until the birth of the prince, the next in line to the throne had been James's eldest daughter, Mary, and her husband William of Orange, both of whom were resolutely committed to the Protestant faith. In 1685 William had contributed troops to Monmouth's rebellion and continued to work closely with exiled English conspirators. After Monmouth's failed attempt to depose James, William and his allies set about planning how best to neutralise the Catholic threat, both in England and in France. At first the plan was simply to pressure James into reversing his policies; but this quickly escalated to a full invasion. In April he sought a formal invitation from the leading opposition figures in London. By the height of summer William had received all the assurance he needed that his English allies would support the invading force with auxiliaries and extra finances. The birth of the Catholic prince, who leapfrogged William and Mary in the line of succession, was the final straw. The Dutch assembled a fleet of more than 400 ships in record time. William boarded his flagship on 26 October. The ship's standard bore a simple motto 'Pro Religione et Libertate': for religion and liberty.

William's army landed at the small fishing town of Brixham on 5 November, emboldening apprentices to commit fresh acts of violence in the capital. On 11 November, they tore down the Catholic chapel in Bucklersbury, where one priest, 'sneaking off with one of the silver candlesticks, had his hand, candlestick and all, cut off by a goldsmith's apprentice'. Another night the mob attacked the chapel at Lincoln's Inn Fields, razing it to the ground, and did the same with those of St John's and Clerkenwell. Struggling to break into the chapel on Lime Street, the young men cried 'they would down with it, were it as strong as Portsmouth'.

Having levelled the religious houses, the apprentices moved on to the printshop of Henry Hills, who had served as Warden of the Stationers' Company at the ceremony when Edwards was sworn in five years earlier. Having recently converted to the Catholic faith, Hills was 'served in like manner' by the mob. The same gang of 'boys and youths' seized cartloads of paraphernalia from another Benedictine establishment and paraded through the street 'in mock procession and triumph, with oranges on the tops of swords and staves, with great lighted candles in gilt candlesticks'. In the chaos some 'boys threw stones, and had cudgells, and so provoked the guards that they shott bullets, and killed some of the boys, and with their swords wounded others'. In retaliation, a splinter group of apprentices schemed to attack the papal ambassador's London residence, dispersing only after they found the house had been abandoned in a rush. On the front door was a note saying, 'This house is to be lett'.

Yet James was not entirely without allies among London's apprentices. Many of the loyal petitioners of the previous decade remained true to their king, escorting him back into the city upon his brief return in December 1688 with 'some shouting' and 'some huzzas'. After his flight to France at the end of the year, and the declaration of William and Mary as joint sovereigns in the following February, many young Londoners remained doggedly loyal. In July, one Thomas Page was accused of being 'in a caball against the government' and charged with speaking these treasonable words: 'God dam him he would murder King William and Queen Mary'. Prominent Jacobites, as James's supporters became known, continued to urge 'the brave apprentices, journeymen, and honest porters, labourers, and others' to 'assist your old master' and 'kick these damn'd Dutch tubs out of the nation'. These lower social groups were among the easiest to mobilise against authority.

Edwards observed all these tumultuous events up close. Likely as not he directly participated in them, chanting and yelling and brawling with his fellow apprentices. Even from the printshop floor he could hardly fail to feel the rumble of change, with new pamphlets and manuscripts on political affairs passing through his hands every day. And as he went about his master's business in the city, he learned more of the new political order and his place in it. By the time he returned with Braddyll to Stationers' Hall, to be 'sworne and admitted into the freedome of this Company' in the spring of 1691, he had learned much about the operations of a busy printing house. He had also immersed himself in the sordid underworld of the London book trade: anonymous printing, political activism, and betrayal were all part of his diet. He had lived through revolution and rebellion. Now his education was complete. In due course he would marry and set up his own workshop with his own press. He would take on apprentices and employ journeymen. Under Braddyll's guidance, he had taken the first steps on a path that would lead him through poverty and punishment, to the corridors of power and interrogation chambers of Whitehall. Whatever vision Edwards had of a blazing career in the book trade, his future would prove very different.

CHAPTER TWO

Messengers After Supper

Early in the evening on Monday 17 July 1693 two figures edged their way through Westminster's narrow alleys to the Blue Posts tavern in the Haymarket. According to John Evelyn, the previous morning had seen torrential rain in London and many of the city's streets remained waterlogged. But it was now a mild evening and the glow of the setting sun was still visible on the swollen river.

The two men were printers. One of them, William Newbolt, was a 'well set middle sized man' of around thirty with a 'short brownish perriwig' on his head. As a child he had suffered from smallpox. The scars were still visible on his neck and cheeks, though now masked behind a rugged, dark brown beard. He probably wore his trusty old 'dark coloured brownish cloth suit', the better to disguise the splashes of mud which were unavoidable during rainy conditions. The other man was Edward Butler. He carried a nondescript package under his arm. Unlike surrounding streets, Haymarket was wide and recently paved with good stone. Debris from the Saturday market lay rotting against the shops and taverns on the west side of the street and the newly built houses to the east. Farmers from across Middlesex and the surrounding counties were already arriving for the Tuesday market. It had been a difficult harvest. Rain had largely spoiled the local crop of wheat and corn. Prices were on the rise.

The Blue Posts was known to put on a good supper. The Duke of Norfolk's butler would regularly be dispatched there from his London residence to fetch dinner for the duchess. In a satirical pamphlet of 1688, Tom Brown joked that even Adam and Eve would be cured of

their 'contemptible frugality of feeding upon sallads' by being treated
to 'a fasionable oglio' at the Blue Posts. Rakish characters in the plays
of Thomas Otway and John Vanbrugh were said to dine there. John
Wilmot, the Earl of Rochester, was another customer, though for him
the main attraction appears to have been the wine. Remembering one
evening of drinking at the Blue Posts in his youth, Rochester lamented
how intoxication 'drew fornication after it; and these two sins in wicked
conjunction begot a most undutiful child'. Like any of London's
taverns, though, the Blue Posts could become a dangerous place in
the early hours of the morning. Two years after the printers trod their
way through the sodden Haymarket, in July 1695, one John Moare
was convicted of killing his drinking partner here after 'words were
heard to arise between them' at around two o'clock in the morning
concerning the bill.

Newbolt and Butler had little time for debauchery and none whatsoever for murder. They were here on business. Several weeks earlier,
over a dinner of haggis in the Ship tavern in nearby Covent Garden,
Newbolt and Butler had been offered a job. Their client was a shifty
individual called William Chaloner. He was seeking forty copies of a
recent Jacobite declaration by the exiled King James, which he whispered were 'not to be dispersed' in a public manner 'but sent to a
private gentleman in the country'. He had been assured by some
mutual contacts that Newbolt and Butler specialised in such dangerous,
clandestine work, and might be willing to help him. At first the two
printers were wary. In the eyes of the government, this declaration
was treasonous. Only the previous year a woman had been imprisoned
for having copies of similar declarations in her possession, and had
been sentenced to death. Newbolt and Butler barely knew Chaloner.
Could he be trusted? Eventually, however, Chaloner persuaded the
printers 'at the expence of several treats and some money' to come
around to his way of thinking.

The drop had been arranged for this evening. It would take place
over another dinner in a private room at the Blue Posts. Having arrived
and enquired at the bar, the pair were directed upstairs to where their
confederate was waiting. It is not difficult to imagine Chaloner's reac-

tion when he saw the package cradled in Butler's arms. He smiled. Little did Newbolt and Butler know, their luck was about to run out.

Earlier that day, less than half a mile across town in Westminster, another meeting had taken place. Having received information from a new source about the handover that evening, the secretary of state, Sir John Trenchard, issued a warrant to his most trusted agent, John Gellibrand. Gellibrand and his colleagues were known as the king's 'messengers'. His orders were to 'make swift and diligent search for William Newbolt and Edward Butler printers and them or either of them having found you are to apprehend for high treason'. Gellibrand would not have known what to expect upon arrival at the Blue Posts. The tip-off only placed Newbolt and Butler at the tavern for supper and claimed that they would be delivering a packet of newly printed treasonous papers. Printers were not usually prone to violence, but there was always a possibility that the arrest could turn nasty. As Chaloner and the two printers settled into their supper, Gellibrand stormed upstairs with a small group of armed constables. 'Instead of grace after meat', joked one contemporary pamphleteer, Newbolt and Butler were entertained 'with messengers and musqueteers.'

Outmanned and with no obvious means of escape, the trio surrendered to their captors. It was every printer's nightmare. Gellibrand was the messenger whom printers most feared, for he had started life as a printer himself. Two years earlier, after several brushes with the law, Gellibrand first offered to 'discover the printer of a scandalous libel' for the House of Lords. His talent for clandestine work was obvious to his superiors and he was promptly assigned a specialist role as messenger of the press. His remit was massive, granting him authority to 'make diligent search in all printing houses, booksellers and bookebinders shops and warehouses' in order to hunt down 'all authors, printers, bookesellers, bookebinders, hawkers, and others as shall be found to print, stitch, cry and sell, or privately convey, or any way disperse such unlicenced, seditious, false, and scandalous books'. Drawing on his years of experience, he penetrated the underground press with ease.

As darkness fell after the raid on the Blue Posts, Gellibrand relinquished custody of Newbolt and Butler to his colleague Richard Hayward, who escorted the prisoners back to his lodgings in Westminster. The apartment doubled as a government safehouse. Though common practice among the messengers, the use of private homes as off-books holding cells often backfired. According to messenger Nathan Wilcox, one of his prisoners once became so angry in confinement that he 'toare my wife's hedclothes and haires of her hed, and went to push her out of the window and called her ould bitch and beast'. Other agents complained of offenders bringing in fleas and vermin. More frequently, though, the prisoners simply went missing, as, the next morning, did Newbolt and Butler.

An experienced operative such as Gellibrand should have known better than to trust Hayward with such important captives. Gellibrand's diligence and expertise were not shared by many of his colleagues. An independent investigation into the messenger service in 1695 exposed a startling number of crooked agents. For instance, the messenger William Jones reportedly received 'gratuities' from a club which assembled at the Dog tavern and worked as 'the common intelligencer to the Jacobites'. There was Benjamin Maris, whose 'wife is a papist, and communicates all she knowes to that faction'; Francis Clerke, who 'keepes company with the Jacobites and is much commended by all that party'; and John King, whom the investigator wrote 'has done so many ill things, that I know not where to begin'. The same inquiry labelled Hayward as 'a carrelesse drunken sotte' with a reputation for duplicity. By 1699 treasury officials were brandishing his name as a byword for corruption among the government's enforcers. Bribery was routine among the messengers of the crown; but in Hayward's case it was impossible to turn a blind eye and he was promptly dismissed from the service. In a begging letter to the queen, Hayward blamed 'the negligence of others' for Newbolt and Butler's escape. Possibly he sought to shift responsibility for the incident onto his fellow messenger Peter Tom, with whom he shared his rooms at Strutton Ground. By 1695 the truth had emerged. Not only was Hayward drunk; he had accepted a bribe of £20 from his captives.

Despite its vast size, London could become a small town when one needed to keep a low profile. Understandably, Newbolt and Butler's initial instinct upon escaping their captors was to run. But first they would need cash, which was kept by their colleague Thomas Farr. As the son of a gentleman, Farr was an unlikely accomplice for the fugitives. He had served his apprenticeship at the Savoy with the respectable printer Thomas Newcomb, before the 1680s when he sank into the illicit underbelly of the book trade. He had contacts who could help Newcomb and Butler lie low, which they accomplished for an entire month.

Their eventual discovery was pure accident. On Thursday 17 July, a junior customs official based near Woolwich, some ten miles downriver from Whitehall, conducted a routine inspection of a Belgian trade ship headed for France. Possibly he expected to discover undeclared goods or contraband. Finding Newbolt, Butler, and Farr in the hold with 'a great many guineas about them' must have come as a surprise. The newly captured prisoners were dragged back to London and the Gatehouse prison, where they were reconciled with their co-conspirator William Chaloner. Or so they thought. Unbeknownst to Newbolt and Butler, they had been played from the start. Their man Chaloner was a double agent.

Having left Braddyll's workshop to carve out a career of his own, David Edwards found himself in a tricky situation. The climate was perfect for freelance informants like Chaloner, who traded on suspicion and fear. It was crucial that Edwards should learn whom he could and could not trust, and that he should learn it quickly. Within eighteen months of finishing his apprenticeship, in September 1692, the government issued a proclamation declaring a £20 reward for the discovery of anybody involved in printing, transcribing, or publishing seditious libels, and a £50 reward for catching the authors. Although the measure was universally approved by officials, it soon came under fire in the press. One pamphleteer immediately denounced it as a traitor's charter:

He that will Judas-like do any thing against the word of God, and his righteousness, though it here covenanted for twenty or fifty pieces of silver (which perhaps the informer may be yet baulked of, notwithstanding such particular directions are here specified for the certain and speedy payment thereof) may also meet with Judas his doom. It would be good for him, if he had never been born and it would be better for him if he had never touched or meddled with such mony, which is the reward of iniquity; the consequence whereof will be persecution and oppression, if it be not the worst kind of direct murder it self.

But Chaloner had no such qualms and, in Newbolt and Butler, found a pair whose liberty he could trade for money. Upon his release after testifying against the prisoners in court, Chaloner boasted that he had enabled the capture of 'at least thirty persons' and the discovery of 'two printing presses' and 'severall cart loads of treasonable lybells, which would have been dispersed, in order to stir up sedition'. Betrayal was a lucrative business. Chaloner walked away with £1,000 and the promise of further government employment.

Under Braddyll's tutelage Edwards learned the dangers of accepting commissions from new clients, especially shifty figures like Chaloner who asked for runs of seditious pamphlets. It would have been a common lesson among junior printers, though that did not stop some of them falling for the trick. One of the government's most successful and subtle agents, Dr Richard Kingston, had masterminded a similar sting operation in the previous November. Unlike some of his colleagues, Kingston understood the only way to bring down the underground press was to infiltrate it. And so he spent months cultivating assets among the printers, until he was viewed as one of their own. His target was the Jacobite printer working under the alias 'Canon', who used a woman called Anne Merryweather as his chief intermediary. Posing as the author of a treasonous Jacobite pamphlet, Kingston grew close to Merryweather. She came to trust him and, as the weeks went by, he observed how she hid bundles of seditious pamphlets in a secret cubbyhole 'between the seeling of the roofe and the partition wall of the house'.

Merryweather was duly hauled in for interrogation. Under normal circumstances, Kingston's evidence would be leverage enough to make her talk. But Merryweather was a zealot whose faith in Canon was seemingly unshakeable. Daniel Finch, Earl of Nottingham and Trenchard's predecessor as secretary of state, led her interrogation in his office at Whitehall, but to no avail. As one of Nottingham's underlings explained at the time:

> all your honour's threatnings and perswasions (she told him) had no effect, for she had not discovered Canon, nor no other person, nor ever would doe it; having resolved rather to dye honourably than live basely; and this she desired Canon might have notice of, lest he should be surprized.

On Thursday 19 January 1693, the court elected to grant Merryweather the martyrdom she craved, and scheduled her execution for the following week. Women condemned for treason were not hanged, drawn, and quartered like the common men, nor beheaded like the gentry. They were burnt at the stake. Although some executioners had begun showing relative mercy to their victims by strangling them to death before lighting the pyre, by the 1690s this practice was far from ubiquitous. Merryweather would remember women who died in the manner of Sarah Elston, whose recent execution became the subject of a short pamphlet: 'the fire was kindled, and giving two or three lamentable shrieks, she was deprived both of voice and life, and so burnt to ashes according to the sentence'.

In the face of such overwhelming terror it should come as no surprise that Merryweather's nerve eventually failed her. On the eve of her execution she declared her intention to 'discover her accomplices, and those that set her on work, provided she may have her pardon'. Temporary reprieves were issued of ten days at a time, dependent on the quality of her intelligence, until, on 15 February, she received an indefinite stay of execution. Merryweather's information was good.

A flurry of warrants for underground printers ensued in late March and April, following Trenchard's appointment as secretary of state.

On 2 May, Trenchard claimed his first victim. Though still in his twenties, William Anderton had long been a thorn in the government's side. His case was particularly embarrassing for Gellibrand's senior colleague Robert Stephens, a messenger who had been on Anderton's trail for several years. The printer had evaded capture at his workshop in Hoxton in July 1691 and again more recently at locations around Soho and Shoreditch, where he was running a secret press under the alias 'Thomas Topham'. By the spring of 1693 the trail was assumed to have gone cold until, quite by chance, Stephens spotted two of Anderton's known associates lurking in the alleys around Westminster.

Having lost the scent nearly six months earlier, Stephens tailed them back to John Scudamore's carpentry shop on St James's Street. This time Stephens planned his raid carefully. Gathering up some local constables, he stormed the property and found, hidden behind a bed mounted on wheels, 'a private door, which led them into a room where Mr Stephens found a printing press'. Here in the secret printing room, Stephens apprehended Anderton, though not, he claimed, 'without a great deal of trouble and abuse'. Searching further, Stephens 'found in an old trunk, a great quantity of libels, and libellous pamphlets' and, in a desk 'which Mr Stephens knew well to be the prisoner's, because he had seized it before', found two pamphlets containing 'the rankest, vilest, and most malicious treasons that ever could be imagined by any man to be put in paper'. Anderton was duly charged with treason and hauled off to Newgate to await trial.

Robert Stephens was even better known and perhaps more feared than Gellibrand, though not because he was more diligent; rather because he was more corrupt. 'Robin Hog' was his nickname among the printers, the 'Wild Boar of the City of London'. Even by the standards of the messengers, his behaviour was savage. When the bookseller Francis Smith refused to submit to an illegal general warrant in 1679, it put Stephens 'in a great heat, both threatening me and persuading me much to obey'. Edwards was already familiar with Stephens from his time with Braddyll; his old master would have told him about the numerous occasions on which Stephens had tried to barge his way into the workshop, only to be 'reflected upon and abused' by Braddyll and his crew. John Dunton knew that Stephens's loyalties could be bought, and so, whenever he 'printed a book that had no license, [he] took such care to dazzle his eyes, that he could not see it'. Even colleagues loathed him. The shrewd spymaster Kingston thought him a brute whose 'cowardice, treachery, bribery, and entire dishonesty' were so compromising that he ought not 'to be trusted farther than throwne'.

There is no greater example of Stephens's cruelty and dishonesty than his treatment of William Anderton. For the Jacobite pamphlets which Stephens claimed to have discovered in Anderton's desk, the same pamphlets for which he was convicted of treason, were in all likelihood planted there by the wily messenger. When Anderton protested his innocence before the court, the jury dismissed this counter-accusation as the desperation of a condemned man. Stephens had got hold of Anderton's former master, a puritan bully called Thomas Snowden, and convinced him to testify against his former apprentice. Posing as an expert witness, Snowden claimed that the font used for the pamphlets matched the cases of type found in the secret printing room at Scudamore's. Snowden did not, of course, mention his 'notoriously known malice' against his erstwhile apprentice, whom he used to beat regularly for his different religious views, to the extent that Anderton's apprenticeship was eventually transferred to the more congenial Miles Flesher. Such inconvenient information would only get in the way of a conviction.

Anderton's lawyer had no chance to refute this argument in court. Before the implementation of the Treason Trials Act in the spring of 1696, defendants had no right to counsel. Still, one sympathetic pamphleteer soon pointed out the futility of Snowden's reasoning:

> I am assured by a very understanding printer, that there is not a printing house in town, but hath of the same sort of letter or character, so that upon such an oath as this, any or all the printers of the town might have been taken, and whom they thought fit hanged. For there is none of them but had characters as suitable to the book, as that which was sworn to; and if it had been seized, and thus sworn to, they were as lyable to be hanged as

Anderton. At this rate the government need not give themselves the charge of a messenger of the press, nor the trouble of such frequent searches; but as soon as any seditious or treasonable pamphlet comes abroad, it is but going to the next printer's and seizing his letter, and having found some of the same sort of character, to get a couple of rattle-headed fellows to swear to it, and hang him; and thus they may pick and chuse what printers they please to hang.

Close analysis of the typography of the Jacobite pamphlets in court must have unnerved Newbolt and Butler. For Chaloner's later record of services rendered to the government shows that he discovered the same two pamphlets in the possession of Newbolt and Butler's chief pressman David Douglas. Anderton had printed more than his share of treasonous pamphlets over the years, but in this case it seems Newbolt and Butler and Douglas were guilty. What must they have thought when, on 3 June, Anderton was found guilty of high treason 'for printing severall treasonable papers against the government', and, within the week, sentenced to a traitor's death?

Eight days later he was dragged to the hanging tree at Tyburn with 'that calm behaviour and decent courage, as stroke the beholders with remorse and amazement'. As he stood on the scaffold, Anderton muttered some half-hearted words of forgiveness to his 'most false and perjured witnesses, and among them more particularly Robin Stephens, my most unjust and unrighteous judges, and my repenting jury'. Yet he also denounced with his next breath those 'infatuated and blind countrymen' who 'rebell'd against their lawful and injur'd monarch' in the supposed cause of liberty: 'I pray consider where is this liberty and property? Where the rights and privileges of the subject? Nay, where the very laws themselves?'

With which the noose tightened and Anderton dropped spluttering into the air. A hanging was always a well-attended event, especially the hanging of a traitor. Maybe Newbolt and Butler were in attendance, silent and supportive among the braying crowd. If they were, they must surely have feared for themselves as they saw the life drain from Anderton's body. It was common knowledge that the printer had named colleagues in a vain attempt to save his life. On 13 June, the same day Anderton's death warrant was signed, the diarist Narcissus Luttrell recorded that 'orders are given for taking up thirty-six severall persons concerned in the trade of libells'. The literary underground was a tight-knit community. When Anderton's corpse was buried, at eleven o'clock at night on 19 June in the churchyard of St Bartholomew-the-Great in Smithfield, great crowds were said to have attended the funeral. Anderton would probably have recognised the work of Newbolt and Butler's press when he was confronted with the two pamphlets in the courtroom. For all they knew, their names may well have been among the thirty-six he surrendered.

Newbolt and Butler very nearly suffered the same fate as their colleague Anderton. Convicted and sentenced to death for printing the Jacobite declarations, they petitioned the queen for mercy. But Trenchard simply diverted their request to Sir William Dolben, the judge who had presided over their original trial. He was not sympathetic. Trenchard had his own strategy for dealing with the prisoners, dangling short-term reprieves from execution of eight days at a time in return for information. On 23 September, Newbolt finally cracked and 'accused severall who were concerned in printing and dispersing the declarations'. On 4 October, Trenchard stayed their execution indefinitely. The printers would be left to rot in Newgate.

Life inside was tough. Although the prison buildings were new, having been reconstructed by Sir Christopher Wren after the fire of 1666, conditions remained squalid. Daniel Defoe drew on personal experience when he described the 'hellish noise, the roaring, swearing and clamour, the stench and nastiness' of the jail, which combined 'to make the place seem an emblem of hell itself, and a kind of entrance into it'. The overcrowded common cells were a den of typhoid. Raw sewage trickled through a sluice cut into the corridor. Access to beer, hot food, and bedding depended on how much cash a prisoner had to bribe his jailers. If Newbolt and Butler wanted a bed in a private cell, it would cost them three shillings and sixpence a week, plus extra for food and drink and firewood and candles, which were a requirement in the cold gloom of Newgate. Their money would soon run out, at which point they would be back in the overcrowded pit of the common cells with no end in sight. Disease would likely claim them if the hangman did not.

Edwards must have looked on in horror. He and Anderton had over-lapped as apprentices, with Anderton graduating three years ahead. Edwards would have known Anderton and Newbolt and Butler, by reputation if not in person, and surely joined the other printers of London in mourning their treatment. The combined threat of free-lance informers, thuggish messengers, and snitch prisoners made it a dangerous time to be a young printer on the make. If Edwards wanted to avoid the fates of his colleagues, he would need to learn from their mistakes.

In the years before his capture, Anderton had countered the threat of surveillance by keeping on the move, dragging his cumbersome kit from house to house. Vast cases of lead type, composing sticks, galleys, ink, paper, work tables, and the press itself all had to be packed up and transported with minimal fuss. Another who used this strategy was William Cannyn, who in February 1691 abandoned his shop in the legal district of Westminster before setting up a secret press in White Friars. Agents working on his behalf included 'a popish coffee woman in an alley within Temple Bar' who distrib-uted pamphlets wholesale, a lawyer in the Temple who smuggled illicit material through a secret passageway in his chambers, and 'a Jacobite weaver' in Hoxton who sold Cannyn's pamphlets under the counter. They received their contraband from a mysterious middleman, usually spotted 'wearing a long black perrewigg, much disfigured or markt with the small pox' and 'a longish face, of a middle well shaped stature, wearing commonly a sword'. Each link in the chain helped distance Cannyn from any pamphlets being sold on the streets.

While this was a viable strategy, it was altogether easier to have influential friends or patrons. There is a good deal of evidence to suggest that Newbolt and Butler had wealthy patrons of their own. They cobbled together £20 at short notice to bribe Richard Hayward; when discovered fleeing to France they had 'a great many guineas about them'; and soon after he testified against the printers in court,

Chaloner found a £500 bounty on his head. The money must have been coming from somewhere.

Edwards had no such connections when he left Braddyll's workshop. For a while he earned his crust working day to day as a journeyman, labouring at the press for whoever would pay him. Having seen his fellow printers sent to the gallows and to jail, he learned to keep his head down and stay out of trouble. Wherever possible, he avoided the sort of controversial publications that might draw the attention of Gellibrand, Stephens, Kingston, or one of their colleagues. He did not want the messengers on his trail.

One of his most reliable new employers was the widow Thompson, whose late husband Nathaniel had been a notable printer in his day. On his death in 1687, Nathaniel Thompson left all his printing equipment to his wife and stepdaughter, Mary. And they needed reliable workmen to keep the business going. Edwards would have known all about the Thompson press from the earliest days of his apprenticeship. Whereas Braddyll had sided with the Whigs through the crises and plots of the 1680s, Thompson had been an ardent Tory and, more worryingly still, a Catholic. Much as Braddyll sometimes overstepped the mark on his side, Thompson was frequently hauled before the authorities to answer for his conduct, leaving his wife and employees to run the press in his absence. Growing up during a period of intense hatred towards Catholics had forced young Mary to become resilient. At one point, with her stepfather in prison and the family kept under house arrest, her mother had protested to parliament that 'she and her children have no liberty to look after sustenance'. She genuinely feared the family might starve. It is testimony to their grit and resilience that, more than five years after Thompson's death, the mother-and-daughter team was still going strong.

It did not take long for Edwards to warm to Mary. She was sharp, intelligent, and headstrong. And while they diverged on religious matters, with Edwards subscribing to the Church of England whereas Mary was staunchly Catholic, the two agreed on political affairs: that the exiled King James had been treated abominably and that King William was nothing more than a usurper. These were dangerous views to hold and doubtless the young couple bonded over their shared Jacobite secrets, which Edwards had struggled to hide from his old master.

Mary also possessed two things Edwards did not: a press and her stepfather's connections. By the summer of 1694 the pair were married. They found premises of their own, a small house for rent on Nevil's Alley, off Fetter Lane, where the Thompson press was assembled anew. Mary had grown up hawking her stepfather's productions and knew the lanes and alleys around Fleet Street as well as anyone. The workshop on Nevil's Alley was to become a spot for trade insiders, not casual customers seeking to pick up a pamphlet or newspaper, who would instead be directed to Mary's little stall over against the Golden Lion, a tavern on Fetter Lane.

Edwards could see that the collapse of the underground press presented an opportunity for any printer brave or foolhardy enough to grasp it. But unlike Anderton, he refused to live between safehouses, constantly looking over his shoulder and packing up his workshop at a moment's notice. In the coming months and years he would develop a new strategy, balancing above-board printing with the sort of clandestine work for which the Jacobite printers had been jailed and executed. Could he maintain a veneer of respectability while secretly churning out libels? It was a huge gamble. But Edwards was a gambling man.

CHAPTER THREE

A Printer's Progress

By the summer of 1694, it had become abundantly clear that the government's current system of press control was not working. Under the terms of the Licensing Act, two copies of every manuscript needed to be presented to the Surveyor of the Press before it could be printed. One of those copies would then be returned to the owner. The other was retained by the licenser so that he could check the printed text against the authorised manuscript version.

It was an inefficient and time-consuming arrangement, ill suited to the massive growth of topical print. In reality, most publishers of controversial material simply bypassed the licensing system altogether and issued texts anonymously. Technically all those unlicensed books were illegal. But the law needed to be administered on a case-by-case basis, which was simply impossible when hundreds of unlicensed books flooded the market each year. Individual printers could be punished; but this did little to hold back the tide. As one partial commentator observed in 1693, it 'appears the law is far insufficient to the end which it intends. Do we not see, not once or oftner, but weekly, nay daily, that continued Jacobite libels against our present happy establishment, are printed and dispersed amongst us; for all that licensing can do?'

Even when printers did follow the official channels, that did not guarantee an easy ride. The licensor's decision was ultimately subject to the shifting whims of parliament. On 21 January 1693, the official surveyor of the press, Edmund Bohun, was hauled before ministers to explain why he had authorised the printing of a controversial tract entitled *King William and Queen Mary Conquerors*. Despite Bohun's protestation that the argument of the book was legally sound, he was summarily dismissed from his office. His successor Daniel Poplar fared no better. In 1694 he was threatened with prosecution by the Privy Council for approving Robert Molesworth's anti-monarchical pamphlet *An Account of Denmark*, which had caused an unfortunate diplomatic incident with the Danish king. Religious books were the domain of the bishops and their deputies, although those officials were subject to the same pressures as licensers of the secular press. The politician William Stephens always claimed that the Archbishop of Canterbury and the Bishop of London refused to license sermons for publication unless they reflected their own theological and political views. Likewise, in April 1694 the Oxford churchman Roger Altham was forced to apologise for signing off a book that accused his political opponent Gilbert Burnet, the Bishop of Salisbury, of heresy. Such were the risks of rigid censorship, for the censors as well as the press.

At first David and Mary Edwards played by these rules. The earliest-known product of their press at Nevil's Alley was granted its licence by Poplar on 18 April 1694. They took on their first apprentice, John Bowes, a local orphan whom Edwards accepted under the terms of the Relief of Orphans Act, on 10 September; in the summer of 1698 they welcomed a second apprentice, Thomas Baily. Establishing a new printshop entailed considerable financial risk. Thankfully Mary brought her stepfather's old equipment to the marriage, so that major cost was avoided. But wherever possible they would continue to save money on paper, printing broadsides on sheets so coarse that they more closely resembled English packing paper than the imported French or Dutch sheets used by most printers. In the early years much of their income appears to have come from jobbing work: that is, from printing advertisements, sale catalogues, and other ephemera. Ever streetwise, Mary helped out by extracting confessions from condemned prisoners which her husband could print to be sold beneath the gallows.

In the spring of 1695 parliament finally acknowledged that the Licensing Act was unfit for purpose. The current system of prepublication censorship was replaced by a new one of post-publication censorship. In practice this meant that the post of Surveyor of the Press was dissolved. Manuscripts would no longer be sent in for his approval. Instead the book trade would be subject to common law, in particular to the laws against seditious libel and treason. That meant publishers could issue whatever books they liked, but would face the consequences if they stepped over the line. It was a subtle move. Legal definitions of libel and treason remained vague. According to the original treason statutes, merely *imagining* the king's death was a capital offence, though there was no clear guidance on how exactly to police the imagination. From now on, printers and publishers would have to become their own censors. The prudent ones would play it safe, staying well clear of politically dubious material.

Edwards would have vividly remembered the treatment of William Anderton and, for a time, was eager to stay out of trouble. Mary was not so cautious. Her stepfather's old friends among the exiled Catholic community were eager to continue publishing their writings in England. With Anderton and his fellow Jacobite printers now out of action, many were looking for new agents in London. An old family friend was the Benedictine priest James 'Maurus' Corker. During the hysteria surrounding the fake 'Popish Plot' in 1681, Corker had been imprisoned in Newgate, where he acted as confessor to his fellow prisoners and wrote religious tracts in confinement. He was released by James II upon his accession in 1685 and converted the poet laureate, John Dryden, to the Roman faith later that same year.

Although Corker followed James into exile, he had spent much of the last decade sneaking between Paris and London, carrying secret messages from the Stuart court to its allies at home. It was on one such trip that Corker's fellow Jacobite courier, William Fuller, first encountered him. Fuller's memoirs contain a report of their first meeting, wherein he recalls how the swashbuckling priest was dressed 'more like a dragoon, than a ghostly father, having on him a red coat, with a swinging belt above a foot broad about his wast, a terrible large long sword, a campaigne wig, and a laced hat, and he looked most furiously'. Mary quickly persuaded her husband to print two theological works by this intimidating priest, with only the initials 'J. C.' on the title page.

More Catholic titles followed, reflecting Mary's influence over the fledgling business. Catholic prayer books were illegal in England, prompting some enterprising French merchants to smuggle parcels of them up the Thames. But some of the seemingly foreign books were actually coming from Nevil's Alley. At least twice Edwards printed a Catholic *Manual of Prayers and Christian Devotions*, though on both occasions he was careful to cover his tracks. For one of the volumes, he sneakily altered the title page to claim it was printed in Paris in 1692. For the other book he gave the date only, without revealing that it was printed in London. The only connection to his workshop was a decorated capital 'O' which Mary had used elsewhere. Both volumes close with a prayer for the exiled Jacobite royals.

It was not long before the press on Nevil's Alley began to attract unwanted attention. In the autumn of 1694, Edwards entered government records for the first time. Robin Stephens, who had dragged Anderton from his secret workshop the previous year, was always on the lookout for possible offenders. On 14 October he received information that Edwards had engaged in 'treasonable and seditious practices against their majesties and the government'. His orders were to 'apprehend and secure' the printer for interrogation. Within a day the news was out. Sitting in his study the following evening, the diarist Narcissus Luttrell recorded that 'Stephens the messenger seized one Edwards for printing libells against the government'.

Nine months later, in the midst of a major assault on the remnants of the Jacobite community in London, Edwards once again stood 'accused upon oath, for printing, publishing or dispersing seditious and treasonable libells against the government'. This time Stephens's colleague John Gellibrand led the investigation. It took him a fortnight to root out the culprit, but eventually Gellibrand managed to capture 'a private presse for printing in the custody of one Edwards, and with it many scurrilous pamphlets'.

The charges were not presented until 28 August 1695, at which point no further action appears to have been taken. The initial delay and absence of a sentence look suspicious. Possibly Edwards had friends inside the secret service. When Richard Kingston made detailed enquiries into those messengers who also worked for the Jacobites around that time, he unearthed information that one William Jones 'receives gratuities from the club at the Dog near the palace gate Westminster'. According to one of his closest friends, Edwards also drank at the Dog 'with the rest of his brethren', surely a reference to the 'club' served by Jones. A government messenger like Jones would have been a powerful ally for an underground printer at the start of his career.

Later that autumn, Robin Stephens informed the Privy Council that he had finally caught Edwards in the act. He had stormed the workshop on Nevil's Alley and seized a run of Catholic prayer books from the press 'as the same was printing'. The books contained 'severall seditious matters', including prayers for the restoration of the exiled Jacobite heir. The Council ordered Stephens to call on the Attorney General and present him with a copy of the offending book, encouraging him 'forthwith to prosecute the said David Edwards according to law'. And yet, as in all the other cases that year, nothing came of the charges. Precisely how Edwards managed to slip through the net once again is a mystery. Perhaps he just got lucky; the Attorney General had more urgent matters to address. Maybe he greased the correct palms. Either way, this streak of good fortune was not to last.

Mary was born into the book trade; Edwards had only been adopted by it and could just as easily be disowned. His clandestine activities irritated his superiors in the Stationers' Company, who believed illicit work brought the trade into general disrepute. In the summer of 1696 they initiated legal action against Edwards. The Company's representative, an experienced lawyer named Charles Howes, accused Edwards and a pair of rogue booksellers of printing or importing from 'partes beyond the seas' many 'greate numbers or quantityes' of primers and almanacs. Technically the Stationers' Company enjoyed a monopoly over the printing of these primers and almanacs, under the terms of a royal patent granted in 1603. Any unauthorised printing of materials covered by the patent was deemed to breach this contract.

Usually such matters would be handled internally. The problem in 1696 was that Edwards had published these books 'in soe clandestine and fraudulent a manner' that the Stationers' Company was 'not capable to make precise proof thereof' without the assistance of a court ruling. Edwards declared that he was being set up. He had printed the books at the request of one William Spiller, he said, who told him that the order was sanctioned by Company officials. Spiller had since gone back on his word, accusing Edwards of printing the books without the Company's authorisation. It led the printer to believe that Spiller was being paid to incriminate him. His treachery was yet further evidence that senior members of the Stationers' Company 'for some years have had hatred and spleene against' him, he complained.

Edwards had other reasons to be nervous. Legal action might bankrupt him, but perhaps a greater worry was that scrutiny might expose his proximity to certain recent affairs of state. Fears of a Jacobite invasion had been growing steadily ever since Newbolt and Butler were caught printing James II's declarations in 1693. In February 1696 government officials thwarted a Jacobite cell in their attempt to assassinate King William while he hunted deer on the banks of the Thames. A lengthy series of public trials began the following month. Within a year, nine of the conspirators had been executed and several dozen were detained in Newgate without trial. One of Mary's cousins, the Jacobite adventurer James Counter, was among those incarcerated, despite having arrived in England only after the conspiracy had been foiled. With their money spent, the accused inmates relied on charitable handouts. Mary was their saviour, bringing parcels of food and clean clothes to their Newgate cell, and paying off jailers to ensure preferential treatment for them. Without her help, wrote one prisoner, 'I must certainly perish'.

In the aftermath of the discovery, London's pamphleteers went into overdrive. According to one informed source, writing in June, the conspiracy was 'one of the greatest that ever was form'd against our laws and religion'. Writers loyal to the Williamite regime were quick to attribute the discovery of this plot to divine providence, rather than to a combination of treachery within the Jacobite ranks and a sophisticated government intelligence network. They were equally swift in blaming Jacobite printers and publishers for stoking the flames of sedition. Seldom had there been a more hostile atmosphere in which to print texts supporting the Stuart claim to the throne. But this did not stop Edwards from printing a virulent piece of Jacobite propaganda, a poem called *The Anti-Curse* which attacked the 'damn'd rebellious brood' who 'basely did King James depose'.

Edwards's worst nightmares were soon realised. One morning he awoke to the sound of Robin Stephens pounding on his door, two constables by his side, demanding to search the house. Stephens made a beeline for the printing room and, rummaging beneath the press, found copies of *The Anti-Curse* bundled into a cubbyhole. Within three weeks of the Stationers' Company opening its lawsuit, Edwards was dragged before the Old Bailey and indicted for printing this 'most scandalous libel'. Stephens was summoned by the court as a witness and provided gleeful testimony against the printer, whom he boasted to have apprehended 'several times for such crimes, and it always proved to be popish work that he did print'.

Unlike Anderton before him, Edwards did not face the gallows. Stephens's evidence failed to meet the standards required for a treason conviction. Rather he was fined £50 and sentenced to stand in the pillory on three occasions, at the Royal Exchange, Cheapside, and Temple Bar. It was an ancient and humiliating punishment. Having climbed up onto a platform, the captive would be forced to bend forward, sticking their head and hands between two locking boards, where they would be left for hours at a time while being 'severely pelted by the mob'. Sometimes, the captive's ears would be nailed against the board, so that any jarring movements would cause their lobes to rip. Release would come only once their ears had been sliced off by the executioner's razor.

Survival ultimately depended on the temperament of the crowd. Occasionally, they were sympathetic. In 1693 two Catholic booksellers, William Canning and Francis Dormer, were sentenced to time in the pillory at Charing Cross for distributing King James's declarations. According to Luttrell, they were 'favourably used by the mob'. When Daniel Defoe was pilloried for seditious libel in August 1703, he wrote a poem declaiming his innocence, to be given away beneath the pillory. The gambit worked. Journalists hostile to Defoe were appalled by the sympathetic crowd who 'hallow'd him down from his wooden punishment, as if he had been a Cicero that had made an excellent oration in it, rather than a Cataline that was expos'd and declaim'd against'. Unfortunately for Edwards, the backlash against Jacobites in 1696 was severe. One citizen later professed his desire to venture down to hell for a quarter of an hour just 'to see what the devil did' with James II. If a man would go to hell and back simply to torment the exiled king, one can only imagine what he would do to one of the king's supporters laid bare and defenceless.

The experience of the Jacobite courier William Fuller shows how brutal the punishment could be. Later recalling his own spell in the pillory, Fuller wrote in shocking detail: 'I was stifled with all manner of dirt, filth and rotten eggs; and my left eye was so bruised with a stone flung, that it swelled out of my head immediately, the blow deprived me of my senses, and I fell down (not wilfully as some say) and hung by the neck.' Fuller was eventually dragged unconscious from the stocks, though not before serious damage had been done: 'I was a miserable object to behold, and hardly any that saw me thought it possible for me to survive. I was all over bruised from head to heel; and on the small of my back, as I stood stooping, a stone struck me, which being taken up was found to weigh more than six pounds.' He lost the eye.

There is no first-hand account of Edwards's time in the pillory. What happened cannot be known. He kept his ears, but the effects of his trauma can be felt in his professional output over the next two years. Edwards stayed quiet. Barely any texts from his press are known to survive from this period. Those which have survived are mostly ephemeral scraps or gallows pamphlets, although there is always the possibility that Edwards continued to print illegal books in secret. Government records indicate that close oversight of the press continued. In 1697 hidden presses were seized at Beddington House (a decrepit property outside London) and at a cheesemonger's shop on Vine Street in Bloomsbury, where, according to the neighbours, 'a noise like working at a press is heard every Sunday'. But nothing from Nevil's Alley.

The winter of 1698 continued to see illicit Catholic books smuggled into London. Searching the Thames customs house in October,

Gellibrand intercepted a 'great quantity of popish books', including bibles printed in France which were destined for an unnamed 'bookseller in the Strand'. On 18 February 1699, several MPs complained on the floor of parliament about 'great numbers of popish priests and Jesuits' in London who have 'imported great quantities of popish books, and keep schools to breed up and instruct children in the Romish superstition and idolatry'. One year later James Vernon, the new secretary of state, 'received information that great numbers of popish books have been lately imported'. Vernon authorised Gellibrand to seize those books wherever he found them. He would be busy. Another contemporary report neatly summarised the situation: 'popish books are forbidden to be sold, but now the booksellers' shops are full of them'.

Edwards's quiet spell after the pillory was not to last. By 1699 he was back printing controversial pamphlets with renewed vigour. He had another minor brush with the law after printing an anonymous satire about the defector George Porter, who had betrayed his Jacobite co-conspirators to the government three years earlier. When news of James II's death arrived from Paris in September 1701, Edwards rapidly printed a royal elegy sent by one of Mary's contacts abroad. This poem had been written in French by a follower of the Jacobites in France and was now translated into English, Edwards claimed, 'with very little alteration'. Controversially, the anonymous author dedicated this text to James's exiled son, whom Louis XIV of France now acknowledged as 'James III', but whom the English government knew simply as 'the Pretender'.

Further Jacobite documents followed quickly from Nevil's Alley, including two editions of *The Last Dying-Words of the Late King James* and, early in the new year, *The Memoirs of King James II*. In a daring and unusual decision, Edwards attached his own preface to the *Memoirs*, explaining how the manuscript of the French original came to him 'so solemnly recommended, that there is not the least grounds to suspect, but that they are indeed the last remains of this good king'. The translation out of the French, he wrote, was 'very faithful to the original', although the translator's 'being a foreigner, has made him,

I'm afraid, a little deficient in the beauties of our English language'.
Despite these misgivings about the literary quality of the *Memoirs*,
Edwards refused to apologise for publishing them.

> I know the world is base and malicious enough, and but too apt
> to censure falsly, and to make insidious conjectures, but the
> honesty of the design, and the regard every man ought to have
> for the memory of this great prince, will I hope, not only account
> for me, but withal recommend the book it self successfully to
> the publick.

It was a plucky move. Edwards was openly confessing his role in
printing Jacobite propaganda while also alluding to ongoing collabor-
ation with and connection to Jacobites abroad. These connections
were made still clearer by the appearance of *The Late King James His
Advice to His Son* early in 1703, for which Edwards once again found
himself in trouble with the law. Edwards recycled some of his earlier
preface for this new book, assuring readers that 'there is not the least
scruple to be made, but that it was written by the late king's own
hand', and, should any doubts over authenticity remain, 'the original
is ready to be produc'd'.

William III had followed James II to the grave on 8 March 1702,
after complications following a riding accident. Whereas the king's
supporters were reportedly 'overwhelmed with grief' by the news,
oppositional Tories were delighted. It was common knowledge that
William was a religious dissenter, despite his being nominal head of
the Church of England. The new monarch Queen Anne was known
to support traditional high-church values; she believed in the divinity
of monarchy and took seriously her role as defender of the faith.
While some on the Jacobite fringe considered Anne to be another
usurper, like William, most traditionalists thought she represented a
step in the right direction.

Anne had no children of her own, her last surviving son having
died of pneumonia two years earlier, in 1700. Consequently, the issue
of succession dominated her reign from the very start. Technically
Anne inherited the throne because she was named by parliament as

William's successor. But she was also the legitimate daughter of James II, with an impeccable Stuart bloodline: a hereditary queen as well as an elected one. According to the recently passed Act of Settlement, after Anne's death the throne should pass to her nearest Protestant relatives in the Hanoverian royal family. And yet, in a world where blood runs thicker than water, it was not beyond the realm of possibility that she might seek to reconcile with her exiled half-brother. And what then?

Edwards understood that the change of regime was an opportunity to expand the literary and journalistic side of his business. He was already the favoured printer of Jacobite sympathisers such as William Pittis, whose first collection of political fables, entitled *Chaucer's Whims*, he issued late in 1701. Edwards enjoyed a good working relationship with Pittis. Having abandoned a prestigious junior fellowship at Oxford in 1695 to pursue a literary career in London, Pittis soon fell in with an unruly crowd. He was a drinker among drinkers, brash in conversation, and careless in the company he kept at the Rose tavern, where wits such as Ned Ward, Thomas D'Urfey, and Tom Brown made their base, on the corner of Cross Keys Alley and the Strand. According to contemporary reports, the Rose was a 'well customed house with good conveniences of rooms and a good garden' where, in the stifling city heat of summer, patrons could relax beneath an arbour 'where the sun very rarely comes, and has had ripe grapes upon it'.

More importantly, the landlord sold excellent wine. Ward himself described the Rose as an establishment 'where wine, according to its merit, had justly gain'd a reputation'. Besides the usual varieties of weak and strong beers from wooden casks, the Rose sold brandy by the glass and jugs of imported wine: hearty French clarets, fortified port and sherry from the Iberian peninsula, or sweet wines from the Canary Islands and Madeira. Ward and his comrades would haunt the 'snug room, warm'd with brush and faggot, over a quart of good claret', where they would toast one another's health, reminisce, and chuckle over their evening escapades.

Pittis appreciated decent French wine as much as the next man, and probably a good deal more than most. The bookseller John Dunton had almost nothing good to say about Pittis, with the exception of some grudging remarks on his capacity as a drinker: 'I'll say that for him, he never baulks his liquor. He'll guzzle more at a sitting than wou'd keep a family a month. His sound brains are potent, and can bear claret.' Pittis found a kindred spirit in the middle-aged satirist Tom Brown, who was rumoured to have drunk the Devil himself under the table at the Wonder tavern, albeit only after the aforementioned Devil had 'promis'd to discharge his reckoning' – that is to say, agreed to pay the bill. In 1697 Pittis and his fellow 'lads at the Rose' launched the first volume of their new poetic journal, the appropriately titled *Miscellanies Over Claret*, which, the title page of the first issue claimed, would be 'continued monthly from the Rose tavern without Temple Bar'.

His love of the grape could, admittedly, land Pittis in trouble. Dunton himself thought that it was 'a great pity' that he drank so much because 'when he reels, and foams, and swears, he's a blemish to the humane nature, and below the dignity of a reasonable creature'. 'By this practice', he continued, Pittis 'ruines his own health, turns the gifts of providence to a wrong use, and in the end will prove the greatest enemy to himself.' Although Edwards apparently preferred to drink with the Jacobite gang at the Dog tavern, it was at the Rose where he was most often glimpsed with Pittis. In an issue of the *Observator* devoted to character assassination of Tory journalists, John Tutchin singled in on Pittis, writing that he 'never fights but when he's drunk, nor then neither; but when his Welch printer's with him, to fetch him off again'. Tutchin appears not to have known his name, but this Welsh printer who moderated Pittis's loutish behaviour can only have been the man from Flintshire. Within days of this allegation, Pittis penned an article defending his 'old friend Davy' against Tutchin's abuse.

In the summer of 1703 Pittis and Edwards hit on the notion of launching a new periodical. This was not Edwards's first foray into the potentially very lucrative but equally risky newspaper market. His first two ventures in this field had failed spectacularly. He had taken on the printing of *The New State of Europe* in the summer of 1701 with the aim of reaping a quick profit. Advertisement spaces were prominently touted at two shillings apiece, while an annual subscription to the paper would cost a hefty eight shillings and eightpence. Edwards knew the paper needed a quick cash injection from subscribers to become financially viable. By 20 September, however, Edwards had lost his rights to print the title and the job was duly taken over by the reliable jobbing printer John Matthews at Pilkington Court. The following year Edwards launched another short-lived thrice-weekly periodical called the *Poetical Observator*, which, as the title suggests, was designed to challenge John Tutchin's populist Whig newspaper the *Observator*. Surviving copies of Edwards's newspapers are few and far between. These were ephemeral products, doomed to become, in Dryden's delicate phrasing, 'Martyrs of pies, and relics of the bum'.

Yet Pittis had a nose for scandal that could sustain a profitable newspaper on a longer footing. His new periodical *Heraclitus Ridens* immediately established itself as the principal voice of Tory journalism in London. Pittis aimed to combat the republican impulse of Tutchin's journalism with a rival vision of English society. He openly abhorred the radical interpretation of Whig principles espoused by Tutchin, and instead devoted his energies to fostering a doctrine of hereditary monarchy and loyalty to the Stuarts, whose rule he hoped 'may last *as long as the sun and moon endureth*, notwithstanding the wishes of some pretended Protestants to the contrary'. Indeed, Pittis proudly reproduced letters sent from hostile readers who attacked *Heraclitus* on the grounds that it was 'destructive of the principles the revolution stands upon'. He wore such complaints as a badge of honour.

Through the energies of his friend Pittis, and through Mary's overseas connections, Edwards established himself as a specialist in scandal. Despite numerous brushes with the law over the past decade and traumatic periods in jail and the pillory, his business continued to exploit each unfolding controversy. It was how he had been trained. Those years of underground printing under the tutelage of Thomas Braddyll had left their mark. By the reign of Queen Anne, he had established himself as the go-to printer for Tories and Jacobites and, thanks to Mary's association, for Catholics too. He was a trade insider, not a publishing celebrity like some of his colleagues on Fleet Street. Through the anonymous newspapers and pamphlets emerging from his workshop, Edwards made his mark in the coffeehouse and the tavern, in the private salon and around the tea table, on the floor of parliament and in the corridors of power. Beyond his friends and associates in the trade, few knew of his activities and he was happy to keep things this way. Soon, though, his circumstances would change. The name 'David Edwards' would once again be murmured in the coffeehouses and on the streets.

CHAPTER FOUR

Inamicable Collisions

'Was there ever such a time of scribble in England?' John Tutchin asked the question in the summer of 1705, though he was neither the first nor the only one to do so. Each week it seemed as though yet another enterprising printer was launching a fresh journal to grace the tables of London's coffeehouses. 'He that comes often' to a coffee-house, observed another pamphleteer, 'saves two pence a week in gazzets, and has his news and his coffee for the same charge.' It was a meeting point for 'idle pamphlets, and persons more idly employed to read them'. The constant appearance of new titles prompted some coffeehouse keepers to complain that 'when a newspaper is first set up, if it be good for any thing, the coffee-men are, in a manner, obliged to take it in: and a paper once received into a coffeehouse, is not easily thrust out again' because 'customers seeing it once in his house, always expect to see it again': 'every paper in a coffeehouse has its set of partizans, to whose humours and understandings it is better suited than the rest. And if a coffee-man turns a foolish rascally paper out of doors, 'tis ten to one but some or other of his customers follow it, and he sees no more of them.'

All those newspaper subscriptions added up: some coffeehouses would spend more than £20 a year on papers alone, more than the annual earnings of most servants. The more resourceful coffeehouse keepers cultivated links with the book trade to ensure discounts and preferential treatment. Members of the book and coffee trades often lived cheek by jowl. John Shank, the long-time proprietor of Nando's coffeehouse on Fleet Street, was also the major distributor for Abel

Roper's newspaper the *Post Boy*. His next-door neighbour was a deter-
mined young publisher called Bernard Lintot, who would soon poach
the equally young and ambitious poet Alexander Pope from his older
rival Jacob Tonson. Equally, newsmongers relied on the coffee men
to keep their papers afloat.

Some contemporary Whigs lauded the coffeehouse as the key site
of rational, enlightened culture, encouraged by access to printed
newspapers and pamphlets. Through the pages of his periodical the
Spectator, Joseph Addison smirked that he had 'brought philosophy
out of closets and libraries, schools and colleges to dwell in clubs
and assemblies, at tea-tables, and in coffeehouses'. He had, in truth,
done nothing of the sort. The patrons of an establishment like
Nando's would sooner have recognised the coffeehouse as a bois-
terous forum 'where haberdashers of *political small wares* meet, and
mutually abuse each other, and the publique, with bottomless stories,
and headless notions'. One was more likely to encounter vexatious
party rags such as *Heraclitus Ridens* or the *Observator* than the sober
philosophy promised by Addison and his cronies. Rational, 'enlightened' customers were few and far between. An engraving of 'The
Coffehous Mob' published in 1710 captured a typical scene of strewn
newspapers and pamphlets, with one patron hurling a cup of coffee
into the face of his neighbour while another tries to restrain him.
Coffeehouses were less sites of balanced debate than of sectarian
conflict.

In the face of overwhelming public discord, the central question
of the age was how this collection of factious individuals could be
bound together into a single coherent society. Balancing the concerns
of individual freedom and social order proved difficult. John Locke
had died in the autumn of 1704, though his disciples continued to
champion the cause of liberty. Coffeehouse habitués such Addison
and the third Earl of Shaftesbury held fast to the belief that man was
naturally an urbane, sociable, and virtuous animal. Only under proper
conditions of freedom could man fully realise his natural condition.
After all, if men were not free to act by their own consciences, their
actions could never be truly virtuous. Unfettered access to the marketplace of ideas was therefore essential to a flourishing society. 'All

politeness is owing to liberty', Shaftesbury claimed. 'We polish one another, and rub off our corners and rough sides by a sort of *amicable collision*. To restrain this is inevitably to bring a rust upon men's understandings.'

Building on the notion that true public virtue required independent thought, both Shaftesbury and Locke rejected prescriptive religious dogma. The domain of civil government included life, liberty, and property; but religious belief was a private matter which could not be regulated by external authority. Salvation ought to be a concern for individuals, not the state. Equally, they argued, no matter how fervently the state compelled citizens to observe particular religious practices, it could never force them to hold certain beliefs. Punishment and persecution might coerce people to go through the motions, attending church or swearing oaths, but they would do so as hypocrites. Their souls would remain their own. 'A sweet religion, indeed, that obliges men to dissemble, and tell lies to both God and man, for the salvation of their souls', wrote Locke. 'If the magistrate thinks to save men thus, he seems to understand little of the way of salvation.' Attempts to enforce religious uniformity would be doomed to failure, according to Locke. Instead of persecuting those who held different religious views, people ought to embrace the intellectual diversity of their age.

Shaftesbury's faith in human nature was not borne out by the everyday experiences of his contemporaries. Basic assumptions about human nature underpinned the teachings of Locke and Shaftesbury, assumptions that collapsed under scrutiny. There was nothing '*amicable*' about the collisions that occurred in coffeehouses and taverns across London. Tutchin was himself beaten to death at the age of forty-three, probably by thugs hired by his political opponents. With the civil unrest of the previous century firmly in memory, few were inclined to believe that man was a naturally polite animal. It was abundantly clear that Shaftesbury mixed in exclusive urbane circles, with fellow Whigs of impeccable breeding and turgid manners. Real people simply did not behave in the idealised manner that Shaftesbury claimed. His suggestion that society would be more cohesive if citizens were free to follow their instincts could be disproved by the merest glance at the streets of London or at the common parlours of the coffeehouses. Morality and virtue were far from natural urges. Soon critics were dismissing Shaftesbury's theories as 'pompous nonsense'. To the coffeehouse regular, observing his rowdy peers from the corner seat at Nando's, polite sociability was a pipe dream.

Shaftesbury's vision of society emphasised liberty and individual freedom, but offered nothing about how to secure them against external forces. Nobody could be said to have contributed more to the protection of English liberties from foreign powers than John Churchill, Duke of Marlborough. By this time, England had been at war with France and Spain for the best part of three years. Under the terms of the peace treaty signed at The Hague in 1698, upon the death of Charles II of Spain, the Spanish throne was supposed to have passed to the House of Habsburg. Instead, in 1700 Charles left his throne to Philip of Anjou, the Catholic grandson of Louis XIV of France. The balance of power in Europe had been precarious for decades. This action tipped the scales firmly in France's favour. Within days of her coronation in 1702, Anne joined the Dutch Republic and Holy Roman Empire in their Protestant crusade to curb the growth of French dominion throughout Europe.

Marlborough led the queen's armies on the Continent. He possessed a genius for strategy, rallying the allied forces to great victories at Landau, Limbourg, and Blenheim. It did not take long for the general to become a source of national pride. Reports of the war raging across the Channel did much to unite the nation under a single banner. All across the country, people read about Marlborough's exploits in the newspapers, chanted songs about his triumphs, and heard parish vicars lauding his example in their Sunday sermons. Hundreds of poems and pamphlets appeared in praise of the duke. Some of them, such as Addison's famed text *The Campaign*, elevated him to the level of demigod, riding in the whirlwind and directing the storm of war. Excited crowds had welcomed Marlborough back to London in the autumn after the Blenheim victory of 1704, lining the streets, hanging out of windows, and waving banners as he marched in triumph to St Paul's. Marlborough and his soldiers were not merely protecting

English men and women from enemies abroad, cheered the press. He was defending a national institution, the Church of England, from foreign popery.

At this stage all England supported Marlborough's efforts against resurgent Catholicism; but there were also many who believed the church was being subverted by a domestic threat. Ever since the Reformation had torn the nation apart in the sixteenth century, tensions had bubbled between loyal members of the Church of England and the more radical Protestant sects. The same 'levelling' principles that had encouraged religious freethinking during the civil wars of the 1640s were also said to have endorsed republican anarchy and social upheaval, to have encouraged true believers to kill the king and turn the world upside down. Likewise, it was the radical Protestant dissenters who were behind all the skirmishes and riots and plots of recent decades, the legacy of men like Monmouth and Sidney and Ferguson. Their religious beliefs had been tolerated by society, but at what cost?

In her first speech to parliament, Queen Anne nailed her colours to the mast. She gave a rousing performance, declaring that, while she would 'be very careful to preserve and maintain the Act of Toleration' which protected the civil rights of Protestant dissenters, her own principles would always keep her 'entirely firm to the interests and religion of the Church of England' and encourage her to 'countenance those who have the truest zeal to support it'. For the Tory press, talk of true zeal suggested that Anne was opening up a second front in her religious crusade; Marlborough would protect the interests of the church abroad, while her parliament would be called to defend it at home.

This question of religious allegiance went to the core of the problem identified by Locke and Shaftesbury. In the eyes of the churchmen, the only means to forge a peaceful society was by imposing and enforcing spiritual uniformity. Flush with their landslide victory from the general elections of 1702, the Tories immediately targeted the religious freedoms enjoyed by Protestant dissenters. Technically, legislation made it impossible for a citizen to hold a government post without also conforming to the practices of the established church.

And yet because Catholics were the real target of this legislation, Protestant dissenters could bypass the penalties by taking communion once a year, a practice known as 'occasional conformity'. True churchmen hated this loophole and seized their moment to introduce a new bill that would outlaw occasional conformity. In their eyes, this action would herald a new era of unity in church and state.

The government had other ideas. For all the overtures Anne made to the churchmen in public, she handpicked her ministers from the political centre ground. Though a nominal Tory, the doddery Lord High Treasurer, Sidney Godolphin, was broadly sympathetic to the Whig interest. As generalissimo of the allied forces, Marlborough was Godolphin's deputy and likewise despised party factions. The Speaker of the House of Commons and newly appointed secretary of state, Robert Harley, gravitated towards the same middle ground. This triumvirate of ministers lived by the watchword of 'moderation'. They believed that, far from binding the nation together, imposing religious conformity would merely alienate the dissenters. In their estimation, unity could only be brought about by compromise, toleration, and cooperation. These domestic religious tangles were a needless distraction from the pressing issue of war with France. And whatever the intentions of backbenchers, the three ministers held all the real power.

A complex series of parliamentary skirmishes ensued between the hard-line Tories and a coalition of moderate MPs and ministers. With the House of Lords on its side, the government managed to dismantle the Tories' occasional conformity bill twice, but only after it passed the vote in the lower house. On the third occasion Tory MPs attempted to 'tack' their legislation against occasional conformity onto a separate bill raising money for the army. The thinking behind this convoluted scheme was that the Lords could not vote down the bill without also endangering army supplies. They must either accept both or reject both; and to reject the bill would put the army in grave danger. It was an ingenious plan, legally and morally dubious, and brazenly partisan. One insider labelled it 'too wild to succeed'.

So it was. By some dextrous parliamentary management, bribing and blackmailing the more pliable backbenchers, Harley managed to block the legislation before it could pass the lower house. Nobody had a greater knowledge of arcane parliamentary tricks and procedures than Harley. He was a politician to his fingertips, born with a natural talent for backstairs intrigue that, among friends, marked him out as 'a mystery, and a very great man'. He was 'sagacious to view into the remotest consequences of things', recalled one supporter, 'by which all difficulties fly before him'. But to enemies, Harley's powers of prognostication and love of secrecy made him little more than a devious and ingenious trickster. One of his political rivals, the straight-talking Lord Cowper, had little patience for 'that humour of his, which was never to deal clearly and openly, but always with reserve, if not dissimulation or rather simulation; and to love tricks even when not necessary, but from an inward satisfaction he took in applauding his own cunning'. Nonetheless, Harley's cunning could be extremely useful when directed against his and Cowper's mutual enemies on the Tory benches. His success in thwarting the bill drew a line under this particular attempt by the churchmen to muscle their way into government.

In the following spring of 1705, the general elections signalled a new opportunity for the Tories to strengthen their core of party loyalists. They campaigned on the basis that, whatever the Catholic threat from abroad, the Church of England was more seriously endangered by home-grown dissenters and their abettors in government: the self-proclaimed 'moderates' who had thrice blocked their legislation against occasional conformity. 'Church in Danger!' and 'No Moderation!' were emotive slogans, chanted by mobs of Tory activists and scrawled across banners. On the other side, Whigs smeared their opponents as extremists who would forget the war against France in pursuing their hostile policies against English dissenters. Emotions ran high. 'Parties draw up in little armies in the streets', reported Defoe from Coventry, 'and fight with all the fury and animosity imaginable', resulting in 'broken heads, bruised and broken limbs.' All across the country, sectarian violence erupted on the streets.

Partisan conflict was stirred by the press. One of the loudest voices was Dr James Drake, a Tory extremist who had previously been hauled before the House of Lords for writing incendiary pamphlets. His advice to voters during the previous elections had been to boycott candidates who subscribed to policies of 'moderation', for 'it is absurd to pretend a true love and zeal for any faith, discipline, or worship, while we knowingly labour to put those into power, who wish the destruction of 'em, or such as particularly favour those that do'. For Drake, the 'history of the last threescore years here in England, sufficiently inform us how little we are to trust to the mercy of any of our Protestant dissenters, of whatever denomination, whenever in power, and how little candour or justice we are to expect whenever they have but a dawning of hope to arrive at it'. Dissenters had not shown moderation or mercy to Charles I, when they executed him on that frosty January morning in 1649. The sin of rebellion was a stain in their blood. Drake saw no evidence to suggest they had changed.

His advice was much the same in 1705, though in his periodical *Mercurius Politicus* he had a new vessel to reach his public. The journal quickly found a receptive audience in the Tory corners of London's coffeehouses, where readers pored over Drake's assault on moderation. Under the current administration, Drake explained, the church was in danger. Any danger to the church was also a danger to the state, for the church was so interwoven with the constitution that 'the government can't long survive its fall'. He believed that dissenters, 'whose pride and conceit of their own gifts made 'em impatient of subordination in the government of the church, wou'd exert that levelling, republican spirit against the civil state likewise'. In short, those who openly opposed the authority of the church must also be 'secret enemies of the crown'.

Satirical poems followed, transforming Drake's words of sectarian violence into jingling rhyme. In his poem *Moderation Display'd*, the Tory MP and amateur scribbler William Shippen denounced the influx of new moderate-men into parliament:

> Be these, and such as these, discharg'd from court,
> The better genii that the crown support:
> Then in their stead let mod'rate statesmen reign,
> Practice their new pretended golden mean.

A notion undefin'd in Virtue's schools,
Unrecommended by her sacred rules.
A modern coward principle, design'd
To stifle justice, and unnerve the mind.
A trick by knaves contriv'd, impos'd on fools,
But scorn'd by patriots and exalted souls.
For mod'rate statesmen, like camelions, wear
A diff'rent form in ev'ry diff'rent air.

Nor was Shippen alone. His fellow backbencher Sackville Tufton soon published *The History of Faction, Alias Hypocrisy, Alias Moderation*, in which he characterised the dissenters with brutal clarity: 'religion is their cry, but money is their god; liberty and property their pretence, persecution and slavery their design'. Samuel Grascome, who had defended the printers Newbolt and Butler in the press nearly ten years earlier, was even more venomous. Recalling the harsh regime of Cromwell, he suggested that dissenters were out for vengeance:

[They] are so bloody-minded in their way, as to think it doing God good service to kill those who are not of their way, and call murther or rapine the carrying on the work of the Lord? This hath been their trade: and though at present the common cry is, Moderation, Moderation; yet it is meer scaffolding and covering their design, that they may once more get into their power to be at their old trade again.

For all their pleas of moderation and middle ground, Grascome believed the dissenters traded in blood.

In the battle for public opinion, printers and pamphleteers directed their attention to where the fighting was most fierce. One such location was the traditional high-church proving ground of Oxford. There were two incumbent MPs for the university, William Bromley and Sir William Whitelocke. Bromley had led the charge to outlaw occasional conformity, and his Tory credentials were beyond reproach. Whitelocke, on the other hand, was no thoroughbred churchman. Fifty years earlier his father had been a servant of the Cromwellian regime and, if contemporary gossip was accurate, he was truly a Whig dressed in Tory clothes. Nobody thought he could hold the seat.

Whitelocke's challenger was an industrialist called Sir Humphrey Mackworth. Mackworth was currently the MP for a minor constituency on the Welsh coast but now fancied himself a contender for the opening at Oxford. He had already made a name for himself in parliament as a hot-blooded churchman. Among his chief supporters in the university was Henry Sacheverell, a swaggering young don at Magdalen College. He had admired Mackworth since he first rose to prominence during the occasional conformity debates, when he had spoken 'so eminently' in defence of the church. It was even rumoured that Sacheverell had begun instructing his students to read Mackworth's political pamphlets rather than spending time on the works of Cicero.

Sacheverell understood the intricacies of university politics and was not above using dirty tactics to install his man. A few choice words whispered in the right ears, and soon groundless rumours began to circulate that Mackworth had the support of the highest Tories in the land. Pamphlets defending Mackworth's conduct were secretly printed locally by Leonard Lichfield 'at his private press in Oxford'. Other papers arrived from London, accompanying cases of good claret to help sway the undecided. Sacheverell masterminded some of these publications, though Mackworth himself also took a coordinating role, writing a public letter boasting of his past experiences and enviable connections in parliament.

The publisher George Sawbridge was well known as a supporter of the Tories, and contributed funds towards printing Mackworth's campaign materials, including £20 and 'a hamper of wine' for Sacheverell. It was a busy season for Sawbridge. He issued a full array of Tory propaganda, including Samuel Grascome's *Moderation in Fashion* and the colossal *The Ax Laid to the Root of the Tree*, in which an anonymous troublemaker denounced religious dissenters by asserting the importance of 'unity' in church and state. According to one advertisement for Sawbridge's shop in Little Britain, he reissued Charles Leslie's explosive tract *The New Association of Those Called Moderate Church-Men with the Modern Whigs and Fanaticks*, which claimed to unearth a plot by dissenters 'to undermine and blow-up the present church and government'. Even more incendiary was the anonymous *An Essay upon Government*, where another of Sawbridge's hacks savaged the emerging discourse of religious tolerance championed by John Locke: 'under the prolifick influence of an abus'd toleration', this writer spat, dissenters have begun 'crawling forth like locusts, first to darken, and then to devour the land'.

Such a prolific publisher as Sawbridge had cause to rely on multiple printers, David Edwards among them. Looking back on that spring, Edwards remembered Sawbridge asking him to carry an advertisement for Sir Humphrey Mackworth to Abel Roper, editor of the Tory paper the *Post Boy*, 'which was to admonish the university and town of Oxford to choose four churchmen'. The printer kept his activities for the Tories secret, refusing to put his name to any of the pamphlets he manufactured. But keen-eyed readers would have spotted that some of Edwards's decorative ornaments reappeared in a cheaply produced satire called *A Kit-Kat Club Describ'd*, which accused Whig grandees of tampering with the election results and which deployed the slogan 'O Monstrous Moderation!' Another pamphlet, anonymous but very closely resembling Edwards's output, attacked moderation as 'a kind of stalking horse, now made use of by the enemies of the church, till they get in gunshot of us'. And yet another, *The Countryman's Remembrancer*, praised Mackworth and other MPs 'who were most for promoting the bill against hypocrisie, heresie, and schism'. Through these slim, antagonistic books, Edwards found himself close to the heart of the action.

Robert Harley had been keeping an eye on several constituencies, but was particularly interested in Mackworth's campaign. He had done the arithmetic and knew that the Oxford election would be crucial to maintaining the balance of moderation in parliament. The government needed a safe pair of hands in the university. Harley had good reason not to trust Mackworth, who was a sly politician. Several years earlier, in 1701, Mackworth had dedicated his treatise *A Vindication of the Rights of the Commons of England* to the Speaker of the House, hoping to gain his 'favour and protection'. But his loyalty was short-lived. Only three years later, after Harley's appointment as secretary of state in 1704, Mackworth was implicated in a Tory conspiracy to oust him from the speakership. His untrustworthiness, combined with his prominent role in the occasional conformity debates, made him a particularly dangerous candidate for the Oxford seat.

At first Harley toyed with proposing a candidate of his own, a mild-mannered career civil servant called George Clarke, before refocusing his energies on securing a second term for the donnish William Whitelocke. Barely a fortnight before polling day it was being widely reported that 'Mackworth it is supposed will desist, for it is certain he will not succeed'. But Sacheverell had campaigned furiously and Mackworth's election had become a very real danger. Unlike the reactionary dons who bought into Mackworth's inflammatory rhetoric, Harley had observed Mackworth up close in parliament. He knew Mackworth could be a formidable opponent. To beat him, Harley would need to play dirty.

As one of the queen's chief ministers of state, Harley had access to senior university officials. Mackworth was a bundle of contradictions, he explained to them. Despite Mackworth being a high Tory, his father and grandfather had been ardent republicans; he was no true gentleman, having earned his wealth through industry and financial wheelings; nor was he even a true churchman, for his private views on godliness and theology were completely at odds with his public stance on the necessity of religious and political conformity. Harley laid out the situation in simple, stark terms. Should Oxford elect Mackworth as one of their representatives, the university would become a laughing stock overnight. It is testimony to Harley's mastery as a political operator that his persuasions worked. The university leaders rallied behind Whitelocke, whipping their subordinates into line. When the votes were tallied on 9 May, Bromley and Whitelocke were returned to their seats in parliament, with Mackworth only a distant third.

As though to underline these bitter divisions across the nation, the returning parliament was neck and neck between the parties. With no clear majority on either side, the House of Commons was gridlocked. For Harley, this was a victory. He was convinced that the electorate's failure to return a strong Tory majority would ensure only moderate, bipartisan bills would make it onto the statute books. However, the dissident grumblings in the nation's coffeehouses and taverns continued unabated. The elections may have solved the immediate legislative problems Harley faced in Westminster, but the question of how to unify a broken society remained unsolved. With the press amplifying fears on both sides of the political divide, it was a question that was becoming more urgent than ever before.

CHAPTER FIVE

Break All

A month later, just a short walk from Nando's coffeehouse, across Fleet Street and up Fetter Lane, David Edwards sat reading the manuscript delivered by the woman in the vizard mask. It was entitled *The Memorial of the Church of England*. When the woman first presented him with the loosely stitched bundle of papers, he had skimmed quickly through the opening five pages but no further. Now she was gone, he had the opportunity to study its contents in more depth.

At its core, the *Memorial* was an attempt to answer the same question that had puzzled Locke and Shaftesbury. How do you unite a broken society? The Whig philosophers saw the root of the problem as too much authoritarianism, too much power being exerted on an instinctively free people. The *Memorial* offered a wholly different diagnosis. All faction, all wickedness, all conflict could, it argued, be traced back to split religious loyalties. With so many wildly contrary religious sects preaching their message across the nation, of course English society was divided. Toleration would only make the problem worse. And the idea of 'comprehension', reforming the established church so that dissenters could be brought back into the fold, was an option that satisfied nobody.

The *Memorial* offered a third way: outlaw occasional conformity and cast the dissenters out of society. But first the churchmen would need to examine their own ranks. The manuscript begins:

Those that look no deeper than the surface of things, are apt to conclude without hesitation, that the Church of England is in a

very flourishing condition. Its dignities and preferments make a
very goodly shew and the patronage of the queen seems to
promise a continuance of prosperity. But for all this fine
complexion and fair weather, there is a hectick fever lurking in
the very bowels of it, which if not timely cured, will infect all
the humours, and at length destroy the very being of it.

The 'hectick fever' that endangered the church was no external force:
not the Catholic threat from abroad nor even the radical dissenters.
It lay in the 'bowels' of the church itself. Lest this seem like code, the
Memorial was warning readers not to be distracted by the radical
fringes of dissent, for, it argued, the real enemy lurked within:

The dissenters are not yet considerable enough for their numbers
(however they boast of 'em), wealth, or quality to bring about
any great change in the constitution of church or state. And our
church is too strong to be shaken, but thro' the treachery, or
supine negligence of its own members, or those at least that
pretend to be such.

Who were those treacherous 'pretended' members of the church?
None other than the moderate triumvirate of Harley, Godolphin, and
Marlborough, whom this author denounced as the 'abettors' of that
'old seditious, rebellious race of fanaticks and Whigs'. If the *Memorial*
was to be believed, these ministers were corrupt and venal liars who
were secretly engineering the downfall of the church, and possibly
even the collapse of all social order. It was a dangerous claim.

Although figures like James Drake and Henry Sacheverell had
attacked the forces of moderation and nonconformity, and a few bold
satirists had laid bare the negligence of particular government officials,
nobody dared accuse the ministers of such a pernicious, insidious
scheme. Such accusations were, in effect, a declaration of war between
the Tory backbenches and the ministry. Under the present government,
the *Memorial* argued, England teetered on the brink of chaos.
Insurrection was the only solution to this growing crisis. Once they
had managed to overthrow the moderates, the backbenchers could

begin their programme of religious persecution, casting the dissenters beyond the pale. With the dissenters gone, English society could be rebuilt according to the religious and political principles of the churchmen.

Having digested this material and fretted over the political implications, Edwards proceeded with caution. In preparing the manuscript for the press, the first task was to calculate how many sheets of paper would be required for each copy of the *Memorial*, a process known as 'casting off'. It was one of the most important aspects of any printer's work. Paper was his single largest expense. In order to make a decent profit from the edition, Edwards needed to calculate precisely how much paper was needed for each copy, which he could then multiply up to estimate the quantity of paper required for the entire print run.

While working his way through the manuscript with his pen, marking where each new sheet would begin, Edwards was forced to reckon with some of the author's more explosive claims. The seventh and eighth pages of the manuscript made him especially uncomfortable. The author had listed the names of several MPs who changed their stance on the occasional conformity bill, asking what 'wrought this wondrous change in 'em?' Edwards blotted out the names with heavy, looping scribbles. Then, for good measure, he scratched over the lines with fresh ink and, in the margin, jotted 'out with a blank'. Although the text was packed with incendiary material throughout, the printer was keen to avoid an unnecessary libel suit. The overall polemical thrust of the pamphlet would not be affected by his removing some of its less discreet flourishes.

As usual, the first set of proof sheets to come off the press was riddled with minor errors in spelling and punctuation. The process of eighteenth-century proofreading is usually invisible three centuries later. Because paper was so valuable, the waste sheets would almost always end up being recycled or repurposed. The proofs of the *Memorial* were duly cast aside, but, unusually for his time, Edwards kept notes on the process. He recalled how his 'particular friend', another Welshman named Mr Hughes, stopped by his shop each afternoon to help out. He would read the manuscript aloud while

Edwards cast his expert eye over the printed sheets: he would 'hearken while I corrected it, and all that he did was, after I read the first proof by the eye, and gave it the servants to amend the faults, I desir'd him to look upon the copy, and I read and corrected it a second time, as we usually do before we put it to the press, and his looking upon the copy was to prevent words being lost out, which will happen otherwise'. He would only trust a close friend with the manuscript, not some journeyman outsider.

Edwards took all the standard precautions to protect his identity as the printer of the *Memorial*. The title page bears no name, provides no information. For decoration he used the fleur-de-lis ornaments that had graced some of his most controversial books of recent years, including the Jacobite poem *The Golden Age* and Ned Ward's *Hob Turn'd Courtier*. He never used these decorative flowers on any book that also bore his name and address; they were for clandestine publications only. Maybe Edwards remembered the trial of William Anderton all those years earlier, when the prosecution had mounted their case on a skewed analysis of typography. There was no reason why the authorities could not also use ornaments to track down and prosecute those responsible for controversial pamphlets. Adding to the confusion is the fact that Edwards obtained all his ornaments second-hand. Other printers active in London also owned items of the same stock, including Jeremiah Wilkins, Charles Bill, and the music specialist John Heptinstall. It would be difficult for anybody to prove that the *Memorial* sprang from Edwards's press and not from any of those other three.

Two weeks passed before the woman in the vizard mask came knocking once again. By now the books should have been finished, she said. Almost, but not quite, explained Edwards. While the sheets were indeed all printed and dry, they were not yet stitched. That would take a couple more days and cost the masked woman five shillings. According to the printer, on hearing this news the woman was suddenly put 'out of order'. Edwards fetched some brandy to help calm her nerves. Before lifting her mask to take a sip, the woman asked him to turn his back while she drank. She explained that she still couldn't reveal her identity, though cryptically assured him that he might yet 'see her hereafter in publick to his advantage'. Edwards later recalled that 'she seemed frightened' on that evening. Before leaving, she urged him to 'burn the copy' she had brought to him a fortnight earlier: 'for God sake Mr Edwards', she begged, 'break all'. He ignored her warnings.

As he walked the masked woman to the door, Edwards noticed another woman waiting for her in the yard, unmasked and alone. Judging by her clothes, he guessed that she was of lower standing than the masked lady, possibly a servant. Casting back his mind to the original visit, he remembered his wife telling him how the masked woman had previously brought another woman with her to Nevil's Ally. Was this the same one? He stood in the doorway and looked a while as the pair scuttled away down Fetter Lane, pondering who they could be.

When the masked woman returned the following evening, this time unattended, Edwards questioned why she was in 'so great a fright' the night before? She did not answer him directly, but instead looked nervously out of the window. Something, or somebody, had distracted her. 'I hope you will prove honourable to me, for I see a man standing at the Swan door, which I am afraid is to dog me'. It was an odd reply. Was this shady figure an innocent bystander, in the wrong place at the wrong time? Or did the masked woman correctly believe she was being tailed? If so, had she also been followed the previous evening? In what capacity was the second woman involved? Edwards peered over her shoulder to the doorway of the Swan tavern. He saw nothing suspicious, just a few men huddled together, though he knew he could easily be mistaken. The books were still not ready, he explained. Once again, the masked woman would leave empty-handed. As she disappeared into the night, Edwards began to wish that 'he had not meddled with the book'. The woman never returned.

It took Mary another couple of days to finish folding and stitching the sheets into pamphlet form. Late in June, a ticket porter named John Fox stopped by her bookstall on Fetter Lane. He was the first of four to visit over the coming week. Porters were a ubiquitous presence on London's streets. Their principal work was as couriers, delivering parcels, letters, and cargo to and from any merchant ships at the docks. It was unskilled labour, though tightly regulated by the city. Members needed to pay for admittance into the formal brotherhood of porters, and would also need to shell out for a tin badge – the eponymous ticket – displaying the wearer's name. This had to be carried openly at all times, identifying the wearer as an approved worker. Ticket porters plied their trade at official stations dotted across the city, often near to coffeehouses and taverns. Fox's base was at one of the oldest stands, on Fleet Street. Like any other member of his profession, Fox carried his 'great badge' and a bag, from which he produced a letter requesting delivery of the pamphlets. Unfortunately, Mary was forced to ask Fox to return to his master, whoever he may be, and tell him that 'the things were not redy, but they would be ready by the next day at nine a clock'.

Around noon the following day a second courier named Thomas Gilbert arrived at Nevil's Alley bearing 'a letter and a crown piece' to pay Mary for stitching the books. He carried with him the matching half of the 'scolop'd paper' which the masked woman had given Edwards at their first meeting, to be handed over 'as a token for delivering the said bookes'. Edwards held up the cut edge of this token against his own half. It matched. He nodded and disappeared into the back room for a moment, before emerging with a bundle of loosely stitched pamphlets. Gilbert began to stuff them into his bag. It did not take long for both men to realize that this bag, which Gilbert had borrowed from a grocer on his way over, would not be large enough for the entire delivery. Between them, Edwards and Gilbert decided that he should take just two hundred of the books now, and leave the remaining fifty behind. Before Gilbert left, Edwards scribbled down a quick answer to the letter he had received. He 'apprehended trouble' from these books and hoped the author 'would take care to indemnify him' if the situation spiralled out of control.

Another two porters stopped at Nevil's Alley over the next few days. Finding nobody at home, one of those porters, a bumbling young man called John Davis, went over to Mary's stall with a letter addressed to her husband. The note was short and written in a spidery hand:

Sir,

I have kept my word with you, and have not published, and if you desire it will forbeare some time longer to give you opportunity further. Pray send by the bearer the remaining fifty which the bag would not hold the other day: Let that be the token, and in so doeing you may engage one, who may serve you more publickly hereafter.

Yours

The letter was unsigned. Mary did not want to hand over the remaining books without her husband's approval, especially not to a stranger bearing a letter of unknown provenance. Besides, Davis, evidently a newcomer to this line of work, had forgotten his bag. The following afternoon yet another courier, one Robert Povey from over by Lincoln's Inn, visited Mary with instructions to pick up the books. This time she relinquished them. Although there had been some 'refreshing showers' of late, the weather was still remarkably hot. Mary later remembered giving Povey 'a pott of drink' before he 'carryed the books away down Fetter Lane'. Running deliveries across town was thirsty work.

The remaining books were promptly delivered to all the major distributors: to Benjamin Bragg at the sign of the Blue Ball on Ave Maria Lane, to John Nutt at the Savoy, and to George Strahan, whose shop was located against the outer walls of the Royal Exchange. Bragg and Nutt were two of the major trade publishers in London, with more extensive distribution networks than any bookseller. They were middlemen, wholesalers who liberated retail booksellers from the financial risk of stocking large quantities of topical pamphlets. Printers would sell to the trade publishers in bulk, usually via an intermediary, and they would then sell pamphlets on in smaller quantities, and with a slight mark-up, to the retailers. Bragg and Nutt knew better than to ask too many questions. If Robin Stephens or another government agent inquired after the printer or author of an anonymous pamphlet like the *Memorial*, it was easier for all concerned if they knew nothing.

George Strahan was different. He was a young Scottish bookseller with a neat little shop at the sign of the Golden Ball, next to the Royal

Exchange. Since opening his business around 1700, Strahan had made a habit of publishing works of a Tory and Jacobite bent – precisely the sort of works that Edwards specialised in printing. The Welshman and the Scotsman were tied together by more than mere business. Edwards's erstwhile apprentice John Law, the son of a tailor, had been transferred over to Strahan in 1702, after a year at Nevil's Ally. More recently, Strahan had loaned money to Edwards to support his workshop, so the pamphlets were given in lieu of payment. At some point in the first week of July, Edwards dispatched a porter with a hundred copies of the *Memorial* to Strahan's shop. It would have been a familiar transaction.

On 7 July, the books went on sale. The *Memorial* was not advertised in any of the newspapers. That would have been foolhardy; dealings with journalists always leave a paper trail. But there were other, equally effective ways of touting a new publication. Going about his daily business at the Royal Exchange, a gentleman named Nathaniel Powell heard the title being 'cryed' on the streets. Wondering what the fuss was about, he dropped into Strahan's shop at the sign of the Golden Ball, where he found the *Memorial* displayed behind the counter. Complimenting Strahan on the pamphlet's 'very pretty title', Powell, a churchman to the bone, fished for information on the author's identity. Jonathan Swift had recently joked about precisely this situation: 'when a customer comes for one of these, and desires in confidence to know the author; he will tell him very privately, as a friend, naming which ever of the wits shall happen to be that week in the vogue'. Of course, Strahan could simply have lied to Powell, in the manner of Swift's imaginary bookseller. Or he could have made an educated guess. By the close of business on that first day, Strahan had sold a good chunk of his hundred copies of the *Memorial*.

The following day, Edwards called on Strahan at his shop. It was busy and the pair needed to discuss matters in private. Leaving customers in the care of his assistant, Strahan led Edwards down to the river. As they approached the water, the cries of tradesmen were slowly replaced by the cawing of gulls and the clattering of small watercraft. Handing over a few pennies, they hopped onto a waterman's boat and were rowed out into the Thames, beyond prying eyes.

Once on the water, the Scotsman 'pulled out' a copy of the *Memorial* from his bag and asked Edwards for 'more books'. So long as there was not to be 'any danger in it', Strahan proposed that they partner up on a second edition of the pamphlet. He would provide the funds. Edwards declined. He did not know why, he told Strahan, but the bookseller 'was particularly excepted against' by the masked woman. The *Memorial* must already have enjoyed exceptional sales for Strahan to suggest printing a new edition.

Assuming that Edwards and Strahan travelled upriver, towards Westminster, they would soon have passed by the confluence of the Fleet and the Thames. Watermen knew better than to approach the entrance of this stinking tributary, into which the butchers of Smithfield flung carcasses and other waste on a daily basis. In his satirical poem *The Dunciad*, Alexander Pope memorably used this intersection as the location for his contest of dunce publishers:

> To where Fleet-ditch with disemboguing streams
> Rolls the large tribute of dead dogs to Thames,
> The King of Dykes! than whom, no sluice of mud
> With deeper sable blots the silver flood.

If Edwards and Strahan *had* turned up the Fleet and battled their way through the ooze of 'dung, guts, and blood', they would have passed Bridewell prison on the left before gliding under the double arches of Bridewell bridge. Here, right 'by the ditch-side', on the eastern bank of the Fleet, was the seedy little bookshop of George and Anne Croome. They had also taken copies of the *Memorial* to sell. Old master George was a notable printer whom some 'would insinuate as though he favoured the Jacobites'. Although John Dunton believed him to be 'a man of more sense', government records show he was indeed apprehended at least once back in 1693 'for treasonable practices'. Like Mary Edwards, Anne Croome was deeply involved in her husband's business, stitching books and hawking pamphlets on the streets. Sometimes those pamphlets and newspapers were printed by George. More often, though, she acquired bundles of books from a wholesaler.

*

On 10 July, the hot and dry weather finally broke. That same day, with the clouds gathering, Harley was alerted to the presence of a new libellous pamphlet being sold in the city. His agent John Gellibrand had been keeping his ear to the ground. He heard about the *Memorial* during his daily rounds of the coffeehouses and, asking an agreeable gentleman where he bought his copy, learned that Anne Croome had been hawking the pamphlet from her little stall at the Royal Exchange.

Gellibrand immediately rushed over to the Exchange, arrested Anne Croome, and dragged her to Whitehall to be examined by his master. He worried that news of Croome's arrest would spread quickly. 'Sir the book has made a mighty noise and Mrs Croom having been taken from her stall at the Exchange there will be expected a prosecution', he explained to Harley, 'besides this woman has an ill character and her husband is a printer and a nonjuror, a viler fellow does not live.' At first Croome refused to 'bring forth the person of whom she had' the books, most likely because this information would have incriminated her husband. But Harley soon managed to squeeze from her the material he needed.

As Croome was dispatched to Newgate that afternoon, Harley drew up a new warrant based on the evidence she had surrendered. It contained instructions for Robin Stephens and Richard Hayward (now reinstalled as a messenger after the debacle with Newbolt and Butler) to apprehend David and Mary Edwards and members of their press team 'for printing, publishing and dispersing scandalous libels'. Despite their best efforts to the contrary, covering their tracks and working in secret, the printer and his wife had been exposed. Stephens and Hayward moved quickly, taking Mary and three servants into custody. Yet when the two messengers reported back to the secretary's office in Whitehall, Edwards was not among their captives.

Now gainfully employed as a government dogsbody after a career writing satires and political pamphlets, Daniel Defoe suspected foul play. He informed Harley of rumours that, several 'houres before his search, a person was sent privately to all the booksellers' and gathered in copies of the *Memorial*, to prevent them being seized. Defoe thought the leak may have come from Stephens, whose crooked dealings were well known. 'That wretch Stephens makes the govornmt perfectly impotent in these matters and the booksellers and he together makes sport at your orders', he told Harley. 'Indeed sir, I write this without private design or ill will to the man. His being a rogue was usefull to me, and I brib'd him allways to my advantage, but in this case they act under his patronage.' Gellibrand shared these concerns: 'the discovery of this book might as easily have been made as I can now go to Whitehall', he explained, 'if you had not been tricked by Mr Stephens your messenger to the presse'.

The truth of these claims is impossible to determine. Though Defoe and Gellibrand may simply have been casting shade on their professional rivals, both Stephens and Hayward were known as corrupt agents. And while it is entirely possible that they let Edwards escape, Stephens had never shown him any mercy before. More likely, the printer received news of Anne Croome's arrest and, fearing she might know where the books came from, sought to make his escape.

The ideal hiding spot would be distant enough from the city that he would not be recognised, but with decent communication links; he needed to keep abreast of developments in London. The Thames was the most obvious route of escape. When Newbolt and Butler had fled from Hayward more than a decade earlier, they set their sights on France. Edwards likewise had contacts across the Channel. His friends among the Jacobites included experts in smuggling people in and out of the country. Alternatively, he might head south to Portsmouth or Plymouth, or to any one of the many anonymous rural havens in the north. Edwards took a different approach. With his wife and servants in custody, the printer returned to his roots.

Ecclesia

THE
Memorial

OF THE

CHURCH of ENGLAND,

Humbly Offer'd to the

Consideration of all True Lovers

OF OUR

Church and Constitution.

L O N D O N :

Printed in the Year 1705.

PART TWO

The Hunt

CHAPTER SIX

General Detestation

Ever since his relocation to Frankfurt on diplomatic business, Henry Davenant had looked forward to receiving mail from home. His doting father, the famous pamphleteer Charles Davenant, himself the eldest son of the celebrated poet and dramatist Sir William, would regularly send family news and keep his son abreast of developments in London. Henry had not inherited his father's intellect. The court insider John Macky once described him as a 'very giddy-headed young fellow', while Jonathan Swift, in a typically acerbic mood, wrote simply that he 'was not worth mentioning'. But he was a good civil servant: reliable, industrious, discreet.

Today's post was unusual. Besides his standard shipment of official correspondence and a letter or two from friends and colleagues in London, Davenant took delivery of a 'strong box': a sturdy wooden chest, clasped in iron. It had been shipped over by his father a week or so earlier. Having lugged the chest into his private quarters, Davenant quietly closed the door and fetched a key from his closet, inserted it into the lock, and turned. Hidden within the box, an elaborate iron mechanism clicked into place. Davenant opened the lid. There, nestled among other valuables and confidential papers, was a copy of *The Memorial of the Church of England*.

It is not difficult to see why Davenant's father had sent the pamphlet in this covert manner. Despite the recent allied victory over the French army at Blenheim, relations with the Holy Roman Empire were on a tricky footing. The death of Emperor Leopold and accession of his eldest son Joseph put British ambassadors on edge. The new emperor had immediately set about reforming the imperial war council and sought assurance of Britain's ongoing commitment to curbing French military activity on the Continent. The last thing young Davenant needed was for an explosive pamphlet defending English anti-war lobbyists to be discovered on his person. He did not want to cause a diplomatic incident.

A week's march to the west, in a military camp on the outskirts of Corbais, the Duke of Marlborough sat reading his own copy of the *Memorial*. He had moved his temporary headquarters to the Belgian town two days earlier while his army continued to dismantle the French lines, and now found time to catch up on news from home.

> In this camp I have had time to read the pamflet called *The Memorial of the Church of England*. I think it the most impudent and scarolous thing I ever read. If the author can be found I do not doubt but he will be punished, for if such libertys may be taken of writing scandolous lyes, without being punished, no government can stand long.

Marlborough signed off this note to Godolphin by adding that, despite his objections:

> I can't forbear lafing, when I think thay would have you and I passe for phanaticks, and the Duke of Buckingham and Lord Jersey for pillars of the church, the one being a Roman Catholick in King James's reign, and the other would have been a Quaker or any other religion that might have pleased the late king. All these procedings makes me weary of being in the world.

This was a typical sentiment from Marlborough, who resented being dragged into domestic party conflict. Soon thereafter, having read some of John Tutchin's bilious journalism, shipped over from London together with the *Memorial*, he explained that he 'would be glad not to enter into the unreasonable reasoning of either party, for I have trouble enough for my litle head'. Understandable, perhaps, for a general in the midst of a transcontinental war.

Back home, the *Memorial* was provoking outrage. Some of the more ingenious figures in government saw opportunity in the mania. On a trip to Northampton, Lord Wharton 'was mighty inquisitive after the *Memorial*', asking locals 'how it took?' On 13 July, Gellibrand reported to Harley:

> The book is very heinously resented by all the friends of the government and I am of opinion that it is as fortunate a thing as could have happened to my Lord Treasurer and others, for it has animated some people of very considerable figure, who were before cool in the matter now to be extreamly warm in his defense and are become intirely party men for him and to shake off their former indifferency.

Ten days later the minister received a similar missive from his ally the Duke of Newcastle: 'I never saw a pamphlet stuffed with more gall, more falsehoods, and indeed more trivial stuff.' Surely the author must be 'short-sighted' because, far from bringing down the government, Newcastle continued, the only outcome was generating 'a general detestation against the book'. If only Harley would seize the day and catch the men responsible for the *Memorial*, he could tip the parliamentary scales in favour of moderation.

There was one snag in the plan. Edwards's involvement was common knowledge by September, when it was reported by the Whig journalist Tutchin. The printer's flight from London prompted questions about who he had been working for. Who wrote the pamphlet? Men and women swapped accounts in the taverns and coffeehouses. Some said it was a gentleman. No, replied others. They heard it was a clergyman. Still other voices would pipe up and offer their own theories. It was a disgruntled lord, forced out of government by Godolphin. What about one of the new journalists in town? Could the whole affair even have been an elaborate hoax, perpetrated by some unknown mischief-maker? The question was on everybody's lips.

From the quagmire of idle gossip and rumour-mongering, three names floated to the surface. The first candidate was the well-known

Jacobite pamphleteer and high churchman Charles Leslie, infamous
in his day for his scandalous newspaper the *Rehearsal*. Though not a
Catholic, Leslie was a leading 'nonjuror', the name given to those
who refused to take the oath of allegiance to William and Mary after
they took the throne in 1689. Tutchin hated the man. 'Not one of the
heathen priests who on their altars offer sacrifices to devils,' he vented
in the *Observator*, 'ever invented such inhumane forgeries, or vented
such diabolical malice against mankind as has that high church priest
the author of the *Rehearsal*.' While Tutchin stopped short of directly
accusing Leslie of having written the *Memorial*, he certainly implied
that he was responsible.

Leslie had his friends, too, notably among the campaign to outlaw
occasional conformity. 'Lesley, and his brood' would often be invoked
as the chief proponents of traditional Tory values. On 2 September,
the Oxford antiquary Thomas Hearne noted rumours that Leslie had
been 'taken up for being author of the *Memorial*, and that he has given
£1,000 bayle'. A week later Hearne, who sympathised with the views
expressed in the pamphlet, was downcast by this possibility:

> 'Tis said if Lesley be prov'd the author of the *Memorial* the
> Jacobites will be greater sufferers than they have been as yet;
> which makes several, who are well wishers to them (believing
> that the greatest part of 'em are men of conscience) wish that
> it may not be proved upon him, and that he would imploy his
> pen upon other subjects.

Hearne need not have feared. The Whig journalists were spreading
baseless rumours; Leslie had not, in fact, been arrested. Nor was he
the author.

Another possibility was the pamphleteer and Tory propagandist Dr
James Drake, whose screeching had dominated the general elections
earlier that year. Having been raised and educated at Cambridge,
Drake first emerged on the literary scene in 1693 when, according to
a sympathetic biographer, 'he made a visit to London, where being
soon made known to the ingenious, he was very much admir'd at all
places frequented by men of the *belles lettres*'. He did not receive

notoriety as a Tory mouthpiece until 1702, when he was hauled before the House of Lords for writing *The History of the Last Parliament*, a shrill attack on a clique of centre-ground ministers who, Drake alleged, were attempting to discredit the heir apparent, Princess Anne, with 'false and scandalous aspersions; and so far they carried the affront, as to make her at one time almost the common subject of the tittle tattle of almost every coffeehouse and drawing room'. In this, Drake asserted, the 'whole party' was 'instructed' by its leaders. When questioned about this specific allegation by the Lords, Drake answered simply that 'he came not thither as an informer to accuse particular persons nor wou'd he do it'; but also 'he cou'd not immagin that such discourses were so zealously, and so generally promoted without some evil design' at the highest levels of government.

Drake was acquitted after a court hearing but continued to be a thorn in the government's side. During the occasional conformity crisis he came out on the side of the extreme churchmen. Firmly in the mode of the *Memorial*, the inaugural issue of his periodical *Mercurius Politicus* contained an explosive article denouncing the present ministry's policy of moderation as 'a studied cheat, an artifice of a violent faction'. The similarities with the *Memorial*, which likewise assailed 'the specious, deceitful name of moderation', were enough to persuade many readers of Drake's involvement. But Drake's accusers could not have known, as Edwards did, that the woman in the 'vizard mask' had implied the author was both a landed gentleman and a prominent and influential politician. Drake was neither.

Harley was eager to keep abreast of these rumours. With David Edwards on the run, he had seen fit to release the printer's wife and servants to roam the streets of London. They could not be of much help without their master, he thought, and perhaps they might find something. Harley was disturbed by the pamphlet, of course, for its invective against the ministry. But the attack on dissenters was particularly worrying on a personal level, for he alone of the government ministers had been raised in a dissenting household. His father, Sir Edward, had been an oppressive puritan patriarch. And, when Harley first moved to London to take up his seat in parliament in 1689, his instincts had been those of a pious Whig. It took Harley several years to free himself of his father's influence, in which time he was exposed to the cynicism and underhand dealings of the house and discovered his natural talent for the subtle craft of politics.

Even though Harley quietly renounced his background as a Whig and a dissenter, and duly subscribed to the articles of the Church of England, he maintained many old friends among the puritan clergy. Indeed, it was this background that enabled him to preserve links with the moderate Whigs while also reaching out to the cooler Tories. But his upbringing made him a pariah in certain quarters, with the extreme wings of both parties levelling charges of religious equivocation. One Whig journalist even claimed the minister was 'a person who makes a stalking horse of his religion, and consequently an atheist'. And given his links to the dissenters, it was difficult for the churchmen to see Harley as anything other than a false friend, precisely the sort of 'pretended' member of the church against whom the *Memorial* railed.

There was also the possibility that the appearance of the book might be coordinated with other activities. He feared, with good reason, that the *Memorial* might be part of a broader conspiracy to take down the ministry. While Gellibrand was trusted to hunt down scurrilous pamphleteers and printers, Defoe was his man for coffee-house gossip. After a month of trawling for information, Defoe had news to send his master. He was convinced that Leslie could not have written the *Memorial*: 'I am fully possess't with a belief that not him, no nor Dr Drake, but the latter as a tool'. 'I cannot forbear assureing your lordship', he continued in a second letter, that although Drake 'might be the drudge or rather amanuensis in the work – his master the Duke of Bucks is as plainly pictur'd to me with his pen in his hand correcting, dictating, and instructing, as if I had been of the club with them.' Here was Harley's third candidate: John Sheffield, Duke of Buckingham.

In many ways the fit with Buckingham was good. The duke was widely known to have been a prop to the high-church faction in recent years. His refusal to take a new oath of allegiance to William after the failed assassination plot won him the praise of Jacobites such as John Dryden, who dedicated his translation of Virgil's epic *Aeneid* to

Buckingham, and he continued actively to oppose the government throughout the remainder of the 1690s. After the accession of Anne, whom he had courted decades earlier in the flush of youth, Buckingham emerged as a leading Tory peer, enjoying two years of policy-making before he was forced from court after the failure of the final occasional conformity bill in 1704. His recent change in circumstances was even mentioned in the *Memorial*, where the author listed those 'great patrons and asserters of the interest of the church' who had recently been 'turn'd out' of office. Buckingham had good reason to be disgruntled, then, and the means to support Drake's pen.

The story that Buckingham and Drake were in cahoots spread quickly. 'I don't know particularly what Drake has written,' wrote Godolphin to Harley, 'but I can easily imagine his great patron and his great zeal together may have encouraged him to meddle too much.' Newcastle described the 'style of this scandalous libel' as being 'as imperious as King John [i.e. Buckingham], himself, full of groundless assertions'. The ardent Whig propagandist Arthur Maynwaring soon penned a manuscript treatise responding to the *Memorial*, accusing Buckingham and his followers of declaring war on the dissenters. Even Thomas Hearne believed the rumour at first, writing in his journal that ''tis said the Duke of Buckingham is author of the pamphlett call'd *The Memorial of the Church of England*, and that he has sent to the Lord Treasurer to desist from making further search concerning that particular, being ready at any time to defend what he has said in it'.

Yet ultimately the weight of evidence was against Buckingham's involvement. Charles Davenant was a close friend of Buckingham at the time and 'was alwais satisfied of the contrary from his grace himself'. Buckingham's ejection from office was not so acrimonious as the Whig pamphleteers suggested. He retained his seat on the privy council. Moreover, Buckingham was in the midst of an ambitious and expensive building project, constructing a palatial home for himself on the former site of Arlington House in St James's Park. Later to become the main royal palace in London, Buckingham House was a time-consuming project. The duke's surviving account book meticulously records every expense from iron railings and 'brass knobs for windowes' to 'crimson velevet for chairs' to furnish his salon. Buckingham went to great lengths to secure valuable works of art to display in the salon, in which he was assisted by the pioneering art critic Bainbrigg Buckeridge.

Responding to accusations that he now spurned the court by 'staying in town at a season when every body else leaves it', Buckingham described his daily routine of rising 'about seven a-clock, from a very large bedchamber (intirely quiet, high, and free from the early sun) to walk in the garden; or, if rainy, in a salon filled with pictures, some good, but none disagreeable' where he would conduct all his 'small affairs, reading books or writing letters.' 'I am never in the least tired', Buckingham remarked, 'by the help of stretching my legs sometimes in so long a room, and of looking into the pleasantest park in the world just underneath it.' According to the ledger, he spent upwards of £5,060 on art for the salon alone, and a further £164 on pictures for the hall: well over £1 million in modern currency. Construction of the house itself cost above £34,000. Harley could not believe that so vain a creature as Buckingham would involve himself in the vicious and grimy world of clandestine polemic, especially not with a lowly printer like Edwards. He would need to look elsewhere.

Facing a confusing array of potential suspects, conflicting messages from his informants on the streets of London, and a printer who had seemingly disappeared into the wind, Harley had no option but to rely on his intuition. The minister was an inveterate reader of newspapers and pamphlets: well informed, articulate, penetrating. It was part of his duty as secretary of state to know who was saying what, a duty which required him to comb through texts looking for distinctive stylistic tics. He knew that ideas could be like fingerprints: the tiniest variations in form or expression render them unique. And, sitting in his Whitehall study reading through the *Memorial*, he was certain the pamphlet contained some ideas which he had encountered before.

One of the most curious features of the *Memorial* was that its argument for the importance of the church was grounded in the writings of Thomas Hobbes. Most churchmen believed that the state of nature was one of servitude to a divinely appointed monarch, whose authority over church and state was derived wholly from God. Consequently, in the mainstream Tory imagination, religious dissent and political rebellion went hand in hand as equally heinous acts of blasphemy. And yet the *Memorial* was no simple high-church rant. For though the fate of the church was at the heart of the book, God was barely mentioned. The pamphlet argued for the church's importance to society entirely in civic, secular terms: as the cornerstone of order and stability.

Harley had a sharp memory and would immediately have recognised Hobbes as the intellectual source of this position. Although the old philosopher had died more than thirty years earlier, his ideas remained shockingly relevant. So important that the radical printer John Darby had recently produced a new, clandestine edition of his masterwork, *Leviathan*. Unlike the orthodox churchmen, Hobbes conceived the 'state of nature' as, in his notorious phrasing, 'solitary, poore, nasty, brutish, and short.' Having witnessed the chaos of the civil wars, Hobbes understood that society was a purely artificial construct, created to lift man from his naturally brutish condition. He believed the pillars of this artificial state were civil and ecclesiastical power, channelled through the actions of the sovereign. In all Hobbes's writings, sovereignty was not a matter of divine sanction, but of strength. If the sovereign were to relinquish command or lose control of those same civil and ecclesiastical powers, man could not be kept in check. Society would collapse. Using similar language to Hobbes, the author of the *Memorial* argued that, in order to escape the 'state of nature', 'civil government was invented, and magistrates created, to terminate differences among one another, and by joynt force to repel and punish that violence, which separately they were not able to resist'. Here, as in Hobbes, the function of the state is to prevent sectarian conflict.

For the same reason, Hobbes famously took issue with the idea of independent religious groups, which he believed diluted the power of the state. His particular bugbear was the torn allegiance of Catholics, whose loyalties were split between their sovereign and the Pope. Split loyalties would always lead to faction, and faction to war. Equally, though, he knew the dissenters were guilty of using their theological principles to destabilise society. Dissent not only weakened the unity of the established church, but was often used as grounds for political resistance. The rapid growth of unestablished religion, spurred on by the seditious or borderline heretical teachings of some radical preachers, laid the path for what Hobbes called 'the kingdome of darknesse', where deceitful sects would use their 'dark, and erroneous doctrines' to corrupt the minds of the people and erode the power of the state. Yet there was still hope that the established church, as a fully incorporated arm of the state, might consolidate power and keep the darkness at bay.

One classic objection to enforced conformity was that genuine spiritual coercion was impossible. Locke had famously argued that no amount of force could persuade someone to surrender their sincerely held beliefs. Framing the debate in civic terms helped sidestep this complaint. According to both Hobbes and the authors of the *Memorial*, religion was not a matter of souls but of bodies. Salvation would remain a private concern, whereas the church was a political instrument for the regulation of public behaviour, the final line of defence against anarchy. Only by extinguishing heterodoxy, pluralism, and sedition could the nation be brought together. Dissenters must conform or face persecution.

Harley would have spotted the *Memorial*'s debts to Hobbes instantly. But he had also noticed similar arguments used recently, while studying the electoral activities of Sir Humphrey Mackworth. Although Mackworth liked to present himself as a doctrinaire Tory, his published writings betrayed some very unorthodox views. In one of his more successful books, *Peace at Home*, published in 1703, Mackworth had illustrated the necessity of 'unity and uniformity in the church and state' with the example of that 'long and bloody civil war in this kingdom', which arose from 'a mixture and confusion of men of opposite principles in one and the same administration'. Conflicting interests had led to faction, he wrote, and faction led to war. History was now in danger of repeating itself:

> We see a nation divided into parties and factions, and are assured that a kingdom divided can never stand, when we see by experience that churchmen and dissenters can never draw well together

for the publick good; that therefore *it is absolutely necessary to preserve uniformity in the state, as well as in the church.*

Mackworth attributed the growing discord within parliament to lurkers and republican infiltrators, set to 'undermine our constitution both in church and state'. In Mackworth's fevered imagination, Hobbes's vision of darkness was becoming a stark reality.

Though Mackworth focused overwhelmingly on what he viewed as the problems brought about by tolerance and pluralism, he was also interested in solutions. He thought citizens could fulfil their obligation to maintain peace and order in two ways: firstly, by choosing MPs to represent their interests in parliament; and, secondly, by conforming to the Church of England. Church and state were so intricately woven together that both those obligations must be fulfilled or none. If dissenters had the right to vote, how could their interests possibly be served alongside those of established churchmen? If the House of Commons was to govern with a single, unified purpose, how could it admit dissenters or their allies to its ranks?

Time and again Mackworth grappled with those questions in his published writings. Time and again he came to the same conclusion. Religious dissenters should not be represented in parliament. They ought to be stripped of their right to vote and cast from the franchise. Far more important that the House of Commons be unified than that it represent diverse and conflicting demographics. Mackworth repeatedly stated that there could be no peace in England unless the nation was united under one church as it was under one monarch. Mackworth endorsed precisely this stance in *Peace at Home*, which opened by arguing that dissenters, like Catholics, ought to be political outcasts. He gave the example of the Huguenots in sixteenth-century France: those who did not flee the country were either forcibly converted to the state religion or were subjected to heavy persecution. A similar ultimatum could work with the dissenters in England, thought Mackworth. Conform or pay the price.

These were unusual statements to come from a Tory mouthpiece. But Harley knew these ideas were not without precedent. He remembered the clerics and dons who supported Mackworth's parliamentary campaign, several of whom had warned how religious dissent would clear the path to a 'field of blood'. They worried not about the salvation of men's souls but about their earthly deeds. James Drake had written similarly about the civic importance of religious conformity. For him, matters of theology and doctrine were utterly unimportant when compared to the social and political utility of the church. 'Religion seems even by God himself to be calculated principally if not only for the sake of government', he argued with startling bluntness, 'that is for the better regulation of men's actions towards one another in this world.' Salvation in the world to come was irrelevant, Drake suggested; in *this* world, government came first; religion served government by regulating social behaviour.

Harley could see that the *Memorial* offered a variation on this theme. Besides its unusually personal salvo against the ministers, the pamphlet's emphasis on religious uniformity purely as a civic good set it apart from the dozens of anonymous high-church squibs which entered the market each week. Just like Mackworth's pamphlets, the *Memorial* was grounded in a thoroughly cynical view of human nature. The only way to prevent MPs from squabbling over religious policy was to ensure they were all 'men of fix'd and settled principles of religion'. Whereas Harley had devoted his career to the middle ground, seeking to legislate through compromise and negotiation between rival factions, the *Memorial* argued that parliament ought to be of one religion, one party, one purpose. If the authors were to achieve their aims, Godolphin, Marlborough, and Harley could not be allowed to continue in government. The ministry would need to change.

From his office in Whitehall, Harley could see the pamphlet was calling, if not for violent insurrection, then certainly for a ministerial coup. The question was whether or not such a scheme was already in motion. If so, Harley would need to move quickly. His political survival depended on it.

CHAPTER SEVEN

A Most Just Doom

Just north of the old city walls, where St John's Lane met St John Street, enclosed within a picket fence loomed an elegant Jacobean building. Hicks Hall was home to the Middlesex sessions court, hearing cases from all across London and Westminster. The Cross Keys tavern stood opposite and the famous cattle market at Smithfield was a stone's throw to the south, at the end of the street. Usually the area around Smithfield stank from livestock. But on the morning of 1 September 1705, the residents of St John Street smelt smoke.

A crowd gathered around a bonfire outside the Hall, where a masked hangman was tossing copies of the *Memorial* into the flames. The pages curled and blackened. Little flakes of charred paper were borne upwards by the heat until, caught on the breeze, they fluttered into the distance. Although this was a very public act of censorship, someone was missing. Seventy years earlier the radical polemicist William Prynne had been forced to stand in the pillory, choking in the smoke as his tract *Histriomastix* was burnt before his eyes. Nobody was pilloried outside the courthouse today. Both the author and the printer of the *Memorial* were conspicuously absent.

On the previous afternoon, the court's judgment had been unequivocal. The *Memorial* was deemed to have been

secretly, but industriously spread abroad, to advance and accomplish traiterous and wicked designs, highly impeaching the truth and sincerity of Her Majesty's royal resolution and pious assurances to support and preserve our government, both in church and state, the rights, liberties, and properties of all her people; and also craftily designed to reproach and scandalize her wise and faithful ministry, divide her councils, create variances, disputes, and discords in her parliament, and to raise and foment animosities, fears, and jealousies amongst all her people.

Having judged the *Memorial* to be a 'false, scandalous, and trayterous libell', the court 'ordered it to be burn't before them by the common hangman' and again outside the Royal Exchange and Westminster Palace in the following week.

Burning the book had not been Harley's idea. It was a significant gesture, but hardly effective as a mode of censorship. As the orthodox churchman Philip Skelton pointed out, the printers of condemned books often 'made twice as much by the retail of their counterband wares, as they lost by the prosecution'. Members of the House of Lords previously complained that 'a great number of books, the same with that ordered to be burnt yesterday, were dispersed and publicly sold in Westminster Hall, and other places'. Indeed, Harley's fear was that burning the book would rouse its supporters against the government. His concerns were shared. Even while Daniel Defoe was lauding the destruction of the *Memorial* as a 'most just doom', Thomas Hearne recorded one of his more temperate colleagues wishing that the *Memorial* 'had not been burnt', reflecting the concerns of the political centre ground.

Exactly as Harley and the moderates feared, the church party cried foul before the ashes were cool. One widely circulating manuscript newsletter, by the notorious John Dyer, brazenly accused the government of packing the jury with its allies. Of the dozen men who presented the *Memorial* to the court, ten of them were dissenters, Dyer alleged, and 'only two of the pannel churchmen, who refused to sign the said presentment'. Defoe promptly dismissed Dyer's accusations as nothing but 'impotent slander!' But that did not stop Hearne, who got much of his information from Dyer's newsletters, believing the prosecution was 'not at al to be wonder'd at, if we consider of what persons the juries consist, and who are the presenters'.

Within days of the *Memorial* being torched outside Hicks Hall, seditious 'elegies' on the now notorious pamphlet were circulating far and wide, with one manuscript having reached Oxford by 14 September:

> But we can you, immortal leaves, restore
> To former life; nor the hard fate deplore.
> Sure from your smoak some miracle must rise,
> As when an angel mounted to the skies
> And sanctify'd the flame in Manoah's sacrifice:
> Spight of thy adverse chance, thou shalt be read,
> Nor dye, till principle and truth be dead.

A few days later, on 18 September, an issue of William Pittis's new periodical, the *Whipping Post*, appeared containing a similar poem under the title 'Fire and Faggot'. As Edwards's old friend and drinking partner, Pittis had good cause to stand up for the *Memorial* and its printer. His doggerel made the connection between the destruction of the pamphlet and religious martyrdom even more explicit:

> Some would have had her all besmear'd with tar,
> And carry'd into Smithfield from the bar,
> Where saints of old eternal truths confess'd,
> Mounting from earthly flames to heav'nly rest.
> But wiser heads, who soon foresaw a tartar,
> Judg'd she from thense might have been stil'd a martyr,
> And sent her to th' Exchange, to make her sad departure.
> Since no one there cou'd be suppos'd to die
> Or for religion, or for loyalty,
> Virtues unknown (their practices a shame on)
> To such whose idol's gain, and God in Mammon.

Both these verses drew on contemporaneous descriptions of Protestant texts being burnt by Catholic oppressors in previous centuries. 'Books have souls as well as men, which survive their martyrdom,' wrote one Protestant chronicler, 'and are not burnt but crowned by the flames

that encircle them.' The same could be said of the *Memorial*. By relo-
cating the book burning to Hicks Hall and the Royal Exchange rather
than the site of past religious burnings at Smithfield, Pittis alleged,
the authorities had attempted to draw a veil over this association. If
that had been the government's plan, it failed. Soon the *Memorial* was
being touted as the 'manifesto of the Church of England' and the
'oracle' of a resurgent Tory party.

'Spight of thy adverse chance, thou shalt be read', promised the poems.
So it was. With Edwards on the run, his former business partner
George Sawbridge rushed out a cheap reprint, virtually identical except
for a handful of misprints. Although Harley's minions were quick to
seize this scrappy new edition, eager readers did not have to wait long
for another. Within two days of Sawbridge's version being confiscated,
Hearne gleefully noted that the *Memorial* was 'now againe publickly
sold about streets at London' with 'pretended remarks that are printed
with it [that] strengthen and not confute the assertions of the author'.
He was referring to a new pamphlet devised by William Pittis, *The
Memorial of the Church of England, Consider'd Paragraph by Paragraph*,
which reprinted the original text in full with commentary.

On the eve of its publication, Defoe alerted Harley to the tract. He
knew that Pittis's sympathies lay with the churchmen and guessed
this new pamphlet was 'done purely to sell' the *Memorial*, 'which the
town is eager for, and which I think the govornment is highly
concerned to prevent'. The idea of reprinting a scandalous book with
commentary was not new; often the government would turn a blind
eye because the commentary was hostile, written to expose the blun-
ders and inaccuracies of the original text. But in this case, as Defoe
informed his master, the 'answers are allways triffles'. It was enough
for Harley to order his men to hunt down the printers and 'search for
the author'.

When Gellibrand eventually managed to trace Pittis to a garret on
the outskirts of the city and make the arrest, the pamphleteer was
brought before Harley to answer for his crimes. Before Pittis was
interrogated, he was hopeful that Harley might be merciful. Such

hopes were misplaced. He was persuaded to sign a confession of his misdeeds and Harley, having secured this information, mounted a prosecution. Pittis later claimed to have been deceived by the guileful minister, who had promised 'that such a confession should be of no prejudice to him'. If Harley did indeed make such a promise, it had been a lie. In the following spring, Pittis would be dragged before the court of Queen's Bench alongside George Sawbridge, fined a hundred marks, and sentenced to stand in the pillory at Charing Cross and by the Royal Exchange, on the very sites where the *Memorial* had been burnt the previous summer. In the paranoid nightmares of some Grub Street hacks, Harley had now become a menacing figure, the 'president of the pillory'.

Prosecution and punishment were only one side of Harley's plan to counter the *Memorial* and its supporters. The second part of his strategy entailed persuading friendly writers to denounce the book. If he could not suppress satirists and mischief-makers through prosecutions alone, Harley reasoned he might also administer an antidote to the poison.

Ever since Harley recruited him to the secret service, Daniel Defoe had deployed his pen at the secretary's bidding. He owed his liberty to Harley's intervention two years earlier, following a spell in prison. Back in 1703 he had been exposed as the author of a pamphlet called *The Shortest-Way with the Dissenters*. Much like the *Memorial*, Defoe's pamphlet was an anonymous publication calling for the persecution of dissenters; but Defoe was in masquerade, for his true intention was actually to alarm moderates away from Tory policies. Through the guise of a fabricated high-church manifesto, he suggested the Tories were out for blood, that they secretly wanted the dissenters killed. It was an ingenious plan and very nearly succeeded. But once he was exposed as the author by his middleman, an unscrupulous wretch called Edward Bellamy, life became difficult for Defoe. Soon after it was published, *The Shortest-Way* had been censured by parliament, denounced as a seditious libel, and a reward issued for the author's arrest. The Tories whom Defoe had misled wanted to see him punished. Like so many writers before him, Defoe was pilloried and imprisoned until he found sufficient sureties to guarantee his behaviour.

Newgate was precisely where Harley wanted Defoe. The longer he was left to suffer the more desperate he would become. Defoe had already proved himself a gifted pamphleteer and the recent case of *The Shortest-Way* proved his cunning was compatible with Harley's own. How useful might Defoe prove if he was writing on behalf of the ministry rather than against it, as an off-books government propagandist offering a continuous stream of favourable press? 'I find Foe is much oppress'd in his mind with his usage', Harley informed Godolphin, 'and if his fine be satisfied without any other knowledge but that he alone be acquainted with it that it is the queen's bounty to him and grace, he may do service.' Soon thereafter Harley extended an offer of partnership, that Defoe would go free if he agreed to write according to Harley's instructions. The imprisoned writer grasped this opportunity with both hands.

It was Harley's idea that Defoe should begin publishing a weekly digest of news on behalf of the ministry, which launched in 1704 as the *Review*. While most newspapers were party rags, the *Review* was from the start an organ of moderation. Harley's initial aim was that Defoe's journalism could buttress support for the war against France, of which many Tories were already weary. But the remit of his mission expanded quickly. By the summer of 1705, Defoe's intentions were to draw the fringes of both parties towards the political centre ground. The extent of his success in this matter was disputed by Harley's enemies, though nobody could deny the newspaper's reach. Ned Ward grudgingly admitted that the *Review* was 'read most by cobblers and by porters'. And Charles Leslie, who feared the *Review* was secretly indoctrinating the public with Whig principles, noted that although many among the lower sort 'cannot read at all', they would 'gather together about one that can read, and listen to an *Observator* or *Review* (as I have seen them in the streets) where all the principles of rebellion are instilled into them'. Defoe's audience was broad indeed.

Naturally, when Harley needed to return fire against the *Memorial*, his first move was to contact his loyal writer. On 10 July, within days of the pamphlet going on sale, Defoe sent Harley the draft of a hastily scribbled response. He included a note stating that he would revise the text according to 'any hint' Harley should provide, adding that 'it should be in the press today if possible'. Two days later the *Review* ran a column urging the government to prosecute the authors of this 'virulent pamphlet', the *Memorial*. 'Of all the lampoons, invectives, satyrs, or defiances that these latter ages of scribbling have produc'd, I may challenge all the nations in Europe, to shew me the fellow to it.' And Defoe's full-length riposte, *The High-Church Legion*, was published within the week.

Defoe's pamphlet was caustic in tone, countering the venom of the *Memorial* with its own strain of acid sarcasm. A more dignified response was in progress. In his lifetime John Toland was a massively controversial figure. An Irishman by birth, Toland's unusual religious views and republican outlook united him with the radical printer John Darby, who would print many of his works. He and Harley had come into contact during the previous reign, while Harley was still a junior politician rising through the ranks. The two men had agreed on many things: on the importance of governing without parties and of resisting corruption. But Toland's ambition and academic pretensions eventually drew him overseas to the elite intellectual circles of the Hanoverian court.

When Toland returned to England in 1704 he was eager to offer his services as a thinker and as a writer to the government. The latter skill would prove more useful to Harley. Unlike Defoe's hurried scribblings, Toland's response to the *Memorial* was a measured tract of more than a hundred pages, titled *The Memorial of the State of England*. Clear of expression and persuasive in its reasoning, Toland's rebuttal emphasised the importance of a unified Protestant front against the Catholic threat abroad. The only way to achieve this, he explained, was through the moderate principles advocated by Harley and other members of Godolphin's cabinet. Compromise and cooperation were the English way, whereas the churchmen's hard-line calls for religious and political uniformity smacked of French absolutism. Naturally, Toland was thrilled to learn that his defence was favoured by the queen and the ministers, describing their endorsement as 'no small satisfaction to me'. But given the book's content, he could not have been surprised.

*

Harley had additional reasons to want Defoe and Toland working to his brief. Ever since he had been appointed secretary of state in 1704, backbenchers had been murmuring about the incompatibility of this post with his other role as Speaker of the House. It was a conflict of interest, they complained. How could Harley be both a servant of the court and a servant of parliament? With the newly returned House of Commons evenly split, Godolphin believed it would be necessary to secure additional Whig support for the ministry. This support came at a price: that Harley should resign the Speaker's chair. Having always tried to build his coalition from moderates across both parties, Harley was not pleased by the arrangement. But he understood that the current numbers were unfavourable to his scheme and duly stepped aside for a new candidate to take his place, one who would receive the support of both Whigs and moderates.

The candidate on whom Godolphin eventually settled was an undistinguished and wearisome courtier called John Smith. Technically Smith belonged on the Whig benches, but he was known to be pliable to the interests of the ministry. Godolphin's friends among the Whigs would promote his candidacy in their party, while Harley would be called on to persuade the Tory moderates to break ranks and vote for Smith. Harley had his work cut out. After he had worked so industriously to sink the occasional conformity bills, many among the Tories now viewed him as a turncoat and had proposed their own candidate for the position: William Bromley, a pompous churchman and long-standing university MP for Oxford. Bromley had been one of the primary movers behind the Tory attempts to outlaw occasional conformity during the previous parliament and was known as a champion of the church.

Going into the opening session of parliament, Bromley's supporters seemed buoyant. Lord Paget was informed in late September that 'the high church party amongst us are very confident that Mr Bromley will be chosen Speaker of the House of Commons'. Around the same time, Lord Thanet wrote to his friend James Grahme: 'I find by your calculation you conclude Mr Bromley is sure of it.' The tide of public opinion was behind a high-church candidate, they thought, although Thanet himself was less certain: 'it will be so near that one vote may save or lose it'. Having lost their majority in the general elections, Bromley's selection as Speaker was the churchmen's last hope of thwarting a moderate government. Only three days before the first sitting of the new parliament, 'a great number of loyal church' MPs was reported to have met at the Fountain tavern 'to consider of their strength for the choice of Mr Bromley to be Speaker'.

James Drake led the press campaign for Bromley. He used the pages of *Mercurius Politicus* to explain the qualities that a good Speaker ought to possess, and the vices that should disqualify a candidate. His arguments were characteristically controversial. He opened with the cynical suggestion that it was ultimately futile to judge a prospective Speaker on matters of political principle, since 'interest, faction and other ingagements have so divided mankind, that no certain principles can be establisht either in religion or politicks, which one party or other will not condemn'. Every man 'will probably follow his own humour, interest or faction' in the vote, so the whole matter of principle ought to be cast aside. Instead, a candidate should be judged on two criteria: their character and their obligations.

Corruption was the issue at stake. Though neither candidate was exposed as crooked in his dealings, Smith's position as a courtier made him vulnerable. 'Court places, though they do not imply corruption, yet they do influence. A place man is not at liberty, his resolutions are tether'd, and he is not likely to vote freely, who may be punisht for it with the loss of his place.' Even if the ministers did not directly put pressure on Smith to act against the interests of the Commons, the very fact of his dependence on them for his position and salary meant he could not be trusted to 'vote freely', for fear of being cast from court. He was a mere puppet, Drake argued. Far better to select the independently minded Bromley, who could be trusted to fight for the rights of parliament against the ministry.

It would take all Harley's considerable skills to sink Bromley's candidature. One of his more ingenious schemes was to reprint Bromley's personal account of his tour through Europe as a young man. The book had been out of print more than a decade. Without asking Bromley's permission, Harley financed a new edition with a spoof table of contents drawing attention to the author's youthful pompositties and, some whispered, to his possible Catholic sympathies. 'Have you not seen Mr Bromley's *Travels*?' he would ask guests after dinner, before fetching copies from the parlour to share around his table. When Bromley finally got his hands on a copy, he scrawled across the title page in fury: 'This was a very malicious proceeding; my words and meaning being plainly perverted in several places.'

Responses to the *Memorial* would be another crucial weapon in this campaign, for the *Memorial* had itself been an early strike for Bromley's supporters. It had already spoken of the need for a leader of church principles, one who could steer the path to outlawing occasional conformity and casting the dissenters from public life. Now Bromley was claiming to be the hero foretold by the *Memorial*. By exposing the pamphlet as ill-conceived and vulgar, and praising the statesman-like moderation of Harley and the ministry, both Defoe and Toland played their part in the campaign for the Speaker's chair. When the new parliament met in October, Bromley was forty-three votes short of his court rival Smith. The ministry had won.

Harley knew this victory was only temporary. Nearly half the Commons had rallied behind Bromley. Whoever was behind the *Memorial* would not rest. And in campaigning for Smith, Harley had lost many of his allies in the centre-ground of the Tory party. It was still necessary for him to discover who was responsible for the book, perhaps even more so now than before. Could the *Memorial* be connected to Bromley? What about its strange blend of political and religious ideas, drawn equally from the writings of Thomas Hobbes and from the coffeehouse banter of the Tory fringe? To find answers, more covert means of investigation would be required. Harley needed to track down the printer of the *Memorial* and discover what he knew. But first he would need to find someone who could carry out his orders, a loyal servant with an intimate knowledge of the book trade. He would not be looking for long.

CHAPTER EIGHT

In From the Cold

Robert Clare was down on his luck. Ostracised by colleagues for informing government agents of their activities, he was now a printer without a press. Recently he had been working for Edward Jones, who printed the official ministry newspaper the *London Gazette* from his workshop in the Savoy. Yet Jones's business had been uncertain of late. He had not called on Clare's services for several weeks. Now it was September. Clare was down to his final pennies and, to support his young family, had turned to creditors. Unable to find new employment or pay his debts, he seriously considered theft or begging as a last resort, and would have followed that path sooner had not the very thought shamed him to his core. He was a desperate man with only one choice: to pick up his pen and write the most important letter of his life.

'To the Right Honourable Mr Secretary Harley', began the letter in a flowing, neat, respectable hand. 'May it please Your Honour, I have known the printing trade now fifteen years, having serv'd nine years apprenticeship thereto, and been six years for my self: in which business (before I serv'd the government) I gain'd no small character, and liv'd in a tolerable circumstance.' Clare dipped his quill and began a new paragraph. 'But now I am reduc'd to great necessity, having no other business to do, but what I serve Your Honour in.' Throwing himself on Harley's mercy, Clare explained his impoverished circumstances: that Jones has 'had nothing for me to do for these many weeks'; that he had 'been oblig'd to live upon my credit, which is now grown extinct; having but few friends, who have serv'd me so far as they were able'; that he had 'not (and am sorry I'm oblig'd to confess it) a shilling in the world'. Nowhere did Clare precisely outline the nature of the work he was offering to undertake. It was assumed that Harley would understand and he did. From now on Clare was going to be his man on the inside.

Harley desperately needed good intelligence on the underground press. Not only was Edwards's whereabouts still unknown, but hidden workshops across London continued to churn out anti-government pamphlets and newspapers. Harley's undeniable investigative prowess was handicapped by his lack of training. He had no experience in the book trade and was not well equipped to deal with the technicalities. His best bet was to rely on his own intellect and on trusted operatives, seasoned men such as Clare. The advantages of having a printer on the inside were obvious: Clare knew all the offenders and the location of 'every printing house in town'. More intriguingly, his years as a compositor had furnished him with an ability to 'read the metal as well as the print', he said. In other words, he could decipher the text of pamphlets before they were even printed, while they were still slabs of uninked lead type set in reverse on the compositor's workbench. That could be a very useful skill in the right hands. Through these means, Clare promised to 'make such discoveries as would be well pleasing to Your Honour'.

Harley's interest was piqued. His reply to Clare's petition included a set of instructions according to which, Clare responded on the following Wednesday, 'I have endeavour'd to act; I hope to some satisfaction. If not', he added, 'I shall still endeavour to do better'. Attached to the note was a meticulously compiled list of all the newspapers currently operating in London with two columns outlining the 'Authors' Names (Real or supposed)' and the 'Printers' Names (Real or supposed)'. Most of the names on Clare's list were common knowledge. Everybody knew John Tutchin wrote the *Observator*. And many of the printers remained unidentified, with Clare promising to 'satisfie Your Honour fully in my next'.

Clare was eager to please and his new career in espionage got off to a promising start. Over the coming weeks he discovered that Edwards's old master Thomas Braddyll had printed a controversial pamphlet by Samuel Palmer, that Ned Ward was responsible for two roguish satires entitled *Hudibras Redivivus* and *Hob Turn'd Courtier*, that James Drake wrote the new *Mercurius Politicus* beloved by passionate Tories. Edwards's old friend William Pittis was outed as the author of the *Whipping Post*, although in this case Clare was still unable to unearth the printer.

Clare was not Harley's only source of information. Besides ad hoc informants, there were also the salaried professionals of the messenger service, which was an intelligence agency in all but name. Its most effective spy, John Gellibrand, had, like Clare, originally trained as a printer. So had its most notorious rogue, Robin Stephens. Though neither a messenger nor a trained printer, Dr Richard Kingston remained a formidable adversary to the underground press well into old age. He was widely and rightly feared after evidence he gathered against Anne Merryweather in 1692 led to her prosecution for treason. Kingston lived for the chase. Once he caught the whiff of conspiracy, he would not stop until he found his man. While most agents were content to surveil the literary underworld of London, skulking in the city's taverns, Kingston ranged far from home, planning covert missions to 'a nobleman's house in the country' where servants were printing 'great numbers' of Jacobite engravings. 'I had not troubled Your Honour with such a trifle', Kingston told his master at that time, 'but that 'tis possible at the same house may be a printing press, as well as a rowling press, oft in such a house may be found more than is lookd for.'

Harley's principal agent was Defoe, who began spying for the secretary of state a few months before Clare. On 16 July, armed with an official pass endorsed by Harley, he set out on his first extended undercover mission: to observe and gather information on the nation's mood, particularly in the West Country, where the churchmen held strong. As he travelled, Defoe learned to juggle the new and exciting responsibilities of espionage with his existing duties as a propagandist, churning out three issues of the *Review* each and every week. His primary task was to recruit a solid network of informants – mostly dissenting pastors – who would keep him abreast of local events. If discovered by hostile authorities, his task could become dangerous. So he travelled under the alias Alexander Goldsmith, keeping his true name and the identity of his employer secret. But no amount of care or preparation could protect a spy from bad luck.

On his departure from London, Defoe left instructions for all official mail to be forwarded to his contact at Weymouth, Captain Turner. He would pick up the letters once he arrived at the seaside town. In a bizarre twist of fate, the letters were delivered to the *wrong* Captain Turner, a privateer whose ship, the *Diligence*, had just anchored in the harbour. Defoe explained the mishap in his next dispatch to Harley:

> The ignorant tarr when he found things written darke and unintelligible shows them to all the town. At our comeing however he restores the letters, drank a pint of wine with us and calls for one himself, which it seems afterward he went away, and never paid for.

Summoned the next morning by the landlord to pay his bill, the sailor vented about the cryptic letters to anyone who would listen. Soon rumours of spies from out of town reached the mayor, who contacted the local magistrate in nearby Dorchester, a meddlesome official by the name of Hugh Stafford.

Meanwhile, Defoe continued westwards through Totnes and Dartmouth towards Plymouth. Having recruited the dissenting minister Peter Baron to his network, Defoe spent one more night in the port. That same evening, Stafford received news of his activities and issued a warrant for his arrest. The document accused Defoe of ferreting about Devon with the intention of 'spreading and publishing divers seditious and scandalous libels and false news to the great disturbance of the peace of this kingdom'.

By the time local constables began the search, raiding Baron's house, Defoe had already skipped town. The first he heard of the matter was when the magistrate at Bideford ambushed him and attempted to make the arrest, only to relent when Defoe showed his official pass signed by Harley; 'here was the first and onely time I show'd your pass', Defoe informed his master, 'takeing the hint from your letter of useing it with caution'. Despite his brush with the authorities, Defoe was confident in the success of his mission. 'I think I may say I have a perfect skeleton of this part of England and a settled corres- pondence in every town and corner of it', he reported: 'I have visited every town so securely by being lodg'd among friends that I am now under the nose of the Justices concern'd in the enclos'd warrant and yet out of their danger.' One senses the glee Defoe took in disguise and deception. His ability to run rings around pompous local officials amply demonstrated his talent for clandestine government services.

While a government official such as Gellibrand or Kingston could bribe or strong-arm information from his sources, secrecy was the casual informant's chief asset. Printers were usually reluctant to speak out against their colleagues or employers, particularly journeymen who relied on word of mouth for employment. A printer who sided with the authorities against co-workers risked being branded snitch, traitor, or reprobate. Unfortunately, Clare's defection to the govern- ment was becoming common knowledge. Before long his utility as a spy wore thin. The book trade responded by shutting him out of its inner workings. And an informant without access could not be of much help to the government.

By the end of November, Harley was heaping pressure on his agent to make further discoveries. Clare attempted to allay Harley's fears in his weekly reports and in face-to-face meetings:

> As to the objection Your Honour seem'd to make, *That I was not sharp enough in my quest, &c.* I did then give something of a reason for it: but could Your Honour (conveniently) at this time give me audience for a minute, I should in few words clear the doubt, by giving Your Honour an account of the methods I shall make use of.

Whatever 'methods' Clare employed, they were failing. His reports were becoming increasingly erratic and were often accompanied by apologies for his shortcomings: without a warrant, for instance, he was 'oblig'd to make a more secret enquiry, in which having not the success I could wish or desire'; and 'I wish I could do more; but I hope you will accept of my honest (tho' poor) endeavours. I think it not only needless, but impertinent in me, to repeat what I have said before, by way of excuse, for my not doing better'.

Soon Clare was reduced to acting as a petty thug. On 29 November, he and an agent called Mr Brown received orders to seize John Bradford, one of the more crafty underground printers operating out of various premises across London, for counterfeiting official documents. 'We went immediately to Bradford's house', Clare reported that evening, 'where we were deny'd entrance (tho' power was shewn) and threaten[ed] to be pistol'd.' Finding it 'an impossibility to take Mr Bradford', Clare sought instead 'a warrant for Bradford's wife, who is known to be an ill woman, and is the chief orderer and director in everything she undertakes; keeping her husband as a prisoner, to protect her in her ill practices, which are known to be many and very prejudicial'. The following day Clare and his accomplice broke into Bradford's shop through the windows and, 'after a small scuffle, seiz'd Mrs Bradford, and search'd the house throughout for the papers, but could find none of them'.

Despite Clare's limited success as a government agent, he did manage to unearth some new information concerning the printer of the *Memorial*. After lurking in the Dog and some of the seedier taverns outside the city walls, quietly making enquiries and overhearing whispered snippets of conversation, Clare learned that David Edwards was 'with his mother (or some other relation) in Flintshire in Wales'. Clare was reluctant to reveal his source, but confided to Harley that the 'person that gave me this information told me, he could not get out of the person that told him, the particular name of the place or town in the said shire'. Clare was certain that he would be able to track this person down and bring him to Harley for interrogation, if that was what he commanded. But the order never came. Whether Harley distrusted Clare's motives or simply did not believe his story is unclear. He did not pursue this line of enquiry any further. Bodfari was a long way away.

*

Nonetheless, pressure was rapidly mounting on Harley to make an arrest. As the weather got colder, journalists continued to demand answers. Even Defoe, who was directly working for Harley, expressed a hope that 'the authors of *Memorial* principles, as well as the author of that book in particular, will be voted seditious, mutinous, and rebellious, and perhaps be us'd accordingly'. He was disappointed that this had not happened already.

Even the queen was forced to respond. She had opened the new parliament on 27 October with a speech against those 'amongst us, who endeavour to foment animosities', which reserved special attention for those who have been 'so very malicious, as even in print to suggest the Church of England, as by law established, to be in danger at this time'. This was an unmistakable reference to the *Memorial*. Prompted by Anne's speech, the House of Lords debated the verity of the accusations made in the *Memorial*, that the church was in danger under the present government. They eventually moved that the church was 'in a most safe and flourishing condition' under Anne's steward-ship, and that 'whoever goes about to suggest, and insinuate, that the church is in danger under Her Majesty's administration, is an enemy to the queen, the church and the kingdom'. It was the resolution Harley had hoped for, with several of the bishops venting against how 'mens minds are debaucht from the press, by pamphlets and libals', repeatedly referring to the *Memorial* by name. One of the Whig lords even denounced the *Memorial* as a book so stuffed with nonsense that it resembled nothing so much as an assortment of deranged 'charms and spells'.

Two days after the Lords passed the resolution, on 8 December, the government initiated a similar debate in the Commons in an attempt to smoke out those who were, as Defoe put it, of '*Memorial* principles'. Several notable Tories spoke against the motion and the debate went on late into the night. One country squire urged that while the government's war against France might help to rescue the church from Catholicism, it would also 'open a door to dissenters' who, he charged, were even 'more dangerous' than the Catholics in their levelling politics. Predictably, William Bromley urged that the church was more threatened by the 'libels [and] pamphlets' published by dissenters than by honest books like the *Memorial*. Another prominent speaker in the Commons was Sir Humphrey Mackworth, who was horrified that 'it should be criminal to say the church in danger' when hordes of Scottish dissenters and French Catholics were poised to invade. Harley could see his enemies at work.

One result of the parliamentary debate was that the queen was finally persuaded to issue a reward for Edwards's capture, notice of which was published in the *Gazette* on Christmas Eve:

> We do hereby further require and command all our loving subjects whatsoever, to discover and apprehend the said David Edwards, and the author or authors of the said libel, to the end they may be dealt withal and proceeded against according to law.

Not only did the proclamation outlaw the further publication of the *Memorial*, but it also, reported Narcissus Luttrell with some shock, 'command[ed] all magistrates to prosecute such persons who shal suggest that the Church of England is now in danger'. The reward for apprehending the printer was £50; for the author, still unknown, it was a staggering £200 – and some members of the government were actively lobbying to set it at £500. Such high sums would catch the attention of London's bounty hunters, men who operated on both sides of the law. £10 was the usual rate of reward for capturing a robber or burglar, £40 for a highwayman. So high a prize as £200 was usually granted only for the capture of plotters or would-be assassins, never for pamphleteers. The implication was that the *Memorial* was being treated very seriously as an attempt to bring the government to its knees.

This proffered reward soon gave Harley's investigation the injection of energy it so desperately needed. Early in the new year Godolphin forwarded to Harley an anonymous tip-off from Dublin. Having spotted the reward advertised in the *Gazette*, this source was reminded of a youthful printer who had recently moved to the city and who was rumoured to have worked for three years 'with this

Edwards during which time severall things were printed against the interest of the government'. According to this young printer, during the time he worked for Edwards 'a certain lord and another person' would visit the workshop 'to read and correct the things the said Edwards was printing'. These two men were rumoured to have been among the 'chief patrons' of the *Memorial*, the letter continued breathlessly, if not 'to have a hand in penning the same, which together with the unsoundness of this printer makes me believe he worked the said *Memorial* for Edwards and that he can if he pleases make a very large discovery'. The information was, however, time sensitive: 'the said printer finding work scarce', the source reported, he 'designs for the west of England which makes me consious that if your lordship judges the examination of this man might be for the publick service I must contrive to come over with him pretending some business'.

The identity of Harley's secret informant remained a mystery, though clearly this was not his first time performing clandestine government services. The letter itself was packed with hints. The informant negotiated acceptable terms in advance: that his expenses would be paid by the secretary's office and he should keep the £200 reward if his information led to an arrest. He also tantalised Harley with additional intelligence: 'if I have the honour to see your lordship I shall courier something els [that] may be for the government's interest to know'. What was this secret?

Mail was frequently intercepted by the postmaster and Harley's informant could not risk becoming known to local officials, many of whom were in thrall to prominent 'gentlemen of the highest rank' who, he reported, 'have been great zealots to the partie of the Memorialists'. To keep his identity hidden, the informant did not supply a return address. Instead, if his 'offer of putting the printer into the government's hands to be examined may be a servis', Harley was to place an enigmatic note acknowledging the letter in the *Gazette*, asking its author to 'come as soon as may be'. Such tradecraft was common among Harley's underlings around this time: similarly cryptic notices addressed to 'S. W.' and 'R. S.' and 'G. D.' are littered throughout the January papers.

Harley waited before making his own inquiries. Ever the cynic, he suspected that the letter was not from Dublin at all, and that the talk of expenses was a ploy to extract money from secret-service slush funds. Even so, it gave him a lead, and one that would require no payment. It did not take long to work out the identity of this young printer in Dublin: he was Edwards's erstwhile apprentice Thomas Bailey, whom Gellibrand and Hayward had briefly seized during the summer. Digging deeper, Harley's agents confirmed that, after his release, Bailey had moved to Dublin and was now making his way to Bristol, where he would be taking up a job with an older printer called William Bonny.

During his London years, Bonny had enjoyed mixed success as a printer before setting out for Bristol in 1695, where he established a local newspaper, the *Bristol Post-Boy*, late in 1701. John Dunton remembered Bonny extremely fondly: 'The frowns of fortune may make him poor, but never unhappy. He was always generous to those he dealt with (as myself have found in several instances); and, upon receiving a sum of money, he would treat so nobly that one could not forbear loving him.' In another twist of fate, Dunton recalled, Bonny had recently lost his eyesight completely: 'I hear he is stark blind'. Young Bailey, 'finding work scarce' in Dublin, heard of Bonny's misfortune and spotted a potential opening to work for him on the *Bristol Post-Boy*.

Harley could not spare Gellibrand and did not trust Stephens with a mission to the West Country. Luckily he had a man on the scene, for the local MP for Bristol, Robert Yates, was a distant cousin and a keen supporter of the moderate principles being pursued by Harley and his ministry. Harley wrote to Yates explaining his situation:

I understand one Baily who was servant to Edwards, at the time hee printed that libell, is in your city with one Bonny a Printer. I desire therefore you will closely examine Baily upon oath (but with great privacy) what hee knows concerning printing the *Memorial*, who brought the copy, the circumstances of it, who corrected it, whither the books were sent; and all other questions that occurr upon this subject. You may give him encouragement

incase you finde him ingenious, but you will please to take such
precaution that hee may not gett away.

Precisely what Harley meant by 'encouragement' was unclear. Perhaps
he was authorising Yates to bribe the young printer? Perhaps 'encouragement' was a euphemism for more sinister modes of interrogation?
Harley also requested that Yates interview any 'people in Bristol who
have an intimacy with this Baily', particularly one Arthur Bedford,
whom Harley had 'reason to believe to bee a very honest man and a
well-wisher to the queen's government'. Whatever transpired in Bristol
is a mystery. Yates kept no paperwork. But Harley's silence on the
matter would suggest that Bailey was a dead end.

Bailey may or may not have known that his former master was close
by. He and the other apprentices had been released on bond soon
after their capture in the summer, as had Mary. Edwards was still in
hiding. The printer had taken the western road out of London. He
covered his tracks well, hiding out in the family home at Bodfari before
heading south to the sleepy coastal town of Newport, just across the
estuary from Bristol. He was in Newport when he received news of
the reward for his arrest. The note came from his brother, Thomas,
who held a junior clerical post in Whitehall. On 29 December he sent
his reply, disguising the paper trail by enclosing his note to Thomas
inside another letter, 'which I have sent to a friend, who will convey
it to the gentleman that comes to you'.

Thomas had blamed their Catholic sister for embroiling Edwards
in the affair, an accusation that the printer was eager to refute: 'I beg
of you not to be so violent against your sister, poor woman! Because
it adds still more afflications to the heavy burden of sorrow which
she bears.' Rather, Edwards asked, 'if it lies in your power, endeavour
to comfort and assist her; that's the part of a Christian, and not reviling
and indignation. I declare before almighty God that she's altogether
innocent of bringing me into any trouble, there being no people of
her religion concern'd with me.' There was nobody to blame but
himself:

You and all mankind that know me can justify that I never was addicted to partiality or lying, but rather too much sincerity for these times, which is like to prove my ruine. I us'd all the means I cou'd by arguments, to evade doing the thing: but it came to me with that face and applause that being, as you know, in my principle always for the Church of England, was overrul'd in it.

However warm Edwards's feelings towards his family, principally this was a begging letter: '[I] desire of you, dearest Tom, to make use of what friends you have to interceed with my lord, whether I may come with safety'. Godolphin's title never appeared in the *Memorial*, claimed Edwards, with the exception of two letters 'which might stand for anybody'. It was a feeble excuse that he knew would not bear scrutiny. He even mentioned the mysterious 'blank' on page five, which he had scribbled out so thoroughly in the manuscript. Here, Edwards claimed, he had actually done the ministry a service by erasing a 'heavy charge' against it.

Most intriguing, though, were his hints about the pamphlet's authorship. With all his leads having dried up, Harley's investigation had hit a dead end. Edwards claimed to know the men responsible:

I am willing to satisfy my lord to the utmost of my power, so far as I know of, whose concern'd in it, and shall do it with all the sincerity that can be desir'd. But suppose there be greatness and wealth in the case, tall trees, which may prove very difficult to clime up to the top of, and perhaps I can't prove I saw it writ; I can prove the delivery of the books, the place, and to whom, by several credible witnesses, and consequently who writ it; it may be done by things printed for the same party, by hand and stile, &c. The whole matter, if done as I shall direct, will be fully prov'd: but a miscarriage in management of affairs may happen. I humbly hope, that if great trees be pull'd down, his lordship will not destroy a shrub.

The curmudgeonly Godolphin was unsure how to act when Thomas Edwards shared this message from his brother on 9 January. So he did

what he always did in such matters and shrugged off the business to
Harley. 'This letter will be given you by Thomas Edwards, brother to
the printer,' explained the Lord Treasurer, 'who brings me a man that
comes from his brother to tell me it will be necessary to seize some
persons before the noise of his brother's coming in or being taken,
or else they will run away. I would not speak with the man myself,
and therefore I lose no time in sending the printer's brother and the
man to you, that upon your speaking with them you may give such
order as you think proper.' This was an extraordinary breakthrough.
In the last six months Harley's agents had discovered nothing. Their
information led nowhere. For all the printer may have been a mere
'shrub', Edwards's hint that 'greatness and wealth' and 'tall trees' were
involved in the case must have intrigued the ministers.

Edwards followed his letter to London before the year's end, taking
a ferry over to Bristol, where he joined the icy road. Before her husband
arrived in the city, Mary arranged a safehouse in which he could spend
the night. On 10 January, the printer contacted Harley to confirm that
he had all the information necessary to start making arrests:

> I have sent an account of persons and papers to my wife. I have
> given you really and truly the naked truth as far as I know at
> present. She can tell you more, being at liberty. She shall wait
> upon Your Honour whenever you think fit. My friend wou'd
> have brought an account of particulars to you, but that can't be
> done by any but her self. She'll go herself, and show the messen-
> gers their houses, because she has not their Christian names; and
> if she shou'd go to enquire for one, it will make a suspicion, and
> she may miss of 'em.

Mary could be trusted. For now, Edwards would not come in without
a guarantee of his security; he did not want to 'be mark'd out for the
slaughter' but would 'return to town with all the speed' only once he
received 'his lordship's honour that his lordship will be pleas'd to stop
the outlawry and prosecutions against me'. Harley lost no time. On
12 January, he drew up a temporary reprieve for Edwards: if he 'shall
within four days after the date hereof discover or cause to be discovered

the author or authors of the said lybell, he and his wife and servants concerned in the printing thereof, shall be pardoned, and indemnifyed and free from any prosecution for or on account of the same'. The clock was ticking.

CHAPTER NINE

Recollect Yourself

On 14 January 1706, snow began to fall. It was not the usual miserable London sleet, melting to slush underfoot. According to Evelyn it was a swirling blizzard, sweeping in from the east and engulfing the city in a drift of 'deepe snow'. Along the riverbank, the burnt-out ruins of Whitehall Palace – accidentally razed to the ground in 1698, when a maidservant left a brazier unattended – were hidden beneath a thick blanket of ice stretching out into St James's Park. The Cockpit buildings in Whitehall were cold and draughty at the best of times. Having originally housed a cockfighting ring and other amusements for the Tudor court, the complex now accommodated civil servants.

Through the gloom and snow of the afternoon could be seen a warm glow coming from an upstairs window. In one of the long, narrow offices overlooking the street, a welcoming log fire crackled behind a grate. The corners of the room were brightly lit with candles. Harley sat warming his hands while his ministry colleague, Charles Hedges, kicked the snow from his boots and stepped into the room. Harley's undersecretary Erasmus Lewis was already huddled in the corner, carefully taking notes. They sat discussing court business and affairs of state until there was a knock on the door. David Edwards had arrived.

Nobody recorded Harley's first words to the printer who had eluded him for the past seven months. Though they had never met, the two men had been dancing around one another for years. They were near contemporaries. During the period of Edwards's apprenticeship, Harley had been training as a lawyer at the Inner Temple, just south

of Fleet Street. After the lapse of the Licensing Act in 1695, just as
David and Mary Edwards were setting up their printshop in Nevil's
Alley, Harley was busy preparing new legislation to regulate the press.
When Harley had been drafting the Act of Settlement in 1701, securing
the Protestant succession in law, Edwards had been printing satires
deeply critical of this statute. Edwards was used to attacking the
ministry from a position of secrecy. Now he was forced to look Harley
directly in those little, dark, unfathomable eyes. He was to be assisted
by no lawyer and assessed by no jury. This was not a trial. So far as
the government was concerned, Edwards was already guilty. The
question was whether he had enough information to be of use.

At Harley's request, Edwards sat in an empty chair by the fire and
began to speak. His story was, by now, familiar: the masked woman
and the manuscript, the second woman outside, the indented paper,
the numerous visits from porters. Harley was already acquainted with
most of these details. He had interviewed Mary two days earlier.
While her husband was hiding out in Wales, Mary had been running
her own investigation. Having grown up in the underground book
trade, performing odd jobs for her mother and stepfather, she was
intelligent, well-informed, courageous, and persistent: qualities which
had granted her greater success than the secretary of state over the
past few months.

Her first line of inquiry, she had told Harley, was to find the porter
John Fox, who came in June with a letter requesting delivery of the
pamphlets. She had since managed to track him down at his favoured
drinking den. After a little nudging, he revealed that the letter was
given him upstairs at the Devil tavern on Fleet Street, 'by a gentleman
in a light peruke and light coloured cloaths, who came out of a room
from seven or eight other gentlemen'. When first she asked Fox if he
could discover their names, he 'seemd very ready to enquire and give
her an account'. But he never returned. When she finally pinned him
down several weeks later, his demeanour had shifted: 'he seemd
reserved', Mary told Harley, 'and desired her to go her selfe to the
Devil tavern' and ask Tom the landlord, for otherwise 'he should be
looked upon as a kidnapper of gentlemen if he should tell who they
were'. Somebody had warned him to keep his mouth shut.

Mary's next port of call was another tavern on Fleet Street, the Mitre, where the porter Thomas Gilbert plied his trade. Here Gilbert confided to Mary how he had been instructed to collect copies of the *Memorial* by 'a little man in black cloaths and a tall man in light cloaths and a light wigg'. They seemed to be gentlemen, he thought, but could not say any more. Mary's last hope was another young porter, John Davis, who had come looking for the remaining fifty copies of the *Memorial* at the end of June. His story bore striking similarities to Gilbert's: 'a gentleman in a light peruke and light coloured cloathes, called him at the Temple Gate, and gave him the said letter, and bid him carry it to Mr Edwards the printer in Fetter Lane, and bid him bring an answer to Nando's coffeehouse'.

Did he know the name of this gentleman, the tall one in the pale clothes? asked Mary. It had to be the same man. Davis shook his head. He had never seen the man before; but he did have another possible lead. The tall gentleman had instructed him to ask at Nando's for another man. Davis was told to wait in the lobby until a tall figure with pale skin and dark, sunken eyes stepped through the door. Davis had seen him around before. He handed the man the letter and waited. The man's eyes flicked across the page. After a minute, he looked up and told Davis to hold fast while he jotted down a note of his own. A few moments later, he was folding the letter tightly and instructing Davis to carry it to a lawyer at Lincoln's Inn. He handed over a few small coins with the sealed letter and, without another word, turned and walked back into the bustle of the coffeehouse. This man was called Sir Humphrey Mackworth.

Harley's ears pricked up. Ever since he first read the pamphlet, with its curious blend of political ideas, Harley had half suspected Mackworth could be involved. But Davis's story immediately complicated matters. While it would be easy enough to catch and convict a literary hack like Pittis on grounds of seditious libel, to arrest a sitting MP was altogether more difficult. The ministry's grasp on power was fragile enough and might not survive another assault from the backbenches. Mackworth had links to Bromley, to Sacheverell, to all the ministry's enemies. Harley was also conscious that, in addition to his position as one of the leaders of the Tory opposition, Mackworth was also a prominent industrialist. In 1698 he had established the Company of Mine Adventurers, raising £125,000 through lottery subscriptions and from prominent members of the gentry. Nobody could take down Mackworth without also risking the financial investments of some of the most important men in the land. Harley would have to proceed with caution.

Mary suffered no such constraints. To her questioners' amazement, the printer's wife related how, having discovered his name, she marched over to Mackworth's house at Angel Court on Snow Hill and demanded to see him 'severall times'; but 'he was always denyed to her, and she could never see him'. Finding no joy, she moved on to the London residence of Sir Humphrey's cousin, Thomas Mackworth, on King Street in Bloomsbury. While Mary waited for the man of the house, she peeked through to the kitchen. There, 'frying puddings' on her own, was the very same servant woman who had accompanied the masked lady to Nevil's Alley in June. There was no mistaking her, Mary told Harley.

Mary's snooping came to an abrupt end when another woman stormed past into an empty chamber and slammed the door behind her. Thomas Mackworth followed a moment later and introduced himself to Mary. The servant woman poked her head out of the kitchen and asked her master, 'what does madame shutt herself out for?' Thomas Mackworth said nothing in reply, merely 'winking' at the servant woman. Then she spotted Mary. 'Oh! I know now', she exclaimed, looking apologetically at her master before returning to work. 'I thought to my selfe that it was the gentlewoman that brought the *Memorial*, that shut herselfe out', Mary told Harley. She did not manage to get a better look at this lady, but remained convinced that she could have been the woman in the vizard mask.

Soon thereafter Mary visited the Lincoln's Inn lawyer whom Davis named, Henry Poley, who was also, like Mackworth, a leading Tory backbencher. Although Poley had been crippled by ill health as a child, resulting in diminished stature as an adult and the nickname 'little Poley the lawyer', he had a formidable reputation. Even the condescending Thomas Hearne, who scoffed that Poley was 'a man of a very despicable presence, being deform'd to the highest degree', admitted that he was also 'endu'd with a strong memory and most solid judgment, insomuch that he was accounted one of the best common lawyers in England'. In her own way, Mary was equally tenacious, soaking up names, faces, and snippets of conversation.

Although the door to Poley's ground-floor chambers was locked and the lawyer 'seemed as if he would avoid' her, Mary 'pressed very much' and was eventually admitted by Poley's secretary. Once the door was shut behind her, Mary addressed Poley directly, 'telling him her name and that she was the wife of Mr Edwards, who had printed *The Memorial of the Church of England*'. They had both 'suffered so much' by printing the pamphlet, she added, conveying her dismay that the authors of it 'would take no more care of her husband'. Poley's response was unusual. He did not deny the charge; he did not comfort his distressed visitor. He merely asked Mary what she 'would have' from him. Did she want money? Information? 'Why you are the authors of the *Memorial*', she cried. Poley replied that 'he did not know what she meant', to which Mary responded that 'she would make him know before she had done with him'. In response, Poley 'bid her do her worst'. These were not the words of an innocent man.

Lying to the servants that she was there to pay legal fees, the following morning Mary sneaked into the chambers of another lawyer MP, John Ward, whom 'the discourse of the town' implicated in writing the *Memorial*. If anything, Ward was even more defensive than Poley. When Mary asked the lawyer if his name was John Ward, he replied 'it may be it is, and it may be it is not'. Mary responded sharply, asking 'if he had done any thing that he might be ashamed of his name' and how 'you and Sir Humphrey Mackworth, and Mr Poley, are not ashamed to bring my husband into troble for printing the *Memorial* and taking no care of him'. Ward 'made no reply, but walked backwards and forwards in his chambers in a disorderly manner til she went away'. In all that time, he said only that 'she might do what she pleas'd'. Either Ward was genuinely baffled by Mary's intrusion that morning or he had something to hide.

Once Edwards confirmed his wife's discoveries to Harley, the secretary of state drew up a plan of attack. To hunt down the men responsible for the *Memorial*, he would first need to capture witnesses and gather physical evidence. He started at the bottom. Turning over a scrap of paper, he scribbled down 'Names of persons and messengers to seize them'. Thornburgh, Ravell, Brown, and Dagley – reliable men all – would each seize one of the four porters: Fox, Povey, Gilbert, and Davis. Wilson and Hayward would be responsible for bringing in the bookseller George Strahan. Taking Thomas Mackworth and his servant would be more difficult. Harley assigned the task to five messengers, hoping they could accomplish the task quickly and quietly. He also wanted to speak to the tavern keepers at both the Devil and the Mitre, to see if they knew what was going on in their private rooms. He could not possibly bring in Sir Humphrey Mackworth or Henry Poley at this stage without firm proof of their involvement; but at some point he would need to question Sir Humphrey's chief servants, William Shiers and Nathaniel Powell. 'With all submission to your better judgement, I am persuaded that the business must be done, as 'twere, at once, or otherwise not effectual. For if one of 'em is touch'd, 'twill run like thunder all over the town', Edwards told Harley. It would only take one tip-off for their entire network to go to ground. The prisoners would need to be detained in safehouses rather than held in jail, where word might get out. It was essential that the operation remain off-books for as long as possible.

Arrests were made on 16 January and the interrogations began in earnest the following morning, a little after dawn. Matters started well enough. Gilbert verified that he had indeed taken a letter and payment from two gentlemen in a private room at the Mitre: one 'a little man in black cloaths', the other 'a tall man, in a light wig' who paid him eighteen pence 'for his bag and for his pains'. John Fox's story was almost identical. He was called into a private room upstairs in the Devil tavern – 'No. 31 as he thinks, or No. 30' – where the same 'tall man, in a light wig' stepped outside 'from severall other gentleman' and gave him a letter to carry to Edwards's shop. But he did not know the gentleman's name and 'never saw the gentleman that gave him the said letter, before or since'. Young John Davis was likewise very helpful, confirming that a 'tall man about six foot high in a light wig' outside Nando's coffeehouse had given him a letter to carry to Nevil's Alley, and that he had taken further letters to Sir Humphrey Mackworth and Poley, the latter of whom was, he said, 'a little man'. Could Poley be the same 'little man' who had hired Gilbert's services at the Mitre, the one in black clothes?

Two days later, having left him to squirm in captivity, Harley and Hedges called Strahan the bookseller to their chambers in the Cockpit. Harley, in particular, knew how to keep secrets; he also knew how to uncover them, how to sniff out lies and bluster. He had interviewed Strahan briefly already, at which point the bookseller denied Edwards's story: that Strahan had pulled a copy of the *Memorial* from his pocket while they were on the river and hinted 'that he knows the author, who was a base man'. Harley was not persuaded by Strahan and wanted to interrogate him again. Before this second interview, he and Hedges quickly checked Edwards's version of events. The printer reiterated that Strahan had smirked when he named Mackworth, adding that 'there were more concerned' with the book than Edwards knew, possibly even a club of like-minded Tories. 'I am positive, very positive on that', Edwards nodded to his interlocutors, before being ushered out of the room. It was time to test the verity of both men's stories.

'Mr Strahan', Harley opened. 'You have had a great deal of time. You have been treated with great indulgence; I must own that you have not been candid. Severall circumstances are certainly true that you have denied; there is proof in two or three particulars, and in others, there are circumstances.'

'Whatever circumstances', Strahan sneered in response, 'I cannot tell what false witnesses may say—'

'You must not use them so', Harley interrupted. 'Do not mistake your selves; none shall protect you.'

After allowing Harley's warning to sink in for a few moments, Hedges broke the silence. 'You have taken great liberty to charge other persons with saying false things, when we know them to the contrary.' From this point onwards Hedges and Harley took turns at the prisoner, confronting him with Edwards's detailed account of what transpired on the river, including the charge that Strahan knew the identity of the author. It was not long before Strahan began to wriggle.

'I solemnly declare, I do not know the author.'

'What did you say the other day, of what passed between Edwards and you upon the water?' Hedges asked. 'It is plain you desired to be let in partner.'

'I did so, when he shewed me the book and desired me to promote it.'

'Recollect yourself.'

'I never said I knew the author, but have had the publishing of it. He sent me some and I disposed of them.'

After some back-and-forth about whether Strahan kept an account book, Harley began to read from the last part of Edwards's written testimony, recounting how Strahan had produced a copy of the *Memorial* on the boat and named Mackworth as the author.

'I do solemnly declare it false', Strahan interrupted. 'He never named Sir Humphrey Mackworth.'

'Did you produce the book in the boat?'

'I do not remember positively. If I did, it is more than I know. If I did then I had got the copy before.'

'Now you take upon you to deny things, contrary to what you said last time.' Hedges repeated his original question. 'Did he ask you if you knew the author?'

Strahan paused for a moment before confirming what the inter-rogators already knew. 'He asked me. I said no.' With that he shook his head. They would get nothing more from him.

Sir Humphrey's deputy, William Shiers, proved an equally difficult nut to crack. The evidence for his involvement was extremely patchy. The brief note delivered by Gilbert from the Mitre was, Edwards alleged, in Shiers's handwriting. Edwards claimed to have recognised the script from previous work they had done together. Having escorted Shiers into his office, Harley confronted him with the letter.

'Do you know the hand?'

'No, I do not,' Shiers replied, glancing over the sheet.

'Consider again. Did you ever see that paper before?'

'Never, sir. No, sir. I never did.'

Harley took back the slip of paper and slid another across the table, looking him directly in the eye. 'Do you know *that* hand?'

Shiers's face dropped. 'Yes, I do', he muttered. It was his own, a letter he had recently written at Sir Humphrey's request, denying authorship of the *Memorial*.

'These two hands are very like.'

'They differ as much as black and white', Shiers yelped. 'I can assure you 'tis none of my hand.'

'The *p*s are alike so are the *e*s the same.'

Shiers denied the charge. 'I never made such an *L* seldom. One hand may be like another, but I can assure you that is not mine.'

'Do you know anything of any books brought to a tavern by a porter?'

'Not one cross syllable.'

On 22 January, Harley's cabinet colleagues were invited to the Cockpit to witness the next round of interrogations, which, according to Luttrell, went late into the night. There were plenty of moderates in the room who supported Harley in his investigation. But the audience also included his critics, particularly the Whig lords to whom Godolphin had ceded ground in the recent reshuffle. They would be watching Harley, waiting for him to stumble. If Harley was seen to go soft on the suspects, they could pounce and suggest he was secretly in thrall to the Tories, that he was deliberately bungling the inquiry. So it was important that everything should proceed according to plan.

David and Mary Edwards initiated proceedings by recounting their side of the story. Then matters began to slide. Five days earlier, Harley's agents had brought in the servant woman from Thomas Mackworth's house, for her to be questioned. Her name, it transpired, was Susannah Gough, a nurse and widowed mother of five who lived near Fetter Lane. Mary had picked her out as the servant who accompanied the masked woman the previous summer, the same woman she had spotted cooking at Thomas Mackworth's house. 'Her face is so remarkable that I can't be mistaken, and I remember her cloaths perfectly well', she swore. Yet when presented to her interrogators in the Cockpit, Gough flatly denied all involvement with the publication of the *Memorial*: kneeling before the panel, she proclaimed, 'I never was with any body out of doors in a mask. I know nothing of any papers, nor do I know Nevills Ally'.

Nor was Gough's testimony the only problem. Robert Povey, the porter who picked up the last fifty copies of the *Memorial* and was known occasionally to work for Poley, denied ever visiting Edwards's shop or having anything to do with the matter. Davis, up until now so reliable in his revelations, likewise veered wildly off script. 'The gentleman did not say anything of bringing an answer', he said; 'but thinking he might expect one, I went back to Nando's to look for him; but he was gone ... I know nothing of the matter. I never knew Sir Humphry Mackworth, or ever went of any errand for him.' 'I have heard that Mrs Edwards is an ill woman', he added, 'and I resolved to have nothing to do with her.'

Davis's volte-face was particularly embarrassing for Harley. Under the circumstances, it was also deeply suspicious. His new line ran directly contrary to the story he had previously spun for Mary. Davis and Strahan provided the only concrete link to Mackworth. Without their cooperation the whole investigation would disintegrate. So what caused this sudden about turn? For a brief period Harley may have suspected the printer and his wife of playing him for a fool. But Edwards soon assuaged such doubts with a theory of his own. The 'messengers lets 'em loose altogether in a room', he complained to Harley later that night. He had seen them all huddled in the ante-chamber, 'for Mr Mackworth to whisper the nurse, and Mr Powell and Mr Strahan to talk together. 'Tis not the way to find out the truth of things', he added in frustration. 'Davis ought to be shut up close. You find that Gilbert own'd what pass'd between my wife and him. You find that Fox own'd too what she had said, tho' not so freely.' Witness-tampering, collusion, and perjury were obfuscating the investigation, the printer claimed. Davis's personal slurs against Mary were calculated to discredit her as a witness. Edwards offered some further advice about handling Strahan:

I know he's a niggardly covetous fellow, touch his pocket, or make him neglect his business, and he'll sqeek presently: I find he has been purloin'd, as Davis has been, to invalidate what we say; but had it not been in Your Honour's presence, I wou'd have kick't him.

One of Harley's challengers among the newly ascendant Whigs, Lord Cowper, shared Edwards's dissatisfaction with Harley's interrogation method. He was 'extream bad at it', Cowper confided in his diary, and managed the task 'neither with cunning nor gravity, to imprint any awe on those examined; by which I believe he spoil'd the thing on his former examinations'.

Three sleepless nights later, on Thursday 25 January, Harley stepped up the pressure, to salvage his reputation as much as the investigation. After Edwards confirmed that 'Nurse Gough is the very woman that came to my house with the gentlewoman that brought the copy of the *Memorial*', Harley acted on Mary's suggestion that the other woman at Thomas Mackworth's house could have been the masked lady. According to Mackworth, the woman was one Mrs Mary Purdon, a guest whom he had been representing in an ongoing legal dispute over the past year. Harley's minions duly hauled Purdon before the committee that same afternoon. She seemed flustered. Thomas Mackworth had already visited her on Wednesday to check whether she had been questioned: 'He told me it was a wonder I had not been before the councill, and said to me, how you will be frightned when you are called before the councill; and he went away laughing.'

Purdon was bemused by Harley's line of inquiry. She remembered Gough as 'the old nurse, that does all works of Mr Mackworth's house', but claimed not to have seen her in months, nor to have been at Thomas Mackworth's house when Mary had visited. Despite Mrs Purdon being 'extreamly like' the woman in the vizard mask, and Edwards even remembering 'her voice to be like that woman's', the printer and his wife were both eventually 'satisfyed this is not the woman'. The revelation came as a serious blow to Harley, who was desperate to resolve the matter and secure a conviction.

In his desperation, Harley grew uncharacteristically slack. He missed crucial evidence. Though she always professed her innocence, Nurse Gough repeatedly testified that she assisted one 'Mrs Jones in child bed about six months ago in Mr Mackworth's house' – that is to say in June, right around the time Edwards was first contacted by the woman in the vizard mask. Mrs Jones was, in Gough's account, 'a jolly, handsome, fair woman, pretty fat; as tall as myself, or taller'; she 'lived beyond Bloomsbury before she came to Mr Mackworth's', the nurse added helpfully. Compare this with Mary's portrait of the masked woman: 'she had fair hair, black eyes, and was something taller than I am, and pretty burley.' Edwards likewise described her as a 'pretty fat' woman, 'oval faced and black eye'd', though of course he could not describe the features hidden by her mask. These accounts paint a remarkably consistent portrait. Of course, Mrs Jones's recent pregnancy would explain her physique. Could the masked woman really have been Mrs Jones and not Mrs Purdon? If so, this was a clue which Harley failed to spot.

Instead of pursuing this line of questioning, Harley returned to William Shiers. He needed to get to the bottom of who sent the letter requesting delivery of the books; once again he slid the original letter across the table. Shiers's response was subtly different this time around: more equivocal than his first answer. 'I don't *think* it is my hand', he stammered; 'I am not sure. One hand may be like another.' His eyes flickered across the page and he rocked a little in his chair. A moment later he looked up, staring at Harley with all his former confidence: 'I am positive I did not write it. I verily believe it. I don't think it is very like my hand. 'Tis a smoother hand than I write. I can be positive I did not write it. It bends more than my hand'. Looking at Edwards's name at the top of the letter, he said, 'I make the *w* another way. The *a* is more set.' At this point he scrawled out Edwards's name on a fresh sheet and showed it to his interlocutors: 'I can't say I should always write it so', he added, but 'I positively deny it to be my hand.'

Shiers was sent out while the panel deliberated. Lord Cowper was in the room and was personally convinced 'by similitude of hands' that Shiers wrote the letter. Summoning Shiers back into the interrogation chamber, he confronted him with 'the opinion of the lords, that he is guilty'. 'I am very sorry for it,' Shiers responded, before restating his position: 'I never saw that hand before I was examined.

I can be positive that letter is not my hand; and that I know nothing at all of it.' Glancing between Cowper and Shiers, Harley offered the prisoner a moment to reconsider his plea. Shiers held his nerve. 'I choose to abide by it', he eventually stated: 'that is not my hand-writing.' Without a confession, Harley had no choice but to release Shiers on bail.

The other, older man under examination was Nathaniel Powell, another assistant in Sir Humphrey Mackworth's mining company. Powell had a long and distinguished career of service to the Church of England. During the 1680s he had worked as secretary to the Bishop of Chichester, before losing his job when he refused to swear an oath of allegiance to the new king and queen after the revolution. Like Shiers, he was duly confronted with the letter regarding the *Memorial* and, when asked if he recognised the script, cryptically replied that 'he thinks he knows the hand, but can't tell whose it is'. Was it that he could not tell or that he simply did not want to?

Powell must have experienced a powerful sense of déjà vu, having been placed in a very similar situation almost two decades earlier, during the trial of the seven bishops in 1688. On that occasion the Lord Chief Justice had repeatedly asked Powell to identify the Bishop of Chichester's handwriting, only for Powell to respond that, although he 'believe[d] it is like my lord's handwriting', he 'did never see him write it' and therefore 'cannot swear positively it is his hand'. Everybody knew Powell was obfuscating. 'He shuffles', complained the prosecu-tion: 'he won't answer whether he believes it or not.' His tactic when confronted by Harley and the cabinet eighteen years later was identical.

Powell appeared before the panel a couple more times. It transpired that George Strahan's older brother, William, used to run errands for Mackworth; the bookseller knew Powell through his brother and, in an offhand comment, revealed to Harley that it was Powell who visited the shop on the 'same morning the Book was first published' and commented on the 'very pretty title' of the *Memorial*. Despite Edwards's protestations that Powell knew the author, the witness said that he had 'never heard of the book' except for when 'it was cryed upon the Exchange' and was duly escorted outside the interrogation room.

Powell was not a young man and the antechamber in which he and the other witnesses were being held was a 'cold damp room'. More snow fell. At midnight, when the cabinet terminated its investigation for the day, Powell was finally released. But the damage was already done. It began with a fever. When he started coughing blood, and the chill seemed to penetrate his very bones, Powell knew his time was up. Thomas Hearne received news of the old man's fate a few days later: the frigid conditions had 'increas'd his distemper to that degree that he paid his last debt to nature within a day or two after, and may justly be reckon'd to die a martyr for the *Memorial*'.

The cabinet did not sit in on any further interrogations. A man lay dead and Harley seemed no closer to discovering the secret of the *Memorial*. He had not even been able to access Sir Humphrey Mackworth or Henry Poley, let alone ask them questions. The nearest they had got were Mackworth's employees and his cousin, Thomas. So far as the cantankerous Lord Cowper was concerned, Harley had wasted enough of their time already; he scrawled impatiently in his diary that the secretary was 'evidently unwilling to prosecute the authors of libells'. Edwards was no less deflated than Harley. His final statement reads like the testimony of a broken man:

> I have nothing further to say. I would have surrendered my selfe sooner but I was willing to make the matter out plainly. My meaning that great men might crush me, was, in case I should offer at the discovery and not make it out. I meant likewise the great party there would be against me.

His offer of service had come to nothing. For all the leads it had generated, the only result of Mary's investigation was that it made them enemies. The printshop on Nevil's Alley was in ruins while Mackworth and the men responsible for the *Memorial* remained at large. Edwards was sure of their intention to topple Harley and instil extreme churchmen at the highest levels of government: 'if I shou'd name it a plot, and no small one, I shou'd not be wrong in my calculation'. But for all his certainty, the clinching piece of evidence remained just beyond reach.

Following the failure of this final round of interrogations, the formal investigation into the authorship of the *Memorial* was adjourned. Harley remained convinced that Mackworth and Poley were in some way responsible for the pamphlet, though surely they had not been working alone. The matter of the tall gentleman with the pale wig remained unsolved. And there was still the chance that, as Edwards claimed, the authors were part of a plot against the ministry. If Harley wanted to catch the men, he would need to release Edwards so that he and Mary could continue the investigation in secret. Harley did not want to lose the printer. It had taken Edwards months to hand himself in and there was very little to prevent him absconding for a second time. But the secretary of state needed hard evidence and was running out of options.

CHAPTER TEN

Mercury and Venom

When Edwards was finally allowed to return to Nevil's Alley in May 1706, the scene was bleak. His workshop had lain empty all through the winter, exposed to the elements. Damp had long since settled in and the timbers and mouldering plaster walls stank of rot. Papers were strewn and upturned cases of type scattered across the floor. Edwards had 'no money'. His clothes were all 'worn out [by] this cursed fatigue'. 'I smell', he bluntly confessed to Harley, but no more so than the 'others coming in too, which comforts my drooping spirits'. Yet Edwards had not returned to Nevil's Alley for fresh linen. He was there seeking evidence.

At length, after much 'inspecting and tumbling in the warehouse', the printer found something he thought long gone: another clue, buried among piles of waste paper. The next morning he scribbled a note to Harley explaining how he had searched for this item once before, when he fled nearly a year earlier.

> I must confess I search'd then for it, and caus'd others to do the same, but cou'd not find it; neither did I expect to find it now; because in August last, I sent orders home to one of the lads to make a diligent search for it, that I might compare it with the little letter you have, but it cou'd not be found, so I gave it over for lost, till yesterday looking for other things, I found it.

What, exactly, had Edwards recovered from his workshop? Enclosed with the letter to Harley were the galley proofs for a short pamphlet he had printed in the summer of 1705, the final iteration of which was published as *Pro Aris et Focis* – for altars and hearths, or, perhaps, for church and state.

The rediscovered proofs were important for several reasons. Back at the Cockpit in January, while questioning Edwards's junior apprentice William Wise, Harley had asked the young man to cast his eye over some letters which had been requisitioned as evidence. Most of the letters confused him. Wise had not been privy to his master's correspondence and was unable to identify the scripts. Confronted with the letter from Mackworth's assistant William Shiers, though, he gave a yelp of recognition. 'He says he knows the handwriting', noted Harley's undersecretary.

Under Edwards's supervision, in the summer of 1705 Wise had assisted with printing two brief pamphlets, the manuscripts of which 'were both written in the same hand, and had the same leaning of the letters'. Wise could not say whose handwriting it was, but he was certain that the same person who wrote the letter on the desk before him now had also written the two manuscripts which he had helped set in type: *Pro Aris et Focis* and another called *A Defence of Liberty and Property*. Edwards agreed with his apprentice's assessment, adding that, although the *Memorial* manuscript was written in a different hand, he 'found the style and pointings to be the same as in *Pro Aris et Focis* and the *Defence of Liberty and Property*'.

Like those other two pamphlets, the *Memorial* had been oddly 'dashed'. The central letters had been stripped out of names, titles, and bodies such as 'Ch—ch of E—nd' and 'H—se of L—ds'. Because libel laws demanded specific names, writers liked to think that a satirical ditty on 'Mr H—ly' or the 'D— of M—lb—gh' would not attract legal censure. It was an oft-repeated literary tip, handed down by veteran satirists to their garret-bound acolytes in Grub Street. Sneering at his literary adversary Richard Steele, Jonathan Swift pronounced 'we are careful never to print a man's name out at length; but as I do that of Mr. St—le: so that although everybody alive knows whom I mean, the plaintiff can have no redress in any court of justice'. Joseph Addison laid the blame for this technique squarely on the shoulders of a prolific drinking companion of William Pittis and Ned

Ward: 'T—m Br—wn, of facetious memory, who, after having gutted
a proper name of all its intermediate vowels, used to plant it in his
work, and make as free with it as he pleased, without any danger'.
Perhaps Addison truly thought Brown had invented this strategy,
though in this matter the satirist was merely a follower not a trend-
setter. Even so, the strong likelihood that Edwards secretly printed
many of Brown's pamphlets shows how immersed he was in this
grubby world of libel and slander.

From his background in printing controversial pamphlets for Brown
and Pittis and company, Edwards knew that the use of dashes was
commonplace. Equally, he was experienced enough to spot patterns
and idiosyncrasies and quirks in how particular authors used dashes
in their writing. The pattern used in the *Memorial* was distinctive
enough to bring back into focus half-faded memories of those other
two pamphlets. 'It is the same stile, the same dashing, the smoothness
of stile that nobody that has been us'd to set it can be deceiv'd in it,
tho' they have put it into another hand', explained one of the men in
Edwards's workshop. The printers were thoroughly convinced that
the *Memorial*, the *Defence*, and *Pro Aris* had all sprung from the same
mind.

Besides their hectoring tone, hostility to the ministry, and similitude
of 'dashing', one of the key features linking the *Memorial* with these
two other pamphlets was a shared focus on recent events at the small
market town of Aylesbury, in the heartland of Buckinghamshire. In
the elections of 1700, a local constable had denied one of the town's
residents his right to vote. The resulting lawsuit threw long-standing
questions of liberty, sovereignty, and political representation into sharp
relief and initiated a lengthy dispute in the courts and parliament.
When the House of Lords overturned the initial ruling of the
Commons on the matter, Tory writers were particularly incensed. By
what right could the Lords intervene in an election to the Commons?
Such an action disrupted the precious constitutional balance of the
three estates – the monarch, the Lords, and the Commons – by making
the authority of the Commons 'precarious and dependent on the
Lords', as the author of *Pro Aris* phrased it. Likewise, when the *Memorial*
addressed the Aylesbury case, it judged that it would be

absurd to imagine, that the Commons shou'd reserve to themselves certain rights and privileges on the full and free exercise
of which depends all their liberty, and yet shou'd leave that
exercise precarious, and at the mercy of the other estates.

In the case of the *Memorial* and its assault on the dissenters, the
Aylesbury ruling was of particular significance. All the Tories' recent
attempts to outlaw occasional conformity had received the sanction
of the Commons before being blocked either by the Lords or by
Harley's underhand manipulations. If the Lords had acted unconsti-
tutionally in the Aylesbury ruling, could the same be argued about
their reluctance to pass Tory legislation? If servants of the court were
working to frustrate the passage of bills through the Commons, might
they be enemies of the people?

When asked by Harley whom he thought responsible for *Pro Aris*
and the other pamphlets, Edwards was ready with an answer. 'I know
Sir Humphrey's style', he explained, 'and I was the more confirmed
that he and Mr Poley [were] the authors, when I read what the *Memorial*
says of the Aylesbury business.' Mackworth had been among the most
vocal critics of the Lords during the Aylesbury affair, in parliament
and in the press. 'This', he declared before his colleagues in the House,
'will be the way to destroy all checks, and to make the House of
Commons depend on the Lords; and then I cannot see upon what
foundation you can be said to sit here to do any service for your
country.' Though dressed in neutral constitutional language, in the
context of Tory efforts to outlaw occasional conformity, this attack
on the Lords had a clear partisan edge. It was an edge that Mackworth
would also exploit in several of his pamphlets, among them *A
Vindication of the Rights of the Commons of England*, which appeared in
1701, and, following in 1704, *Free Parliaments*. The similarities between
these books and the *Memorial* were not lost on William Pittis, who,
in his defence of the pamphlet, recommended Mackworth's writings
for the 'farther satisfaction' of his readers.

Beyond the obvious parallels in thought and style, Edwards had strong
cause to link *Pro Aris* and the *Defence* with Mackworth. He had received

the manuscripts of both pamphlets from George Strahan, whose older brother worked as a menial drudge in the mining office at Snow Hill. Through his brother, Strahan was introduced to Mackworth, who tasked the bookseller with ushering his writings through the press, starting with the six-hundred-page behemoth *The Principles of a Member of the Black List* and latterly with his *Treatise Concerning Providence*. Strahan had often come to Edwards for help, outsourcing the print work to his press on Nevil's Alley.

Strahan did not let Edwards into the secret of who wrote *Pro Aris* or the *Defence*. His duty as a middleman was to protect the author and, though Strahan had been working with Edwards for three or four years now, he still did not trust the printer with that kind of sensitive information. Despite the bookseller's reticence, when Edwards spotted an opportunity to confirm his hunch he took it. The manuscripts he received from Strahan had initially contained even 'more invective than the *Memorial*', he later told Harley; it was only at the late stage of correcting the proof sheets that the authors 'chopt it and chang'd it' and 'made it smoother'. *Pro Aris* went through five or six stages of correction, with Strahan couriering each iteration of the proofs between printer and author. The changes were substantial, as Edwards explained in his note to Harley: 'I told you that the *Pro Aris* at first had more mercury and venom in it than the *Memorial* as you may see by the title of this; the matter I had to go on first suited this title, but was qualify'd by so many alterations.' The title emblazoned across the enclosed proof sheet was *Slavery in Disguise*, a sentiment that captured Mackworth's dim view of the status of the Commons if the Aylesbury verdict should be allowed to stand.

Having taken delivery of the second or third set of proofs for *Pro Aris* at his shop in Cornhill, Strahan asked Edwards to wait for him at a nearby alehouse while he dropped the sheets with the author. Ever suspicious, Edwards waited a few moments before tailing Strahan west onto the broad expanse of Cheapside. He maintained his distance, careful to remain unseen while also keeping Strahan within view. At the end of the road, before St Paul's, Strahan took the right fork along Newgate Street and beyond the city walls. Edwards followed. He saw the bookseller, clutching the folded proof sheets, turn sharply and step into Angel Court at Snow Hill, where the offices for Sir Humphrey Mackworth's mining company were located.

Edwards kept what he had learned to himself for several weeks. Strahan had insisted the printer would not be paid for his work until all the corrected proofs and the original manuscripts had been returned, which Edwards did in July. He was very strict in the matter and Edwards guessed the author had instructed him to tie up any loose ends. When Edwards revealed that he had lost one set of proofs – the same sheet he later recovered from his warehouse – Strahan had 'made a heavy noice' but was at length calmed. So long as the sheets were lost or destroyed, and any trace of the author's handwriting with them, he would be satisfied.

When the handwritten letter demanding delivery of the *Memorial* arrived in the following month, the manuscripts of *Pro Aris* and the *Defence* 'came fresh into my mind', Edwards later recalled. He promptly sent a message to Strahan, asking to meet him for a drink at the Bear tavern on the following afternoon.

'I had a letter about the *Memorial*', he told Strahan, 'which I took to be the same hand' as the copies of *Pro Aris* and the *Defence*. He was sure that Strahan still had the manuscripts hidden away in his shop and asked him to lend them to him so that he could prove the likeness of handwriting. With a sly look, Edwards told Strahan that he saw him go into Mackworth's office with the proof sheets of *Pro Aris et Focis* and that he knew Mackworth must be involved.

'I won't contradict you', Strahan shrugged, before grumbling into his beer that 'he had lost by *Pro Aris et Focis*, for he gave away many copyes and that Sir Humphry was a base man'. 'If I can assist you, I will tell you', he said. But he refused to share the manuscript with Edwards. It was more than his job was worth.

The saga of the *Pro Aris* manuscript continued long after Edwards absconded to Wales. The very day she was released from custody, Mary received a message from Strahan asking for a quiet word. She hurried over to the shop on Cornhill, taking the apprentice William Wise for safe measures. Strahan's questions seemed innocuous enough, asking 'how it fared with her' and 'whether her apprentice had sworn against her husband', which Wise was quick to deny.

Mary returned to Strahan a few weeks later looking for money. It was 'very hard', she told the bookseller, 'for these men have starved my husband and I'. The authors of the *Memorial* had promised to stand by her and her husband, but had left them with nothing.

At this statement, Strahan looked at her curiously. 'Why, who do you think is the author?' he asked.

'You know the author well enough', Mary replied. When Strahan shook his head, Mary looked equally confused. 'My husband told me that you did know.'

'Who do you say it is?'

'Why, Sir Humphrey Mackworth.'

At this Strahan erupted in laughter and gave the printer's wife a look of pity. 'He will never do any thing for you or your husband,' he explained, 'for he is a base principled man that never did a fair thing by any body, nor he wil not do it by you.'

'Oh', Mary gasped, 'he will have more honor sure than to let my husband starve.' This only prompted more chuckling from Strahan and another scornful response.

'He has a great deal of honor indeed, you'l find.'

Mary then reiterated her husband's request from weeks earlier. Would Strahan share the manuscript of *Pro Aris*, just so that it could be checked against the letter sent to Nevil's Alley? The actual copy of the *Memorial* was in a different hand, she explained, but a comparison with the letter might yet clinch the matter.

Taking a moment to consider his options, Strahan struck a bargain. 'If you wil let me see your copy, wee wil compare it with my copy of *Pro Aris et Focis*', he told her. If the hand matched the letter, then Strahan would go to Mackworth, explain the situation, and encourage him to provide hush money for Mary, possibly as much as twenty guineas, 'to do her a kindness'. It was a reasonable compromise, Mary thought, and she was desperate for cash, though she added that Strahan would need 'to call at her house for that purpose, for she would not bring the copy out.' She could not afford to lose her most valuable piece of evidence.

Strahan visited Nevil's Alley in the following week, by which time Mary had been in contact with her husband. He had written with a warning 'that Strahan was a cunning Scotchman and might snatch the copy from her'. Under no circumstances should she hand over the manuscript, he urged. It must remain locked away in his desk.

Walking into the lodgings, Strahan got straight down to business. 'I have brought the copy in my pocket, let's see yours.' Mary explained that it 'was locked up in her husband's desk; and she dared not open it; for that her husband would be very angry with her'. She defended herself briskly, adding that 'she did design to have done it' and, were it not for her husband's insistence that the manuscript should remain under lock and key, would have upheld her end of the bargain.

Strahan was put into a fit of fury by Mary's change of heart and passionately 'urged her to let him see'. The bookseller was a young man and powerful; he could easily have overwhelmed Mary and she later spoke of her fear that 'he would knock me on the head' and steal the manuscript. But he made no attempt at violence, bottling his rage and storming out of the house and away down the street.

Once Harley had his chance to interview Strahan, he was convinced that the bookseller was more deeply involved than he claimed. Though the degree to which he was a mastermind or merely a dim stooge was unclear. Soon after the *Memorial* was published, Strahan had been summoned to Oxford. He was carrying a book, he said; a new edition of Ovid's poems, to deliver to Henry Sacheverell, despite never having met the notorious churchman.

'How came you to carry a book for a stranger?' Harley asked.

'His pupil Mr Mackworth wrote to me for it, and having business there, I carried it to him.' Strahan was referring to Mackworth's son, Herbert, who had begun his undergraduate studies at Oxford under Sacheverell's tutelage.

By the time Strahan arrived in the university, the *Memorial* had already begun to make its mark. Thomas Hearne reported on the pamphlet's favourable reception across Oxford, writing in his diary about the regular occasions on which he and his companions at high table would toast 'the health of the author of the *Memorial*'. When news of Marlborough's latest military triumphs reached England, his supporters across the country strung lights from house to house in celebration. In Oxford, however, only one don illuminated his lodgings. It was joked that 'the chief reason of his hanging out lights was that *The Memorial of the Church of England* might be read by those who walk'd in the street'.

One of the most prominent advocates of the *Memorial* at Oxford was Arthur Charlett, the long-standing master of University College, and a close associate of the university's senior representative William Bromley. Through his agent Samuel Wesley, Charlett had helped co-ordinate Tory propaganda during the summer elections and would go on to have business dealings with Strahan, who occasionally procured books for him from the London market. He was also the key figure distributing copies of the *Memorial* across Oxford and the Midlands. One of his associates, a provincial Northamptonshire cleric called John Hutton, took copies of the *Memorial* from Charlett and shared them among his own friends. When a thin-skinned Whig gentleman rebuked Charlett 'for not burning the *Memorial* by the hands of the common hangman' at Oxford, Bromley leapt to his defence, wryly reminding the gentleman that the university did not employ a hangman.

Early in the new year, in the week following the Cockpit interrogations, Harley received an anonymous tip-off in the penny post. It was a little slip of paper, tightly folded, with an Oxford postmark.

Sir,

Tho I am deterr'd by the character usually fix'd on informers to come before you in person to accuse Dr Charlet Master of University College in Oxford last summer receiv'd by the carrier and dispers'd thro' the university great numbers of *The Memorial of the Church of England*, yet in duty to the queen and government I think myself oblig'd to assure you of the fact, the notoriety whereof in Oxford and particularly in his own college will clear me from the charge of forging this story to his prejudice. A little art us'd would no doubt make the priest squeak (if he knows the author or authors) whose fears for his person and

hopes of preferment by serving *anyone* will work more steadily
upon him to make him discover than his zeal of the church will
to make him hold his tongue.

I am sir your most humble and most obedient servant A. B.

Harley was unable to place the source of this information and could
not risk angering Charlett's friends in parliament, especially Bromley.
Though it was within the secretary's power to make him 'squeak',
the worry was that Charlett would instead scream and the Tories
would come to his aid. As it happens, Charlett had advance warning.
On 22 January he received a letter from one 'John White', describing
how he had 'given Information to R. Harley Esq one of Her Majesty's
principal secretarys of state that you receiv'd by the carrier a great
parcel of *The Memorial of the Church* and distributed them about the
university'. If not a false pseudonym, White was probably the student
of that name recorded at Christ Church, a junior scholar in his early
twenties who had taken his BA in the previous year and would go on
to receive his MA in 1707. White was nervous about being branded a
snitch. Charlett could easily make life uncomfortable. So, he explained
in his letter to Charlett, 'to do you what service I can, I give you this
notice that if you have a mind voluntarily to inform the government
what you know of the author or authors, it may perhaps prevent a
prosecution for what you have already done'.

In the course of his investigation, Harley did not contact Charlett
once. Nor did the don volunteer information. But there was ample
evidence to link him to the authors of the *Memorial*. Harley could not
forget Edwards's revelation that the manuscript had been 'recommended' for publication by representatives of the universities. Charlett
fitted this description. And Mackworth's bid to become the university's
MP also put him close to the centre of the web.

Equally, Harley thought it no accident that Strahan's jaunt to Oxford
to meet with Sacheverell coincided with the *Memorial* making its mark
in the city. Could the bookseller have dispatched or couriered copies
to the university? 'The *Memorial* was not mentioned between me and
Mr Sacheverell at Oxford', Strahan pleaded in January, 'I never knew
him before I saw him there, or corresponded with him.' But when

confronted about *Pro Aris* and the other pamphlets, he grudgingly confessed that 'he did carry a proof to one person who is now in the country, but he does not care to name him without his leave'. The identity of this ally in the country would remain a mystery. This person, too, may have been involved with the distribution of the *Memorial*. Strahan's silence on the matter would suggest so.

When Harley received the proof sheets of *Pro Aris* from Edwards in the spring of 1706, he pored over the corrections scratched into the margins. It was scrappy evidence at best. Strahan had demanded that Edwards return the proof sheets and original copy to him, because he feared the handwriting could be used as evidence against the author. And while this was clearly true of the manuscript, which must have been written in a clear and consistent hand, there was not much to go on in these cramped marginal jottings. Most were simple crossings-out. These were private flicks of the pen, not intended for anyone other than the printer.

Closer inspection would have revealed one or two distinctive features which, if Harley was meticulous, could have helped him identify the scribe. There were some passages added to the text. Despite the limitations of the margin, the capital *L* of 'L—ds' in one such passage was drawn with a round, looping tail, where the vertical downstroke circled back and around into the horizontal stroke. The lower-case *d*s were similarly distinctive, with vertical strokes extending upwards before shooting out horizontally back over the bow of the *d* and any adjoining letters. There was nothing unusual about this general letter formation, which commonly resembles a fishing hook; but these particular *d*s were surprisingly angular, more like the sting of a scorpion's tail.

Harley must have been disappointed by this new evidence. If, as Edwards suspected, Mackworth's secretary Shiers had copied out both the original *Pro Aris* manuscript and the letter asking for copies of the *Memorial*, then certainly he had not written these corrections. The scratchy annotations were just too different to Shiers's neatly coiled hand. If Harley had been able to locate one of the letters sent him by Mackworth over the years – and there were several such letters scattered among his papers – the puzzle would have been solved. For the corrections to the *Pro Aris* proofs had been written by Mackworth himself.

Edwards hoped the proof sheet could be useful evidence in the case against Mackworth. But Harley was unable to make anything of the handwriting and, even if he had recognised Mackworth's hand when he saw it, the sheets merely indicated his responsibility for *Pro Aris*. Everything else depended on the hunches of Edwards and his apprentice printer: that the style and 'dashing' of the *Memorial* were identical to *Pro Aris*, even though the manuscripts had been in different hands; that the *Pro Aris* manuscript, which Strahan now claimed either to have burnt or lost, had been in the same hand as the letter requesting delivery of the *Memorial*; that Strahan had been involved in disseminating both pamphlets in Oxford and beyond. The circumstantial evidence linking Mackworth to the *Memorial* was overwhelming – but it was still only circumstantial. And Strahan's testimony suggested more people were involved than just Mackworth and Poley alone. The secretary of state would need further clues, further tangible pieces of evidence. He would need to investigate the scenes of the crime.

CHAPTER ELEVEN

The Club at the Devil

At the confluence of Fleet Street and the Strand, on the main route from the city to the court at Westminster, stood a gate. It was an unusual gate. London was a walled city, with entry points evenly dotted along the battlements from Aldgate in the east to Ludgate in the west. With the exception of those who arrived by river, all visitors to the city passed through one of these ancient passageways. But this particular gate, known as Temple Bar, sat half a mile outside the city limits. Unlike the squat, fortified city gates, built in brick on ancient foundations, Temple Bar was styled in the fashion of a Roman triumphal arch, a formidable structure constructed from the best white stone. Above its central passageway stood four statues. On the west-facing, figures of Queen Elizabeth and King James I greeted new arrivals to the capital. On the east side, figures of Charles I and his eldest son, Charles II, gazed out across the skyline to the dome of St Paul's. Perched atop the arch were the impaled heads of recently executed traitors. Silhouetted against the sky, they were a grisly reminder of the fate that awaited those who indulged in treason.

The area around Temple Bar was bustling. A steady flow of traffic clattered back and forth between the city and the court. Hundreds of shops lined the surrounding maze of side streets, lanes, and alleys, their owners hoping to profit from the heavy footfall. Jutting out over the road was the famous clock of St Dunstan's church, marking the passage of the day with its loud, insistent ticking. Opposite were the new bookshops opened by Bernard Lintot and the newspaper propri-etor Abel Roper, which catered for the needs of the well-educated and cash-rich lawyers who worked from the local Inns of Court. Down by the entrance to the Middle Temple legal chambers, Nando's coffeehouse was humming with customers. The day's newspapers were usually dropped off early by a porter, much to the delight of the barristers and law students who stopped by for coffee and conversation.

For those who preferred something stronger, there were plenty of options. Writing about the diversions of the town in *Hudibras Redivivus*, no less a drinker than Ned Ward celebrated Fleet Street as 'that tipling street', where rival landlords quarrelled over who could 'with most art and int'rest brew' and deceive their guests by charging top prices for cheap wine. Grizzled old drinkers like Ward knew the best spots. An ancient building on the corner of Chancery Lane, the King's Head was known to serve good claret to the locals, as were the Mitre, the Cock, the Rainbow, and Peele's, at the end of Fetter Lane. Ward and Edwards's old friend William Pittis could often be found just the other side of Temple Bar, lurking over a bottle at his habitual spot in the Rose.

Tucked into the corner between Temple Bar and Nando's was the Devil tavern. Its curious sign swayed over the road, displaying St Dunstan using his blacksmith's tongs to pinch a sinister, black demon by the nose. The Devil was a large establishment, spread across four levels, with a common area for drinking and eating on the ground floor. At one end of the room was a large fireplace, though in this heat it would not have been lit for some weeks. At the central bar area worked a small team of 'drawers' who poured the beer and wine while attendants scurried about taking orders from chattering customers. Food here was good: in later years Jonathan Swift recalled a particularly memorable lunch at the Devil with Joseph Addison and Samuel Garth, when they gossiped about politics late into the afternoon.

No common alehouse, the Devil had been a favourite watering hole of lawyers, artists, and poets for more than a hundred years. During the reign of James I, Ben Jonson and his poetic 'sons' famously congregated upstairs at the Devil. And Samuel Johnson would continue to host his vaunted club suppers here long after the *Memorial* had been scrubbed from memory. In 1702 an anonymous poet recounted an enjoyable evening of drinking in 'a little snug room' on the second floor of the Devil, lit by two candles and enlivened by some 'very good' wine. Smaller groups would be shown to the smaller rooms, where they could eat, drink, and talk in private. One pamphleteer joked about rakish young lawyers seducing ladies in the upstairs rooms here, over pickled oysters and bottles of 'racy' wine from the Canary Islands. If these little rooms could hide an illicit tryst, certainly they could help conceal secret meetings from prying eyes.

It was to one of those snug private rooms that the porter John Fox was summoned on that sweltering June afternoon in 1705. According to the story he told Harley during the Cockpit hearings, Fox had been waiting for a job at the rickety porters' stand by Temple Bar, trying to find some shade, when Tom, the chief tapster at the Devil, poked his head round the door and beckoned him inside. Somebody upstairs wanted a message delivered. Fox hurried up two narrow flights of steps and along a dusty corridor to room number thirty. He knocked on the door. Hushed murmurings could be heard within. After a few seconds the door opened and the rich scent of tobacco drifted into the corridor. For the briefest of moments Fox caught a glimpse of 'seven or eight other gentlemen' muttering to one another in the gloom and pipe smoke.

A man stepped out into the hallway. He was an imposing figure, above six foot tall with a stately, pale wig billowing over his shoulders. He was neither very old nor very young: above forty, if Fox had to guess, but no older than fifty. To a porter who spent his days delivering letters and packages about the muddy streets of London, the man's gentlemanly status was immediately obvious: his clothes were light in colour and immaculate. Doubtless he got around by carriage. The gentleman leaned over, handed Fox a letter, and asked if he had a bag. He nodded, at which point the gentleman 'bid him carry the letter to a printer in an alley in Fetter Lane, and bid him take his bag, and receive what they should give him'. Money for his troubles would be waiting downstairs at the bar on his return.

When questioned about this encounter by Harley and his colleagues, Fox held nothing back. But he had only glimpsed the men inside the room and could not remember their faces. As for the tall gentleman, Fox replied, 'I do not know him, but if I see him again I believe I can give a shrew'd guess at him.' Besides his physical description, there was one other kernel of information that he thought Harley might find useful: 'That room No. 30 I have heard used to be kept for a club', Fox explained. A few months earlier he had 'been sent on a message by a tall elderly gentleman of that club, that lodged in Shier Lane as I think, whose son (as I have heard) was the last year High Sheriff of Salop [Shropshire]'. So who was the tall gentleman in the pale wig, the one who handed Fox the letter? Who were the 'seven or eight' other men, who kept out of sight? Could the *Memorial* have come from a club which met at the Devil?

Harley was not surprised to learn that a secretive clique was meeting in the tavern. He had frequented similar clubs before his elevation to the ministry and was familiar with the arrangements. So was Ned Ward, whose drunken adventures with Pittis often brought him into contact with this world. His comical *The Secret History of Clubs*, first published in 1709, claimed to lift the lid on fictional societies such as 'The Knights of the Order of the Golden Fleece' (packed with stock jobbers and city traders), the 'No-Nose Club' (a group of lecherous sots with venereal disease), and the absurd 'Farting Club', whose members were 'so vain in their ambition to out-fart one another, that they us'd to diet themselves against their club nights, with cabbage, onions, and pease-porridge, that every one's bum-fiddle might be the better qualify'd to sound forth its emulation'.

Beyond the farcical, Ward made some serious comments on the hypocrisy of these societies, remarking on the 'loose talk, mischievous cavels, and inordinate tippling' that he described as the 'principal felicities that ever were enjoy'd by the giddy members and promoters of such suck-bottle assemblies'. Even to a hardened drinker like Ward, the behaviour of some clubs was shocking. And it was not even the excessive drinking that most concerned him, rather the manner in which certain secretive groups fostered sedition and conspiracy. He complained that the true business of politics was being conducted from the back rooms of taverns and coffeehouses. As a direct consequence, the British people 'are often misled into dangerous errors; and tavern clubs have been frequently made the proper vehicle, in which our politick empericks have convey'd their poison into the heart of the kingdom. Nor', he warned, 'have there been any plots, or conspiracies in any reign but what have been first hatch'd, and then nourish'd in these sort of societies.'

Scattered among the fictional clubs of Ward's *Secret History* were a few real ones which he accused of pulling strings behind closed doors, most notably the Beefsteak and the Kit-Cat: the former named after the patriotic diet of its members, the latter after the tavern keeper Christopher Cat, who cooked excellent mutton pies for the club's meetings. Although the chief aims of these assemblies were literary and cultural, both were Whig organisations with members drawn from the highest levels of government: the famed essayist and poet Joseph Addison, the diplomat George Stepney, and the future prime minister Robert Walpole. The Kit-Cat's secretary Jacob Tonson was an eminent publisher who made his fortune with an illustrated edition of Milton's *Paradise Lost*. Although Tonson liked to pretend he was above lowly matters of party politics, David Edwards disagreed. During the general elections he had printed a pamphlet which directly accused Tonson of 'interfer[ing] with elections, when he has no right to give a vote in them'.

And then there was the Calves' Head Club, which may or may not have been an urban legend. If the Calves' Head *was* an invention, then certainly Ward was not the inventor. There had been whispers of such a clandestine society for years. It was rumoured to meet each year on the anniversary of Charles I's execution, 30 January, and feast upon a macabre dinner of calves' heads while singing blasphemous, republican anthems and guzzling from a 'calves-skull fill'd with wine or other liquor'. 'For my part, I was of opinion at first that the story was purely contriv'd on purpose to render the republicans more odious than they deserv'd', wrote Ward, until he got talking to a 'certain active Whigg' who assured him that the club was indeed real. Milton was said to have been a founding member. It was rumoured to have been continued by his modern heirs, men such as Toland, Tutchin, and John Darby the printer. Of course, a grizzled Tory like Ward had ample motive for uncovering the dealings of this secret society. His exposé of the club was framed in such a way as to unmask the modern Whigs as regicides in new clothes.

If not real, then the Calves' Head Club had a close analogue in the Green Ribbon Club, a strident Whig association that met during the reign of Charles II at the King's Head tavern, just opposite the Devil, at the corner of Chancery Lane. Although the existence of this club was an open secret, its members took every precaution to keep its activities under wraps. There were strict rules to guard against government infiltration: members were cautioned against speaking to strangers at club meetings, while new entrants would need to be proposed and seconded by existing members of at least three years' standing. Backsliders were expelled and shunned.

Their behaviour was not simple paranoia. The Green Ribbonites had better reason than most to be careful. During the Exclusion Crisis its members were responsible for numerous plots against the crown. Twenty-four Green Ribbon men were implicated in the Rye House conspiracy; fourteen supported Monmouth's rebellion. Several members lost their heads, most notably Lord Russell and John Ayloffe. Ever the king's man, Samuel Pepys conducted research on the Ribbonites, transcribing minutes of club meetings that undercover agents had managed to intercept. His assessment of the group was scathing: ''twas a club of devils'. Although the club was supposedly dismantled after the failure of the Rye House plot, there were rumours as late as 1701 that 'a certain club of great men' was still being 'held not far from the King's Head Tavern'. Such rumours fed into Ward's sense that these shadowy organisations had infiltrated the government at every level.

Harley would not have subscribed to Ward's conspiracy theories. He was experienced enough in politics to know where the real power lay at court. But he was acutely aware that certain groups posed a threat to his personal status at the heart of government. His spies were already keeping tabs on the various Jacobite associations which convened in taverns across London. The cell which orchestrated the assassination attempt on William in 1696 met regularly upstairs at the

Blue Posts, the tavern where the printers Newbolt and Butler were captured three years earlier. In 1697 a government sleeper agent called Robert Alcock petitioned the treasury for payment for his services, which included discovering 'several notorious clubs and unlawful meetings of the Jacobites in the city, some of which have been convicted'.

Pittis once claimed that Edwards's favourite spot was the Dog tavern, where disaffected Jacobites and papists were known to congregate. Seditious words were always tolerated at the Dog, according to informants who infiltrated the group. Narcissus Luttrell reported that suspected French spies had once been arrested there. On another occasion, the French ambassador himself was said to have met with and 'Bowe[d] to a number of Jacobites that were got together at the Dog Taverne'. Usually these activities went on behind closed doors, but not always. On the Pretender's birthday in 1695, Luttrell recalled that 'several Jacobites mett in several places, and particularly at the Dogg tavern' where, to the sound of drums and trumpets, 'they caroused, and having a bonfire near that place, would have forced some of the spectators to have drank the said princes health, which they refusing, occasioned a tumult, upon which the mobb gathering entred the tavern, where they did much damage'.

Mainstream Tories were not excluded. In the autumn of 1701, three prominent Tory MPs – Charles Davenant, Anthony Hammond, and John Tredenham – were found ensconced with the French attaché, Monsieur Poussin, in a private room at the Blue Posts. Much to their embarrassment, it transpired that Poussin had been formally expelled from the country several days earlier for conducting unauthorised espionage work. Once a few Whig journalists discovered the meeting had taken place, the Tories were forced to issue a rather feeble statement that 'Not a word [was] said of the great pity due to King James the Second, or the great hopes due to King James the Third, nor one jest made on the Bill of Succession'. Another putative Whig discovery was a club of Tory MPs who met at the Vine tavern, including the three 'Poussineers' and dozens of other familiar names, among them Sir Humphrey Mackworth.

Harley's search for a new secretive Tory club to match the Kit-Cat or Beefsteak must have led him back to the Devil, where the largest

Tory fraternity of the 1690s had formerly met upstairs. The club appears to have formed in the aftermath of William's proclamation as king, with the express aim of petitioning the new ruler (a foreign dissenter) to adhere to the principles of the Church of England. From contemporary pamphlets, the club's unifying Tory stance is clear. According to the Whig polemicist George Ridpath, senior Anglican clergymen were involved. Other paranoid dissenters accused the club of harbouring papists: 'We may also lose some of the Devil Tavern club', decided one pamphleteer: 'it were better for us to be rid of them than to be betrayed by them in Protestant vizors.' Yet another anonymous hack thought they were all Jacobite traitors.

Roger Morrice, a well-connected puritan minister who kept a meticulous journal of events around the revolution, had inside knowledge of this Tory club. Its first meeting was on the evening of Saturday 16 March 1689, when 'scores in number being very angery hereat mett at the Devill Tavern'. Over wine and dinner, this cabal hatched a plot. Through subterfuge, they would obstruct the passage of moderate bills through parliament and then blame the Whigs for their failure. If all went to plan, the clubmen would ask their colleagues in the press to 'clamour upon the dissenters as obstinate unreasonable and factious, and so endeavour to raise a new persecution against them'. By the start of 1690 the club comprised 'about 150 Members of Parliament', all with high-church sympathies.

According to Morrice, members of the Devil Tavern Club did not simply plot and scheme. They also wrote together. Besides the 'salvo' compiled by members during the spring of 1689, in the following January members 'agreed to draw up an addresse to give His Majesty thanks' for conforming to the Church of England. Other clubs were more overtly literary, particularly the Whig societies. The Green Ribbon Club was notorious for churning out satirical poems in the vein of Andrew Marvell, putatively written solo by the likes of John Ayloffe and John Freke, but more likely corporate productions. The Calves' Head Club was rumoured to have sponsored Darby's publication of Milton, Sidney, and Ludlow in the 1690s, and to have collaborated on their own pamphlets. Further up the social spectrum, the Kit-Cats were the principal sponsors behind the *Tatler* and the *Spectator*.

Most of the essays were penned by two of its more famous members, Addison and Richard Steele, though both were known to incorporate ideas and essays by their fellow club men.

Although Harley may initially have thought one person responsible for writing the *Memorial*, further study of the pamphlet made it clear there were more involved. Segues between topics were clunky. The text awkwardly moved from its critique on moderation to the failed occasional conformity bills, from Tory backsliders to insidious conspiracy theories, from the 'secret designs' of the Whigs to the legal status of elections. Having read the *Memorial* closely, Harley was left with the impression of several brains working alongside one another, and not entirely harmoniously. His man Toland likewise suspected 'there was a club of them' writing it, as did Defoe. Their rival John Tutchin had still stronger opinions about that group. 'Don't you think the people that wrote the *Memorial* were drunk when they did it? And when they spew'd it from the press what a stink did it make all over the kingdom.'

When Edwards turned himself in, he brought additional evidence that the *Memorial* was a collective work. Because although the manuscript of the pamphlet was written in a single, neat hand, some of the corrections appeared to have been the work of a second, slightly scruffier pen, possibly Mackworth's though it was difficult to be sure. Just as important were the letters received by Edwards, both of which were in different hands to the manuscript: the first likely to belong to Shiers, the second unknown. From the physical evidence alone, a minimum of three people must have been involved. The woman in the vizard mask had mentioned that academics at Oxford and Cambridge had approved the book, which again suggests some form of collective responsibility.

Harley also remembered Edwards's account of his trip on the river with Strahan. At the Cockpit, Edwards had sworn that Strahan told him 'there were more concerned' than Mackworth alone. The porter John Davis claimed to have been given his letter by the mysterious 'gentleman in a light peruke and light coloured cloathes' outside Temple Bar, but to have returned Edwards's answer to Mackworth at

Nando's, and then to have taken another letter from Mackworth to Henry Poley. Thomas Gilbert was sent to Edwards by two nameless men: 'a little man in black cloaths and a tall man in light cloaths and a light wigg'. The impression is of collective responsibility shared between several men.

Assuming that Edwards was correct to suspect Sir Humphrey Mackworth, and that Harley's identification of the 'little man in black cloaths' as the lawyer Henry Poley seems likely, who else was in the upstairs room at the Devil? The tall gentleman in the wig remained a mystery, though his reappearance at several stages would suggest he was deeply involved. Was John Ward, the other MP implicated in the affair by 'the discourse of the town' and who acted so suspiciously around Mary, another member of the group? The woman in the vizard mask promised Edwards that the manuscript had been 'approved' by representatives from the universities. Mackworth had plenty of reactionary friends at Oxford, including Henry Sacheverell and William Bromley. Could one of them have been in the room?

There was one other scrap of evidence. Under questioning, the porter Fox mentioned a 'tall elderly gentleman' at the Devil whom he heard was 'of that club', one who lodged on Shier Lane and whose son was formerly sheriff for Shropshire. Harley had good reason to suppose that Fox's information was patchy; he couched his testimony with the phrase 'as I have heard', which hardly inspired confidence. Yet he also knew the Mackworths were a major Shropshire family. Sir Humphrey was raised in Shropshire and his father was the local justice of the peace before he was elected as MP for the county in 1656. Thomas Mackworth once held office as sheriff, albeit for another county. Moreover, Thomas had lived on Shier Lane until recently. Could Fox have jumbled his information, confusing the two cousins? Could he have stumbled on an elderly relative, on Thomas's father or his uncle?

These would prove difficult questions for Edwards to answer with any degree of certainty. Despite his advising Harley that the chief drawer at the Devil ought to be taken in for questioning, the secretary of state never followed through. When Edwards began asking around in the spring of 1706, nobody had seen the gentlemen in months – or, if they had, they were unwilling to tell him so. Once it became clear that Harley was investigating the *Memorial*, the club had plenty of time to disperse into the wind. The gentlemen were sly and well resourced and patient. Edwards was desperate. The corrected sheets of *Pro Aris* had not been enough to demonstrate Mackworth's guilt. In his heart, the printer knew the man was deeply involved, yet all his inquiries into the club at the Devil tavern had led to dead ends. Only one clue remained, one line of inquiry open to him. He would forget the Devil tavern; he would forget Sir Humphrey Mackworth and Henry Poley and George Strahan. From this moment he would have one priority. Find the woman in the vizard mask.

CHAPTER TWELVE

Study My Ruine

Walking east from Edwards's printing shop, through a labyrinth of tight alleys and side streets, one came to the edge of the River Fleet. As it wound its sluggish path towards the Thames, from the opposite bank, beyond the stinking vapours rising up from the ditch, drifted mournful cries of 'pray remember the poor debtors'. Over on that side was the Fleet prison, where men, women, and children begged passers-by for food, drink, or money, their hands stretching out through the barred windows and into the street. Poverty was their only crime. These prisoners had been jailed for failing to pay their debts.

Even at the best of times, the book trade was not a financially secure business and the Fleet was packed with failed writers, printers, and booksellers. Most were common Grub Street types: the lower sort of hack satirised by Alexander Pope or William Hogarth. But some had once been established stars of the trade, such as Moses Pitt, a well-respected publisher who sold scientific works by Robert Boyle alongside a range of fine bibles and prayer books from Oxford.

In 1678, at the encouragement of Christopher Wren and other members of the Royal Society, Pitt had set out to produce a new atlas of the world, including 'divers late and new discoveries of parts heretofore unknown'. The king himself supported the project. John Dryden, Isaac Newton, and Samuel Pepys were all among the earliest subscribers. They were to be disappointed. Only four of the twelve prospective volumes ever appeared. Costs spiralled out of control and Pitt found himself spending more than £1,000 on the first volume alone. In 1689 he was arrested by his creditors and hauled away to the Fleet, where he would remain for seven years.

In prison, Pitt witnessed horrors. The inmates were all desperately poor, but were forced to pay the turnkey exorbitant sums for basic sustenance. Some were permitted to roam the area around the prison – known as the 'rules' of the Fleet – begging for alms. Many were left without food or drink for days at a time, stuck in the common cells 'starving, rotting with soars, carbuncles, devour'd with vermin, poisoned with nasty stinks, knock'd on the head, and that for no crimes, but for their misfortunes'. Pitt heard stories of prisoners being tormented and tortured by their jailers, of others who survived only by catching and eating rats, of corpses left in corners to rot. Many debtors complained that they were kept in the same cells as dangerous criminals: murderers and rapists and other 'dangerous fellows'. Pitt even wrote a short book, *The Cry of the Oppressed*, outlining the woeful conditions inside. The life 'of a poor imprison'd debtor is far worse than a criminal,' he wrote. At least a convicted felon could hope for a swift death at the gallows, whereas 'a poor debtor is kept a prisoner as long as it shall please God to lengthen out his life'.

There were, of course, stories of government informants ending their days in financial ruin. It took months or sometimes years for individual agents to be reimbursed for their labour, which often required a certain amount of personal outlay in bribes and hush money. One of the most pertinent cases concerned John Dunton, the publisher and bookseller turned anti-Jacobite spy. During his missions for the government, Dunton uncovered specific details of a pending Jacobite invasion plan, at great personal cost. He borrowed and spent hundreds of pounds in the course of his investigations: more than he could ever hope to recover through his publishing business. Despite promises that he would receive compensation from the Treasury, Dunton was seized by his creditors and dispatched to the Fleet. There he churned out pamphlets begging his patrons to intercede, the tone of which became increasingly desperate as the months passed: 'han't I often ventur'd my life and fortune, and spent many hundred pounds', he wrote, 'for no other reward but that lousy jayl (or temporal hell) where I must groan out this just complaint, and should be bury'd alive in a few days (that is, *starv'd in earnest*)'.

The parallels with Edwards's situation were ominous. Life in the Fleet was not far from his thoughts in the weeks after he was released from custody. Edwards's absence had driven Mary 'into an indigent condition, having little or no business, she being indeed not capable to carry it on'. Bills went unpaid. Having been released in May, he at first 'dare[d] not go home' for fear that his creditors would be lying in wait: 'I have where withal to answer the expectations of some that I owe money to; so I must keep away till Saturday; or otherwise, I only go from one prison to another.' Edwards was a hardened scrapper. He had been through much in his decade as a master printer, from prison to the pillory. But the future he and Mary now faced looked bleak.

As the weather grew warmer through the spring, rumours of Edwards's defection and new-found status as Harley's spy began to spread. Since the previous summer, his and Mary's printing business had dried up completely. Nameless men had been calling on his landlord, urging him to 'swife' valuables from the printing house to recover money owed. 'Coming in to serve the government, ha[s] provok'd a restless party that make it their business to study my ruine', Edwards reported. 'They have set all the people I dealt with against me, insomuch; that if your honour stands not favourably my advocate, there's nothing but ruine will ensue, by reason they are so numerous and powerful.' 'I am mark'd out', he claimed. One churchman even accosted Mary in the street, telling her that she 'ought to starve even upon a dunghill in a good cause'. Turning his attention to Mary's husband, he said: 'you see how kind the government has been to him, to keep him all this while from his business, and I am sure,' the man continued, 'they'll turn him poor enough.' 'I have no money in my pocket,' Edwards told Harley, nor 'have any at present to pay for a glass of wine.'

If Edwards was to survive, he needed money fast. By turning his coat, the printer had alienated many of his old friends. Men like William Pittis and Ned Ward, who had defended the *Memorial* in the press at great personal cost, would no longer even look at him. He was left with no choice but to throw himself on Harley's mercy. 'If I had but a little for the present in my pocket, I wou'd prevail with some of my creditors to give me time', ran one note, for time was not on his side. 'I am perswaded that Your Honour will stand my friend, whereby I may be put in a condition to maintain my family', went another. The pleading continued all throughout the summer of 1706, with letter after increasingly frantic letter arriving at Harley's office. 'I beseech you, sir, for God's sake, do not let 'em have that to insult over me, my case being bad enough as it is, not to want an addition.' 'I hope your government will be generous and put me into a capacity to be above the insults of my enemies.' And so on.

It was a dire situation. Harley could be ruthless when he needed to be and was not in the habit of sinking government cash into lost causes. Poor Robert Clare had learned this to his peril in the previous year, after volunteering his services as a government spy. Clare's final letters to the secretary of state were equally pitiful documents, begging for remuneration. Poverty was the price for his defection. From the moment he became Harley's agent, he lost all he held dear: his friends, his job, any prospect of future work as a printer. The government left him with nothing. If Edwards wished to escape Clare's fate, he had only one option. Stay useful.

Although the printer remained the conduit through whom information was passed to the secretary's office, it was Mary who bore the burden of their investigation. While chasing down the authors of the *Memorial* in the previous year, Mary had discovered her natural talent for intelligence work, deftly disguising herself as a client of the lawyer John Ward, claiming she was visiting his chambers to pay a fee before confronting him about the *Memorial*. She only spotted Susannah Gough at Thomas Mackworth's house for a moment, but could recall her features with precise clarity.

Despite having been driven into an 'indigent condition' by her husband's absence, Mary's investigations would soon provoke the churchmen, in her husband's words, to 'curse my papish wife bell, book and candle'. 'She is a very honest woman', Edwards told Harley, bluntly explaining that she 'is able to do more than I can'. Having spent her childhood running errands for her stepfather and his shady associates in the Catholic book trade, it was a part Mary was born to play. Her husband was soon reporting to his master how Mary flew at the suspects 'like a tyger being let loose'. And they ran from her 'as if there was wild fire to their tails'.

Women had long been integral to the clandestine services. The tendency of men routinely to underestimate women's abilities made them hugely useful in the field. Female agents were able to infiltrate households and networks without arousing suspicion, whether that was by posing as a servant girl or a confidante. Whereas men like Defoe or Gellibrand needed to lurk in the shadows, women could be invisible in plain sight. During the civil wars, there was a pamphlet seller named Elizabeth Alkin who sold information about underground royalist printers to the Cromwellian authorities. The royalists knew nothing more than the fact that they were repeatedly betrayed by 'an old bitch' with the ability to 'smell out a loyall-hearted man as soon as the best blood-hound in the army'.

Harley was not intimidated by strong women. His cousin, Abigail Masham, was one of Queen Anne's favourites while also acting as Harley's eyes and ears at court. Masham used her influence over the queen to guide her towards the policies and positions chosen by Harley, at the same time secretly reporting all she learned back to him. Harley recognised that Mary Edwards had an equally keen nose for this line of work. Under questioning, one of the porters, Povey, had dismissed Mary as an 'ill woman', to be avoided. She would be 'a plaguy thorn in their sides', Edwards claimed. Now Harley would put that natural prickliness to good use.

Mary's orders were simple: find the woman in the vizard mask. Having ruled out Mrs Purdon months earlier, during the interrogation sessions in the Cockpit, and seemingly having missed the clue about the recently pregnant 'Mrs Jones' who lodged with Thomas Mackworth, Mary needed to chase down all known associates of Susannah Gough, the nurse they believed had accompanied the masked woman to Nevil's Alley. It was tricky work, relying on Mary's willingness to snoop on potential suspects as they went about their daily business. Yet by the start of October she had traced one witness who was 'ready to swear' that Gough had secretly received fifteen guineas from an unnamed beneficiary. The nurse had apparently boasted to her friends that 'there's a gentleman in the city that will neither let me want for gold nor silver' and 'she was confident she shou'd never be try'd whenever the parliament sate; and that if she had a mind to it, she cou'd discover a great many gentlemen and ladies'. If this witness was speaking the truth, Gough's behaviour was certainly suspicious.

This witness did not know the identity of Gough's mysterious benefactor. Another of Mary's sources did. Speaking secretly with servant girls across town, Mary had learned that one of Gough's closest friends, a gentlewoman called Susan Garrett, had often been visited in her home by 'a crooked, deform'd gentleman with large staring eyes'. Mary immediately recognised Henry Poley from the description, with his bent back and strange looks. Garrett's maid had helped prepare dinner whenever Poley visited and, in the manner of one accustomed to housework, remembered him chiefly for his appetite: more than once she had cooked a fillet of veal for Poley – 'which he loves' – and, on another evening, a pleasant meal of baked fish. The maid also remembered that Garrett had ordered her out of the room whenever Poley visited and that, most tantalising of all, a 'tall gentleman in a light wigg' had attended these intimate suppers on three separate occasions.

Could Garrett have been the woman in the vizard mask? David and Mary Edwards both seemed to think so. Once Harley provided 'suitable encouragement', Edwards promised that his wife 'wou'd soon ferret out Mrs Garret; tho' she has attempted it twice, and finds 'em very shye'. He closed his report with a brief appeal for cash: 'wife is continually abroad about this affair; which is very expensive to her; and I want money at home to carry on business; and scarcely indeed to subsist; wherefore, I beseech Your Honour to consider me.' A banker's draft for £6 arrived from Harley about a week later.

Finding Susan Garrett proved more difficult than Edwards could have imagined. All through the winter and into the following year, the printer and his wife were silent. In March 1707 Harley finally received some good news. A breathless letter arrived from the printer, hurriedly written in Edwards's scrawl. Mary's persistence had, it seemed, paid off.

Rt Honble Sr

I believe my wife has so far brac'd the matter that 'tis now
even fix'd, and 'tis no hard matter to be satisfy'd; but she must
actually be the woman. I hope the difficulty will be consider'd.
I must confess, I did not expect ever to find nurse nor she neither;
but I cou'd not persuade my woman to keep at home, but she
wou'd pursue 'em, and I believe now to some purpose.

Sr, our trade is very dead, and I have nothing to do, and we
must subsist till something is done. If this be the right woman,
as I doubt not but she is, I hope your government will be generous
and put me into a capacity to be above the insults of my enemies
and

> Your most obedient humble servt will ever pray, &c.
> D. Edwards
> Sr pray let my wife speak to you, having a great deal to
> the purpose

Despite Edwards's request for a personal audience, Mary was forced
to submit a written report to the secretary's office, a large folio page
densely packed with her husband's handwriting. Mary had spent the
entire winter on Garrett's trail, she explained. She quickly learned
that Garrett used to lodge with a cosmetician in the city, but the
woman had moved since then and her current whereabouts were
unknown. For all her energy, Mary had been able to unearth only one
nugget of incriminating evidence against Garrett, though it certainly
provided an interesting lead. About two years earlier Garrett had
employed a man called Johnson to deliver some books for her. Could
these have been copies of the *Memorial*, destined for the country?

Mary had finally rooted out Johnson on the previous Wednesday
evening, about nine o'clock, at the Queen's Arms, a tavern by Holborn
Bridge. The meeting seemed innocent enough, though Mary was
lying from the start: 'I told him that I was a servant, and that my
master had given me direction' to deliver a bundle of books, only 'I
had lost the direction; and that nobody could tell me how to write
the direction right but Mrs Susan Garrett; and that I had been to see
for her, but could not find her, which made me come to you, in hopes

you can give me direction'. It was an audacious deception. Johnson
bought it.

'Why', he said, 'what directions can I give you?'

'Had not you some books off Mrs Susan Garrett about two years
ago, to carry down? Four that this bundle that I lost the direction of
is to go to the same place.'

He asked 'where she liv'd, and what her landlady's name was?'

'She lodg'd att Mrs Ball's, a powder shop, facing Red Lion Square',
Mary replied. But she understood the woman had moved since then.

'So she did', he nodded. He had 'carry'd many a cheese, and many
a pot of butter to that lodging to her [and] did about two years ago
carry several bundles of books ty'd up in brown paper, which Mrs
Garrett deliver'd with her own hands to me.'

Mary asked him if they were bound books.

He said 'no, but that they felt like stitch'd books, and that they
were cover'd so close with brown paper, that he cou'd not see what
they were.' But he had also received parcels from Mrs Garrett's own
hands on three separate occasions, 'which he carried down to her
father, a clergyman in Wiltshire; and that he was paid for every parcel
or bundle as he brought them, by the said Mrs Garrett's father; and
that he brought the money to London, and did pay it to Mrs Susan
Garrett's own hands; but whether the money was for herself or no,
he knew not.' Johnson looked at Mary, suspicion in his eyes. Why did
she need to know if the books were bound? Did she work at a printing
house?

Mary shook her head.

'Because', he continued, 'I did use to go to a printing house to fetch
books for Mr Garrett.' Where did Mary's master live?

'I told him that he was a bookseller in Cornhill; and that he was a
very hasty man; and that he wou'd knock one o' th' head if I did not
send the books right: so I desire him to be so kind to find out Mrs
Susan Garrett, for that I did not know whether the bundle was to be
direct to her father or her brother.'

Mary's quickfire lies seemed to satisfy Johnson. 'I will go to Mrs
Crow's at London Bridge, she knows where she is; and if you'll come
tomorrow at one of the clock, I'll tell you where she is.'

When Mary returned to the tavern the following day at the allotted hour, her companion was nowhere to be seen. She asked behind the bar. The tapster had not seen Johnson all morning. Mary ordered a drink and settled into a corner. Three hours later, at four o'clock, he arrived, spotted Mary, and shuffled across the room to greet her.

'I saw Mrs Crowe.'

Mary asked if he had found where Garrett lodged.

He shook his head – no – and looked at her curiously. Something was amiss. 'Do not you live in Fetter Lane?'

'No', Mary replied, thinking on her feet. Was she rumbled? 'I live in Cornhill.'

'At what sign?'

'At the Sun'. Mary shifted the conversation away from her backstory. 'Who is this Mrs Crowe?'

This interjection caught Johnson off guard. Oh, she was Susan Garrett's landlady, he replied, at 'Three Tun Court just by London Bridge'. And Mary had what she needed: a name and an address. Harley only had to sign a warrant for Crowe and Garrett to be brought in for interrogation.

But Mary's line of questioning also revealed a couple more lingering details about the case: Johnson confessed that in 1705 he had couriered 'several bundles of books ty'd up in brown paper' to Everleigh, in Wiltshire, where they were received by Garrett's father, a clergyman named Walter. As it happens, Walter Garrett was a notable high churchman trained at Cambridge. His published works included an eccentric exegesis of the Book of Revelation, holding that the resurrected lamb was not Christ, as conventional scholars had it, but the restored Stuart monarchy and Church of England after the republican tyranny of Cromwell. Like the authors of the *Memorial*, it was his firm belief that the dissenters were 'enemies of the Church of England' who ought to be crushed. Could those bundles of books have been copies of the *Memorial*, destined for the West Country? Could Walter Garrett have been working in tandem with Mackworth and Poley? Could he have been one of the men at the Devil tavern? Mary was making real progress, it seemed. But Harley did not respond. He had more urgent business.

*

Ever since the failure of the *Memorial* interrogations in January, a rift had been growing between Harley and Godolphin, who remained Harley's nominal master. At least in part, this was because they failed to see eye to eye on matters of parliamentary management. Both men were committed to the political centre ground, though by increasingly disparate means. Deadlock in the House of Commons led Godolphin to rely on his friends among the Whigs, particularly the powerful group in the Lords known as the 'Junto'. Godolphin believed he could trust the Whig leaders to put the interests of the nation above those of party.

Harley was savvy enough to think otherwise. While his goal was always to govern without relying on a single party, he had enough experience to understand that no government could rely on the support of cross-bench moderates alone. In these increasingly partisan times, moderate men were simply too few in number. Instead, Harley came to believe that he could exploit the Tories for his moderate ends. Of course, Harley did not trust the Tories any more than he trusted the Whigs. But his experience had taught him that the party was a factious rabble and lacked the organised leadership structure of their parliamentary opponents. While there were hugely respected individual Tory statesmen such as the Earl of Nottingham and the Duke of Buckingham, and extreme lobbyists such as William Bromley and Sir Humphrey Mackworth, there was no coordinated body to match the Junto. Instead, the Tories were led from the backbenches, by individual MPs with individual bugbears. Greed and interest and self-preservation were powerful motives which Harley could use to his advantage. A minor government post here or a grant of land there would be enough to keep them quiet, whereas the Whigs wanted their top men in senior policy-making positions. As the price for their continued support, it was simply too dear.

Despite Harley's efforts to persuade Godolphin that the Junto aimed to dictate policy to the ministry, and that the Tories would be too busy squabbling among themselves to pay much attention to the everyday business of government, the Lord High Treasurer failed to grasp his arguments. On 14 January 1708, Harley called a special meeting with Godolphin and Marlborough in a last-ditch attempt to pitch them his scheme of rapprochement with the Tories.

While Marlborough was encouraged by the plan, Godolphin was cold. He thought that any attempt to reshape the administration in Harley's image would reduce his own status as chief minister, despite the fact that everybody knew Harley had been pulling the strings for the last three years. Godolphin was a simple and austere man. He lacked the talent for backstairs intrigue which Harley possessed in spades. Naturally he resisted the plan. Yet Harley had a more important ally, the queen, whom he was now privately briefing several times a week on political matters. Even though Godolphin had enjoyed the queen's confidence since she was a girl, Anne's loathing of the Junto overrode any feelings of friendship and loyalty. She gave Harley sanction to continue negotiations in secret and secure an alliance of pliable Tories and moderates to oversee the incoming parliament.

With his attention split between parliamentary business and the *Memorial* investigation and a dozen other issues, Harley failed to notice a crisis brewing under his own nose. A junior clerk in his office, William Greg, was working beyond his brief. Greg had come to Harley's attention some years earlier, first as an assistant diplomat in Denmark and then as Harley's man in Edinburgh, reporting on Jacobite activities north of the border. According to friends, he was 'a very ingenious man, understanding some languages', a listener not a speaker: 'in company he was always very thoughtfull; when he went to a coffee-house he would scarce speak a word', useful qualities in a spy.

In 1706 the minister recalled his agent to London and put him to work as a clerk. The salary was meagre. For a greedy man with a history in espionage and debts to pay, the temptations of the office, where it was 'customary to let state-papers be there loose and open', were too great. Part of Greg's job involved sifting through and decoding the correspondence of imprisoned French spies. His daily research showed that the French minister of war, Michel Chamillart, was getting desperate. Chamillart would handsomely reward information on the allied forces. In the autumn of 1707 Greg initiated a

treasonous correspondence with the French court, sending over transcripts of parliamentary debates, copies of diplomatic messages sent
by the queen to her allies, and even military plans drawn up in
Whitehall.

He should have known better. Continental spy networks were no
less effective than British ones. All post entering France was being
monitored. When the letters passed through Brussels en route to Paris,
the local post master duly intercepted and transcribed the lot. On
New Year's Eve, Marlborough received word of Greg's treachery from
the Dutch authorities and informed the cabinet. Greg did not resist
arrest. On 3 January, he confessed to 'the blackest of crimes, which
his necessities, not disloyalty, unwarily led him into' and, after the
briefest of trials, was convicted of high treason and sentenced to the
gibbet and the knife. He died at Tyburn on 28 April, showing, in the
words of one witness, 'a true sence of sorrow for his crime'.

Harley claimed ignorance of his underling's secret activities and
there is no reason to doubt his denials. Regardless, the whole affair
provided the Whigs with precisely the ammunition they needed. How,
they asked, could Harley be innocent in this matter? At the very least
he had neglected the duties of his office and possibly even conspired
with the traitor. Rumours spread that Harley himself had persuaded
Greg to confess because doing so would prevent a trial, 'whereby the
public might have been truly informed of the particular nature and
circumstances of his crime'. The Whigs clamoured for an inquest to
establish Harley's guilt or innocence, which was to be headed up by
one of their own, the Earl of Sunderland. There were efforts to suborn
Greg to produce evidence against his former master, implicating him
in his treason. It was a politically motivated witch-hunt based on no
firm evidence, as Harley's supporters pointed out at the time: 'no arts
were left untry'd, to involve him in Greg's treason,' reported one of
his loyal propagandists. Even so, accusations of incompetence,
treachery, and a tendency to 'solace himself with his friends, and a
bottle' stuck firm.

If the Greg scandal had been all, Harley could probably have wea-
thered the storm. But it was at the same time becoming clear that his

discussions with the Tories were on the verge of collapse. Godolphin's discovery that Harley had proceeded with his secret negotiations, against the senior minister's express wishes, infuriated him, as did revelations that Harley had been bad-mouthing his political competence to the queen. Whatever was left of their working partnership had crumbled by the end of January, when Harley received a venomous note from Godolphin, tearing into his duplicity: 'I am very far from having deserved it from you. God forgive you!'

No mercy would be shown. But how to convince Anne? Godolphin had an ace in his pocket: Marlborough, who as generalissimo of the allied forces could tip the scales against Harley. Without Marlborough's support, there could be no new ministry. On 6 February 1708, Godolphin wrote to the queen explaining that he could no longer serve her while Harley remained in post. Two days later the Duke of Somerset followed, walking out of cabinet after explaining that 'he could not serve' while 'Her Majesty suffered that fellow', pointing an accusatory finger at Harley. Harley relented on 11 February, tendering his resignation as secretary of state. He was out.

With Harley gone, the *Memorial* was allowed to fade from view. Godolphin and his friends among the Whigs had secured their position in the arena of high politics. For all that the pamphlet may have unnerved the ministry during the summer of 1705, two years later the high-church threat seemed to have been nullified. Investigating the authors, whomever they might be, was no longer a priority. Harley's notes on the case, meticulously raking through the evidence, were left to gather dust; David and Mary Edwards were cast aside. But if Harley thought he had seen the last of this troublesome pamphlet, he would be sorely disappointed. Though the *Memorial* had exited the stage for now, it would return.

THE
Memorial

OF THE

CHURCH OF ENGLAND:

Humbly offered to the

CONSIDERATION

OF

All True Lovers

OF OUR

Church & Constitution.

Now first Publish'd from a Correct Copy.

To which is added

An Introductory Preface,

Wherein is contain'd the

Life and Death of the AUTHOR,

And Reasons for this present Publication.

Printed in the flourishing Year of the
CHURCH. M.DCC.XI.

PART THREE

From the Ashes

CHAPTER THIRTEEN

The Flourishing Year

On the morning of Thursday 8 March 1711, John Cass set off from his family home at Hackney to the parish church of St Botolph, just outside the eastern city walls at Aldgate. Cass was an important man. Earlier that year he had secured a seat in parliament as one of the city aldermen, where he quickly developed a reputation among churchmen as a 'worthy patriot'. Today was a special date, both for Cass and the nation: it was the anniversary of Queen Anne's accession to the throne, a traditional day for loyal celebration, and Cass would mark the occasion by opening his new charity school at St Botolph's. His ambition for the school was that poor local children and orphans would be educated 'according to the principles of the Church of England'. Sympathetic journalists lauded his philanthropy in the press. Others dismissed the school as a cynical ploy to indoctrinate the next generation with high-church dogma.

Cass shouldered his way through the crowds massed around Aldgate and into the parish church. To celebrate the new school he had organised a sermon, to be preached by the Bishop of Chester, and afterwards a fund-raising banquet at nearby Drapers' Hall, to be attended by 'a great number of the *loyal true sons of the church*', according to the papers. Yet the chief attraction for those loyal sons was neither the bishop nor the promise of a good dinner. It was the man scheduled to read prayers after the sermon, the man who was rumoured to be in attendance at the feast: Henry Sacheverell. Though no longer young, the Oxford don had lost none of his fire. He was known as much for his fine voice as his scorching rhetoric. Even his enemies admitted that he spoke 'without noise or any harsh grating accent'. One doting admirer wistfully recalled him speaking with 'the most agreable voice, that ever I heard'. On this occasion Sacheverell lived up to his reputation. In his daily journal entry the former rector at St Botolph's noted with dismay that Sacheverell, through his mellifluous voice and startling turns of phrase, succeeded in whipping up the crowd 'to make a mob and noise'.

Precisely a year and a day earlier, Sacheverell had stood in court to defend himself against charges of seditious preaching. On 5 November 1709 he had been invited to preach at St Paul's in London. Traditionally this date commemorated both the failure of the Gunpowder Plot during the reign of James I and the anniversary of William III landing in England. Custom dictated that sermons on this occasion should attack foreign papists and celebrate the nation's deliverance from such foes. Instead Sacheverell warned his congregation against 'the perils of false brethren', recycling a text that he initially preached at Oxford during the *Memorial* controversy years earlier.

In a breathless performance lasting nearly two hours, Sacheverell attacked the dissenters and their allies as an existential threat to the nation. Just as false brethren had corrupted the church with occasional conformity, so the ascendant Whig ministers had corrupted the state. The government was packed with 'professed enemies' to the church, he raved. Much like the *Memorial*, which envisioned this threat as a lurking illness, a 'hectick fever' lodged in the bowels of the nation, Sacheverell saw the Whigs as 'vipers in our bosom', spreading their venom with a bite.

These false brethren in our government do not singly and in private spread their poyson, but (what is lamentable to be spoken) are suffer'd to combine into bodies, and seminaries, wherein atheism, deism, tritheism, socinianism, with all the hellish principles of fanaticism, regicide, and anarchy, are openly profess'd and taught, to corrupt and debauch the youth of the nation, in all parts of it, down to posterity, to the present reproach and future extirpation of our laws and religion.

Sacheverell had already preached on this topic, on 23 December 1705, in a brazen performance just three days after the government issued a reward for capturing Edwards and the authors of the *Memorial*. Back then, an anonymous informant told Harley that the publishers 'will be so wise as not to print it, otherwise the world might be bless'd with a piece of the most exquisite virulence that ever the press produc'd'. Not so in 1709. As Sacheverell's audience flooded out of St Paul's and into the city's coffeehouses and taverns, word of his fiery performance spread. Chatter on both sides of the political divide was all of Sacheverell. Depending on whom you asked, his sermon was either a heartfelt expression of loyalty to the church and the queen, or it was a scandalous and seditious libel. Few could talk of anything else. There was huge demand for a printed edition. Within weeks, tens of thousands of copies were being passed around, shared, and discussed. Among the early readers was the MP and jurist William Thomson, who was quick to link Sacheverell's fevered rantings to the *Memorial* scandal from years earlier:

> from the ashes of that phoenix arose another *Memorial*, with many of the same virulent expressions against Her Majesty's administration, agreeing in the whole scope of it as to the same scandalous purpose, but far exceeding it in malice. And this new Memorialist has presum'd to publish his seditious reflections in the most open manner; first at the assizes at Derby, and after in the great church of this metropolis; and has printed and dispers'd about forty thousand of them over the kingdom.

Sacheverell had sought legal advice before he took to the pulpit. His lawyers had indicated that the sermon was legally sound, despite its obvious political transgressions. But the Whig majority in the House of Commons sided with Toland's assessment and, on 14 December, voted to impeach Sacheverell for high crimes and misdemeanours. The clergyman's trial in the following spring was a sensation. Thousands of spectators crammed into Westminster Hall to witness the proceedings. Partisanship was rife between Sacheverell's supporters and his critics. Outside, the high-church mob turned violent, tearing down and torching dissenters' meeting houses across the city on 1 March. Later that night, a local pawnbroker called Francis Morgan arrived on the scene at Lincoln's Inn Fields to find 'so large' a crowd 'as to extend from the meeting-house to the fire' with 'great numbers running' about 'hallooing' as they threw timber into the burning chapel. Upwards of 5,000 angry hooligans paraded through the West End, demolishing dissenting places of worship at Hatton Gardens, Drury Lane, and Fetter Lane, just across the road from Nevil's Alley. The high-church insurrection predicted by the *Memorial* had arrived. Flames could be espied from all across the city.

Cometh the hour, cometh the man. Although the court found Sacheverell guilty, his sentence was considered so lenient – a mere three-year ban on preaching – that the churchmen decided their time had arrived. Sacheverell was to be their standard-bearer for this new era. Celebrations began in London, where bonfires were lit and church bells rang out; crowds packed the streets of Westminster and the western suburbs, singing and toasting the health of Sacheverell and the Church of England. Soon the fever spread to Oxford, where students and townsfolk burnt an effigy of the notorious low-church enemy of Sacheverell's, Benjamin Hoadly, along with his books.

From Oxford the mania proved impossible to contain: there was tumult at Barnstable, 'headed by a rascally fellow'; a straw dummy of King William was committed to the flames in Cirencester; frenzied crowds at Exeter smashed the windows of the local dissenters' meeting houses and burnt offending books on the cathedral green; a man was killed in a duel at Bristol after a disagreement about the threat to the church posed by dissenters; at Wrexham, effigies of Hoadly and prominent dissenters such as Daniel Burgess, whose meeting house had been razed in the riots, were 'whipp'd, hang'd and burnt'.

When a senior judge and Whig MP called Sir Joseph Jekyll arrived at Wrexham to preside over the local court, he was outraged by the negligence of a local sheriff who 'very unwillingly went' to face down the mob: 'upon his appearing they immediately ran away and dispersed, but about an hour after got together again, whereupon I sent again to the sheriffe and ordered him to goe a second time which he

did and again disperst them but brought no prisoners along with him'.
In Wrexham, at least, local law enforcement was complicit with the
rioters.

Lest this sudden explosion of activity be mistaken for mere high
jinks, consider the testimony of John England, a dissenting pastor
from Sherborne who genuinely feared for his life. He had never seen
'the like in this place, upon any occasion; in divers houses there were
illuminations, many bonfires were made in several parts of the town;
Dr Sacheverell's health was publickly drank in our town-hall'. Anybody who refused to toast Sacheverell when confronted by the mob
'was treated in a rude indecent manner'. Looted bottles of wine were
dispatched to the parish church, where Sacheverell's 'health (as I am
informed) was drunk by both sexes, at the top of the tower, with
lights in their hands, to give notice of it'. As for Mr England and his
fellow dissenters:

> we were excluded from the common joy, being forced to keep
> our doors fast, and this was scarce sufficient to keep us from the
> rabble, who curs'd the presbyterians to the pit of hell, beat a
> drum about the town, threatned to burn or pull down our
> meeting-house; and having guns with them, they made a halt at
> several houses, and fired at them; at my own in particular, to
> the affrightment of my family.

His dismay was palpable. Sherborne had formerly 'been esteem'd a
civiliz'd town, has had excellent preachers, men of piety and learning,
and has been fam'd for religion', he wrote. Now it had become 'the
seat of Satan', a 'very den of devils'.

Nor did these devilish high churchmen show any sign of slowing.
By summer, rumours of a general election gained momentum and,
when it was finally announced in September, the Tories could smell
victory. The churchmen campaigned ferociously. According to the
newsletter writer John Dyer, at the polls in Cambridgeshire a 'professed
dissenter' provoked the mob by 'stabbing' a portrait of Sacheverell;
so they chased down and tackled the offender, ripped off his trousers,
and kicked him in the dirt. During polling in Cheshire, one dissenting

minister was so intimidated by the 'noise of elections' that he refused
to preach at a funeral, preferring to bolt himself in his study. Another
supporter of the Whigs complained that the 'Sacheverell mob' had
obstructed his friends from voting. He described how the crowd
swamped the polling station, pictures of Sacheverell waggling in the
air on the points of their swords. But at least the Whigs in Cheshire
put up a fight. The Bishop of Ely simply gave up all hope for the
Whigs in Cambridgeshire, resigning himself to a Tory victory. Even
cities with a strong base of dissenters, such as Coventry, fell prey to
the high-church revival; the Whigs did not even field a candidate. It
was a bloodbath.

When he fell from grace two years earlier, Harley found himself in
an unusual position. He was at last free to explore his options with
the Tories, who were a key part of his strategy to win back power,
though in his heart he remained a moderate. Ever the political artist,
Harley's plan was both simple and subtle. Behind closed doors he
continued to lobby the churchmen, promising future cabinet positions.
His cousin, Abigail Masham, had become the queen's bosom
companion. Harley used her influence without scruple. He understood
the queen's personality and, for her part, Anne once again came to
enjoy Harley's company more than that of Godolphin or Marlborough.
With Abigail whispering in the queen's ear, Harley managed to
persuade Anne that his former colleagues were dragging out the war
with France, ruining the Church of England, and failing to govern in
the national interest.

   He presented the queen with a solution to the nation's troubles.
At the head of a resurgent Tory party, and if she would accept him,
Harley promised to curb the extreme fringe of churchmen who had
previously proven so troublesome. His plan was to 'graft' the more
moderate Whigs to the 'bulk of the church party', building a governing
coalition that would depend on Harley and the queen's ministers for
leadership. It took many months of delicate persuasion, but eventually
Anne was convinced. On 10 August 1710, she relieved Godolphin of
his duties as Lord High Treasurer and chief minister. Harley was back
in control.

Not for long. When the new parliament assembled in November, following the high-church riots of the spring and summer, it became clear that Harley's plans were doomed to failure. The Tories had ridden the groundswell of support for Sacheverell to victory at the polls. And with a new-found firm majority in the Commons, they had no need of Harley's proposed coalition. Over a quarter of the newly returned MPs had no parliamentary experience whatsoever. These new members proved exceptionally difficult for the more established hands to control. Even while Harley was launching into a tricky political balancing act, the insurgent Tory backbenchers were scheming to draw the new chief minister away from the centre ground.

The first fruit of their labours was electing William Bromley as Speaker of the House, on the promise that he would champion the traditional high-church values of Sacheverell. Soon thereafter backbenchers formed their own pressure group, the October Club, through which they sought to demonstrate to Harley that he could not govern without their support. Members of the club met most evenings in a tavern near parliament where they drank and sang and railed against the Whigs. Within weeks the membership had swollen into the hundreds. 'They are most of them young gentlemen of estates that has never been in parliament before', wrote Peter Wentworth, 'and are not very close, but declare to everybody what they designe, to have every Whig turn'd out, and not to suffer that the new ministry shou'd shake hands as they see they do with the old.' Harley's readiness to work across the aisle, to shake hands and make deals with those whom the new breed of Tories perceived as enemies, marked him out as a backslider.

Although the October Club's main demand was a full and thorough inquiry into the misconduct of Godolphin and the previous administration, the government's continued failure to protect the church from nonconformity was another key sticking point. In December, the MP for Yorkshire explained the club's desire to 'give us that security to the church we have wanted and thought necessary'. The price of their support had not changed since the early days of Anne's reign. The government must once again propose legislation to outlaw 'that scandalous and impious pretext of occasional conformity', urged the club's manifesto, arguing that this old loophole for dissenters was little more than 'an umbrage for atheism, hypocrisy, and prophaness, and an inlet to faction and enthusiasm, and all sorts of dangerous and destructive sects and opinions'. Their inflated language, like Sacheverell's at the pulpit, was drawn almost verbatim from the *Memorial*.

Harley and his supporters found such declarations of hostility deeply concerning. The minister did not want to let himself be bullied into a corner; neither could he afford to lose control of the House of Commons. As Harley's new chief propagandist, Jonathan Swift was worried that the club was 'growing to a party by itself, and begins to rail at the ministry as much as the Whigs do'. Defoe was called on by his old master to write a hasty *Secret History of the October Club*, setting out the traditional Harleian principles that government ought to be 'in the hands of the disinterested honest men of both sides, without respect to Whig or Tory'. For all their rhetorical power, such calls for moderation ultimately fell on deaf ears. In these days of zeal and enthusiasm, nobody was interested in such middle-of-the-road edicts.

And then everything shifted. On 8 March 1711, the very same day John Cass and Sacheverell opened the charity school at St Botolph's, Harley was stabbed in the chest. Nobody could have predicted the event. The minister had been on the other side of the city, in the Cockpit, interrogating a suspected French double agent, the Marquis de Guiscard. As the suspect was escorted from the chamber, he whipped out a penknife from nowhere and sprang at Harley, planting the blade squarely in his breast. Luckily for the minister, to mark the anniversary of Anne's accession he had been wearing his best waistcoat of pale blue silk thickly embellished with gold thread, beneath a heavy woollen overcoat, lined with buckram around the buttons. As the blade sliced first through the wadding of the coat and then the gold embroidery, the force of the blow was seriously weakened. The knife struck into Harley's breastbone, snapping half an inch above the handle. Guiscard managed a second jab before he was dragged away by the guards, though this time the jagged stump of the broken knife failed to puncture the skin.

For several hours Harley's survival seemed to hang in the balance. Gossip pulled the story in different directions. Some whispered that Guiscard had been aiming for Harley's deputy, Henry St John, and that Harley had got between them. Some heard St John had avenged his master by running Guiscard through with his rapier. Some thought Guiscard's desperate lunge was part of a coordinated French conspiracy against the queen. There were even rumours that the wily Harley had devised the whole incident himself, taking the blow in a desperate attempt to bolster his own reputation. Distraught by news of the assassination attempt, the queen wept all through the night with her ladies-in-waiting. Writing to his friends in Dublin, Swift declared 'my heart is almost broken'. He had been playing cards when he heard the news and rushed across town to Harley's bedside. The wound 'may put him in a fever', Swift feared. 'I am in mortal pain for him.'

Within a few weeks of the attempt on Harley's life and of Sacheverell's triumphant prayers at St Botolph's, a new edition of an old book was advertised in the newspapers. The *Memorial* was back.

Londoners were quick to spot the significance of this new edition. For some, the republication of this most controversial book signalled that it was truly 'the flourishing year of the church', as the title page proclaimed. Thanks to Sacheverell and the October Club, the bleak prospect of tolerance and pluralism had been thwarted. Others saw the book as symptomatic of rotten English politics. A virulent column for one Whig newspaper laid the blame squarely on the printer's shoulders:

As to faction, do we not all remember the æra of the *Memorial*; the sermons of the stamp of that at St Paul's; the tumults, riots, rebellions and progresses, that attended and follow'd the tryal of Sacheverel? And even now the very person who escap'd the pillory for printing the *Memorial*, thro the mercy of the court only, has insolently reprinted it.

The suggestion that David Edwards was guilty of reprinting the *Memorial* would not have troubled Harley, lying in his recovery bed catching up with recent pamphlets. Before the minister's fall two years earlier, he had negotiated a new role for the printer. It was at first Edwards's view that he ought to fill the post of messenger of the press, recently vacated by the elderly Robin Stephens, whom they both agreed 'was always look'd upon as the scum of the trade'. He had proved his value as a government agent, he suggested, and deserved the position.

Harley disagreed. After Edwards's bid for the lucrative *London Gazette* contract failed, the minister arranged an opening in the Thames customs office, inspecting and collecting duties on high-value goods from the East Indies, mostly silks and spices. Harley's men in the customs office reported back that Edwards was doing well. He would soon be promoted to the more senior role of 'landcarriageman'. And while Mary continued occasionally to print and sell books from her stall on Fetter Lane, the press on Nevil's Alley was mostly dormant. So the new edition of the *Memorial* must have come from elsewhere.

Few could match Harley's perceptive eye for detail. He had spent enough hours studying the original *Memorial* to notice that the paper, the lettering, the ornaments used to decorate this edition all looked different. But he was not familiar enough with London printing houses to know precisely where the book originated. Had he asked around, he might have found his answer: that this new edition was produced by Thomas Ilive, a mischievous high-church printer who served his apprenticeship alongside the Jacobite martyr William Anderton. Ilive's was a family business and his three sons all followed him into the trade. His eldest, Jacob, was widely known to be 'an expeditious compositor' who 'knew the letters by the touch', though he had a quirk of working in an overlarge dressing gown, the gaping sleeves of which often dragged pieces of type into the wrong slots. He had not fallen into such bad habits when he helped print the new *Memorial*, the text of which is neat and crisp.

The real question was who provided the text. In a preface outlining the rationale for republishing the *Memorial*, the mastermind of this new edition triumphantly claimed that the battle for the future of the church had now come to a glorious conclusion.

The pamphlet which this is introductory to, has been so much talk'd of, and inveigh'd against, under an administration in other hands, that it is hop'd it will not be displeasing to those that sit at the helm of affairs now: since the publication of it proceeds from no manner of apprehension of the church's being in danger at *present*, but is only reprinted to put them in mind of what she has miraculously escaped.

It was an extraordinarily audacious claim. The *Memorial* had argued that the foundations of church and state had been undermined by the government's slipshod attitude towards dissenters. Parliament and the queen had vehemently refuted such accusations. They had outlawed the book and destroyed it by fire. For the pamphlet to be so 'insolently reprinted' was viewed by many in the press as proof that the churchmen behaved without respect for the queen or her ministers. But to supporters of Sacheverell and the church, this new edition appeared nothing less than a declaration of victory.

Harley was not surprised that his opponents should find in the *Memorial* a prophetic vision of this 'flourishing year'. But another feature of the preface must have come as a shock. Despite his previous efforts to hunt down and prosecute the authors of the *Memorial*, and despite his role as the chief spokesman of moderate cross-party government, a lengthy section of the preface concerned Harley himself. It was a fawning account of his career. More alarming still was the suggestion that Harley was not the moderate he claimed to be. Rather, the pamphlet told how Harley secretly supported the high-church insurgency; all his dealings with the Whigs had been duplicitous; he had been working behind the scenes for many years to bring about the victory foretold by the *Memorial*.

This indefatigable patriot was forc'd to conceal his real designs for a while, and seem[ed] to walk hand in hand with those whose practices he had an aversion to, for fear of being suspected, he has prov'd himself such a friend to the constitution both ecclesiastical and civil, as leaves us no room to doubt his good will

... If this cannot acquit him in some men's opinions, the wounds
which he has lately receiv'd by the hands of an assassin, for
detecting his correspondence with our enemies, must; for he
must be a confess'd good man who has his life practis'd against
and sought by the bad; and, after having escap'd from the machinations of private malice, that would have suborn'd accusations against him, stands rescu'd and deliver'd by the hands of
providence from the open and undissembl'd villany of the worst
of ruffians; a name that can never come up to the nature of so
detestable an attempt as that of the Marquis of Guiscard.

Why would the editor of the new *Memorial* be writing these things
about him? As he scanned the pamphlet, Harley must have asked this
question. It made no sense. Harley had worked against the extremists
in parliament and their October Club. He had devoted many months
to investigating the original *Memorial* and interrogating the suspects
– interrogations from which one witness did not emerge alive. How
could these comments be justified?

Despite his injuries and the queen's insistence that he should recover
fully before returning to the fray, Harley was piqued by the appearance of this new edition. The general reaction to the assassination
attempt had been an outpouring of sympathy. 'It is impossible to
express the firmness and magnanimity which Mr Harley showed upon
this surprising occasion', explained St John, for the 'suddenness of the
blow, the sharpness of the wound, the confusion which followed,
could neither change his countenance, nor alter his voice.' In the
public imagination Harley had very nearly laid down his life for his
country. His patriotism and bravery could not be questioned. And as
the preface to the revamped *Memorial* showed, even the new school
of Tory extremists was forced to change tack and express compassion
for the man it had so recently and so viciously assailed. As Bishop
Burnet later recalled in his memoirs, the incident 'was of great use
to Harley; for the party formed against him was ashamed to push a
man who was thus assassinated by one that was studying to recom-
mend himself to the court of France, and who was believed to have
formed a design against the queen's person'. The minister was a hero.

Who now stood to gain from these fulsome remarks about Harley? The minister knew David Edwards could not have been responsible. And the lawyer Henry Poley was dead, having succumbed to ill health in the summer of 1707. Sir Humphrey Mackworth was still alive, though his star had fallen considerably. In the last year Mackworth's mining company had collapsed. Years before, he had made promises of massive returns for early investors: promises which he was now struggling to keep. In essence, Mackworth had sold too many shares. Revenue from the mines was barely £2,500 each year, whereas the interest due to his shareholders was more than three times that. From the start, Mackworth tried every trick in the book, borrowing money and issuing additional shares to raise cash, with which he would pay off his earlier shareholders. His plan was to keep investing in more mines in hope of future profits. But, as debts began to mount, Mackworth and his fellow company directors grew desperate. Their solution was to manipulate the stock price by cooking the books, before selling their own shares to raise funds which they could then pump into the failing enterprise.

The whole business was a sordid mess. In 1710, disaffected shareholders petitioned parliament in an effort to recover their money. The House of Commons had little choice but to censure Mackworth and rule that he was 'guilty of many notorious and scandalous frauds'. The end result, after months of legal wrangling, was an injunction barring Mackworth from working for the very company he had founded. Responding to events, Mackworth picked up his pen once more, firing off a whole series of pamphlets defending his conduct and honour. It was too late. Disgraced, he sauntered off the public stage. He would continue to work in other speculative businesses over the years, but could never escape the taint of his earlier frauds. Nor did he ever return to frontline politics.

It seemed unlikely, then, that Mackworth could possibly be behind the new *Memorial*. But there was another possible clue. The preface had connected the assassination attempt with earlier 'machinations of private malice, that would have suborn'd accusations' against Harley. Though it stopped short of naming names, everybody knew it was suggesting a moral equivalence between Guiscard's desperate lunge and the attempts by the Whigs in 1708 to implicate Harley in the treason of his clerk, William Greg. Had Harley been found guilty of these trumped-up charges, he would have been sent to the executioner's block. It was a link that Jonathan Swift had already forged in his newspaper the *Examiner*:

> it may be worth observing how unanimous a concurrence there is between some persons once in great power, and a French papist; both agreeing in the great end of taking Mr Harley's life, tho' differing in their methods: the first proceeding by subornation, the other by violence.

Even Harley's old foe William Bromley seemed to agree with Swift. In an enthusiastic speech welcoming the injured minister back to parliament, Bromley expressed relief that providence 'has wonderfully preserved you from some unparalleled attempts'.

Many observed the dangling plural, which was widely believed to have implied the connection which Swift dared to state outright. The preface to the *Memorial* did something very similar. Swift was not in the habit of ushering other people's writings through the press. Nor would he have risked angering his friend and master with a new edition of a notorious libel. But Bromley had lurked on the periphery of the *Memorial* investigation from the start. The original pamphlet had been written expressly to support his candidature for the speakership. He had lost the contest in 1705 before winning in 1710. Now that Bromley occupied the Speaker's chair, his primary concern was reconciling the new ministry headed up by Harley with the extreme faction in his own party. Although Bromley was a hero to many of the new Tory entrants in parliament, the feeling was not fully reciprocated. Rumour had it that Bromley 'absolutely refused' membership of the October Club, when offered. Welcoming Harley back to parliament, Bromley signalled a change in tone. He lauded the minister's years of service and denounced the 'unwearied, and restless endeavours against your person and reputation', alluding as much to his own backbenchers as to their mutual enemies among the Whigs. Could this new *Memorial* have been another front in Bromley's attempt to reconcile the ministry with the malcontents?

If so, there was a price to reconciliation. The reappearance of the *Memorial* showed that Harley could no longer afford to straddle the aisle. He would need to renounce his background and commit to the Tories, becoming a loyal defender of the church. Reprinting such a controversial pamphlet in such a conspicuous, unashamed manner painfully exposed the recent shift in the balance of power towards the Tories. It demonstrated that Harley could no longer restrain the wildest excesses of the churchmen, taunting the minister with his own help-lessness. Equally, if Harley wanted a resolution with the October Club, he would need to meet their demands: bring the war to a close, provide government posts for Tories, alleviate the burden of taxes, and launch an inquiry into the conduct of Godolphin and Marlborough. Despite all Harley's attempts to resist becoming enthralled to either party, he was now put in a situation where his only options were either to submit to the extremists or to risk open conflict and potentially lose the office he had worked so hard to regain.

It was a difficult choice, one that would require Harley's full atten-tion in the weeks ahead. But right now, as he lay in bed recovering from the violent wound to his chest, it was another of the preface's revelations that sparked his curiosity. For the editor of the *Memorial* claimed to divulge another piece of information: the identity of the original author. Not Sir Humphrey Mackworth, nor even Henry Poley alone. The author was claimed to have been that prolific Tory pamphleteer Dr James Drake. Harley saw the problem immediately. It would be impossible to renew his original investigation. For Drake, he knew, was dead.

CHAPTER FOURTEEN

To This Day Unknown

At some point in the autumn of 1705, Dr James Drake shared a drink with the rector of St Botolph's parish church in Aldgate, an observant, scholarly vicar called White Kennett. There is no trace of where they met or precisely when. But Kennett did keep a brief record of their 'long conversation' jotted in the margin of his diary. 'As to Dr Drake', he began, concerning 'his politicks, I am a very great sceptick in reference to his merit in such matters, from a notable argument he made use of [to] me, much about the time that the *Memorial* was published.'

According to Kennett, who aligned himself with the Whigs in parliament, Drake was interested only in the supposed threat of the dissenters. With heroic patience, Kennett tried explaining to the doctor that it was simply implausible that a House of Lords 'where there was not one presbyterian, but twenty-six bishops, or a House of Commons where there was not one in a hundred a dissenter from the establisht church, would ever do any thing to endanger it'. In riposte, Drake spluttered that Kennett was 'so far from entring into the knowledge of that matter' as to be 'ignorant of the fact [that] there were a hundred fanaticks' in the House of Commons already. As for the bishops, most of them would gladly surrender their role in parliament in return for a decent pension. Kennett left the conversation with little doubt that the *Memorial* was 'under direction and management drawn up by Dr Drake'.

Kennett was far from alone in this opinion. John Oldmixon, a down-and-out scribbler who had tried his hand at poetry, drama, criticism, and biography before settling his career as a Whig propagandist, recalled a similar discussion with the high-church preacher

Luke Milbourne, who gained notoriety as a firm supporter of Sacheverell. Over a mug of beer Milbourne whispered to Oldmixon that 'the *Memorial* was written by Dr Drake, with the assistance of Mr Pooley in matters of law, and one of the discarded ministers in matters of politicks'. Drake had confessed his role to 'a confident of his, employ'd in the secretaries office', who had in turn told Milbourne. The story was plausible enough. Even though Oldmixon later wrote in his *History of England* that 'the real authors of the *Memorial* are to this day unknown', he also 'thought the style to be like Dr Drake's'.

Some contemporary readers left traces of their own suspicions on copies of the book itself. Late in 1705 a man called Thomas Rud purchased a copy of Pittis's reprint of the *Memorial*, with the drunken satirist's remarks on each paragraph. Having read the book, Rud made a careful note on the title page: 'writ by Dr Drake a physician and Mr Pooley an eminent lawyer in the court of Chancery'. Another reader shifted the balance of responsibility, writing on the cover: 'By Counsillor Pooley and Dr Drake'. One reader of Defoe's *The High Church Legion*, written to Harley's orders, commented: 'This is an answer to Dr Drake's well known *Memorial of the Church of England.*' Yet another, later reader of the first edition of the *Memorial* took up his pen and inscribed the title page 'By Dr James Drake M.D.'. Inside the cover he wrote a neat summary of the book: 'The design of it is to shew that the then ministry were contriving the destruction of the Church of England and countenanc'd its greatest enemies, and that then all places and preferments were possess'd by the Whigs.'

There were two grounds for attributing the pamphlet to Drake: his reputation and his style. Drake's reputation was forged as much by his enemies as his allies. For that Whig controversialist John Tutchin, he was the quack 'Doctor Duck', who 'dives into lies and forgeries as a *drake* does under water, and always brings up some scandal with him'. While Drake's friends could not disagree with the substance of Tutchin's remarks – for Drake did specialise in scandal – they could shift the emphasis towards his skill as a writer. Abel Roper would praise his 'great mastery of the English tongue' and the 'ease and fluency' with which he wrote 'in a manly stile'. Although Drake's enemies attacked his pamphlets according to their 'different humours, passions and interests', Roper noted, 'all agreed in commending his way of writing'.

Certainly the *Memorial* was no stylistic triumph; but keen-eyed readers would have found plenty of parallels between its 'manly stile' and Drake's previous writings. His notorious debut of 1702, a pamphlet titled *The History of the Last Parliament*, had likewise opened with a savage attack on insidious foes. Whereas 'declared enemies are easily provided against', he wrote, 'corrupt friends betray us willing to the snare'. Drake was talking about state finances here, but the *Memorial*'s opening comment on the 'the treachery or supine negligence' of false friends merits close comparison.

There were also numerous instances of phrases borrowed directly from Drake's contemporaneous periodical *Mercurius Politicus*, which was being published at the very moment the *Memorial* was delivered to Edwards's workshop. In the second issue Drake attacked 'the dissenters and their abettors', a distinctive phrase that the *Memorial* echoed precisely: 'The sudden death of the late king disappointed, mortified and humbl'd the dissenters, and their abettors the Whiggs'. No other contemporary polemicist used that combination of words. Readers of *Mercurius* found Drake arguing in a Hobbesian mode about the rational foundations of the state: 'for the better regulation of men's actions towards one another in this world … civil government was invented by man'. And in the *Memorial*: 'civil government was invented, and magistrates created, to terminate differences among one another'. No less than the parallels spotted with Mackworth's pamphlets, this passage too was a direct match.

Perhaps the most distinctive example of shared vocabulary occurs in the same paragraph, which deploys radical arguments against government ministers who fetter parliament. Here the author of the *Memorial* quoted a familiar Latin maxim. It meant, simply, that citizens ought to have both the ability and the right to protect themselves from harm.

> *Data facultate datur jus facultatem tuendi* is the foundation of all the law in the world. For what does property signify if we have no power to defend that property? Because in the state of nature,

men were frequently unable to withstand singly the violence of invaders; civil government was invented, and magistrates created, to terminate differences among one another and by joynt force to repel and punish that violence, which separately they were not able to resist.

The original source of the aphorism was Hugo Grotius's classic work of political theory, *De Jure Belli*. Undoubtedly, though, the author of the *Memorial* was also drawing on a more recent and equally controversial text: Algernon Sidney's notorious *Discourses Concerning Government*, written before his execution in 1683 but unpublished until 1698. Here Sidney had quoted Grotius's line verbatim, in defence of what he viewed as justified resistance to tyranny.

The only contemporaneous writer to have drawn on this specific passage of Grotius, via Sidney, was Drake himself. He quoted precisely the same Latin tag in his *History of the Last Parliament*:

That the House of Commons are the guardians of the rights and liberties of the people of England, is granted on all hand; and by the nature of the trust itself are invested with a power to defend it, and themselves in the discharge of it; *Quia data facultate datur jus facultatem tuendi*. Those that confer the trust, convey along with it whatever right they have to protect and defend that trust; otherwise it were no trust at all, but an invidious burthen.

Here Drake was arguing that the House of Commons had both the ability and the right to defend itself against the encroachments of ministers – the very same argument that would reappear in the *Memorial*. This strange Latin excerpt appeared nowhere else in contemporary pamphleteering: only in Drake and the *Memorial*. In both form and content, the passages are virtually identical.

Harley had initially dismissed Drake as a candidate. Thanks to Defoe's dutiful reports, he knew that coffeehouse murmurings implicated the doctor. But those same rumours suggested that Drake was only ever the amanuensis of the Duke of Buckingham, who had been the pamphlet's true mastermind. And Harley could not seriously believe that a gallant old courtier like Buckingham could have been responsible for the *Memorial* and its torrents of invective and bile.

While the minister appears to have missed these distinctive parallels with Drake's known writings, the last example did not pass unnoticed by everyone. Ironically the one person to spot the peculiar quotation from Grotius was another high-church pamphleteer, Charles Leslie, who had himself briefly come under fire as a suspected author of the *Memorial*. Despite his shared conviction that the dissenters undermined and endangered the values of the church, Leslie hated the *Memorial*. He thought the author of such a pamphlet ought to subscribe to orthodox Tory doctrine: that kings derived their authority directly from God; and that resistance against a sovereign was an act of rebellion against the deity, the very worst kind of heresy. Instead he saw the pamphlet's foundation in radical political theory, its conviction that government was an *artificial* construct and not a symptom of divine authority. Its arguments were grounded not in the Old Testament, he saw, but rather in the blasphemous writings of Hobbes.

Leslie was appalled. So repulsive did he find this line of argument that he suggested the *Memorial* must be an elaborate hoax. Defoe had pulled a similar stunt in 1702 with his faux Tory polemic *The Shortest-Way with the Dissenters*, the very pamphlet which landed him in prison. What was there to stop the Whigs from pulling the same trick twice? Focusing on the line extracted from Grotius and Sidney, Leslie raved about how the 'principles of government' set out in the *Memorial* were 'diametrically opposite to high church and *jure divino*', and 'therefore this cou'd never come from an high churchman'. In his opinion it was quite 'plain that the design of the author was to personate an high churchman, and [he] wrote with that air'. The intrusion of radical political theory was deemed a telling slip. Sir Jeffrey Jeffreys agreed with Leslie's assessment and even took it upon himself to inform Harley that he thought the *Memorial* came 'from the Whiggish party and low church men, and was writ by them on purpose to throw the odium on the honest part of the nation'. Thomas Hearne likewise wrote that 'it plainly appears to have been done by a Whigg, from the odd scheme of government there laid down, which savours of Hobbism or something worse'.

Leslie and his followers had a knack for grabbing the right stick by the wrong end. There was indeed something curious about the use of this quotation in the *Memorial*, as there was in the pamphlet's blend of high-church zeal with unorthodox political philosophy. If Leslie could spot the oddity of this particular recurring Latin tag, Harley really ought to have done the same. And yet he was so invested in proving Mackworth's guilt that this scrap of evidence slipped through the net.

What did Harley make of the revelation that Drake was involved? Had all those months harvesting information against Mackworth and Poley been wasted? Worryingly, Mackworth was not even mentioned in the 1711 preface. Could all the printer's hunches about the style and the handwriting and the couriers have been mistaken?

Had Harley gone back over the evidence from his initial investigation, he would have found much to comfort him. While the new preface did not name Mackworth as a collaborator, it did admit that Drake worked 'in concert' with Henry Poley. And Edwards's labours revealed beyond doubt that Poley also worked with Mackworth. The physical evidence likewise showed that Drake could not have been working alone, for not one of the documents among Harley's cache of papers was written in his distinctive, archaic hand. Somebody else must have copied out the manuscript and letters to Edwards, at the very least. Drake also supported Bromley during his speakership campaign, and Bromley was close to Arthur Charlett, who was caught distributing the *Memorial* in Oxford. They could all be connected.

It all depended on how far the net was cast. Fox the porter claimed to have spotted seven or eight men in the Devil tavern. It is entirely possible that Mackworth, Poley, and Drake were all part of the club, and Bromley too. It could be that Bromley preferred not to dirty his hands and that Mackworth was acting as his agent in Grub Street. Those men all shared the same distinctive vision of impending darkness. They all believed that the pernicious forces of dissent and heterodoxy could only be resisted by enforcing uniformity with an iron fist, that religious persecution was a legitimate and necessary policy. They all were steeped in the same combination of high-church dogma and radical political theory. Such views were not formed in isolation. It should come as no surprise that they might have been working together.

So why did none of Harley's witnesses mention Drake? Maybe they did. Within months of the *Memorial* being published, Drake commissioned a portrait by a successful young artist called Thomas Forster. Like most of Forster's work, this was to be a little portrait, a miniature in graphite, known in the trade as a *plumbago*. The sitter commands the frame: a heavyset figure with plump cheeks, a patrician nose, and the suggestion of a jowl poking out from behind his tightly knotted cravat. He is a big man. There is the trace of a smile in the corners of his lips and a glimmer of mischief in his eyes, which stare directly out of the frame. He wears a finely brocaded waistcoat under his jacket. Billowing over his shoulders is an ornate, pale wig, the tightly packed white curls captured with a flick of Forster's pencil. This little oval miniature would later become the basis of the engraved portrait of Drake which adorned his medical textbook, *Anthropologia Nova*, when it was published in 1707. In its transfer to print, the likeness admittedly lost some of its vitality. His cheeks appeared slightly droopier, his nose straighter, and his eyes and lips joyless. Despite those slips, Drake remained the same imposing, bewigged figure.

The portrait prompts a simple question. Could *this* be the mysterious tall gentleman in the pale wig and light clothes? The same gentleman spotted scheming with Poley in the Devil tavern and outside Nando's coffeehouse? The same gentleman who summoned Fox the porter and handed him a letter to deliver to Nevil's Alley? Could Drake have been hiding in plain sight all along? Unfortunately, Harley could not pursue this new line of inquiry, even if he had wished to. Drake had been scooped up in the autumn of 1705, following the publication of a seditious article in his newspaper *Mercurius Politicus*, and was brought to trial in the same week as William Pittis. But unlike that other Tory wit, Drake escaped on a technicality. His lawyer pointed out that the clerk had made an error in the indictment, transcribing 'not' instead of 'nor', which was enough to trigger a mistrial.

Such a narrow escape ought to have been cause for celebration. Yet the repeated process of arrest and imprisonment, of trial and retrial had played havoc with Drake's health. Much as Edwards had expected the authors of the *Memorial* to stand by him through his troubles, so too Drake was dismayed when his Tory patrons deserted him. *Mercurius Politicus* was finished. He tried to re-immerse himself in the anatomical research he had abandoned to become a Tory pamphleteer. And his final work, the medical handbook *Anthropologia Nova*, shows that his mind remained sharp as ever. But his body could not withstand the stresses of rejection and disgrace. Early in 1707 Drake contracted a fever. By 2 March he was dead. His colleagues in the Royal College of Physicians remembered him as 'a gentleman of very pregnant parts and good learning' who 'deserved a much better treatment from the great world than he met with in it'. A humble legal clerk, when tasked with surveying prosecutions at the court of King's Bench, noted the generally held belief at court that 'the severe prosecution he underwent on account of *Mercurius Politicus* occasioned the distemper of which he died'.

Given the rumours of Drake's involvement, it comes as a surprise that Harley did not question him when he had the chance. Or it may be that Harley was playing an even deeper game than usual. For all the noise and trouble he stirred, Drake was a mere hack, a lowly scribbler. He could be relied on to stick rigidly to his principles, but would never have worked alone or without payment. Harley knew that, if Drake had been involved with the *Memorial*, somebody else had to have laid out the scheme for the pamphlet, the same master-mind behind the coordinated strike in parliament and the press. Defoe had wrongly thought it was Buckingham, but why not Mackworth? By launching a prosecution against *Mercurius Politicus*, maybe Harley thought he could muffle Drake temporarily while he hunted for more evidence against the men he and Edwards believed to be the pamphlet's true architects.

When the *Memorial* was republished in 1711, it was convenient for all concerned that Mackworth should go unmentioned. Neither Bromley nor the leaders of the October Club wanted to be associated with his corrupt dealings, by which many of them had already lost a great deal of money. Mackworth was a rogue and an outcast. Drake, on the other hand, was an old friend who had been driven to his death by Whig persecution. And Poley died within three days of Drake. More convenient, then, to foist the pamphlet on two dead men, both of whom were considered patriots who had devoted their lives to the cause. Mackworth would be left to sink into obscurity.

Transferring responsibility from Mackworth to Drake was a gradual process. Changing opinions about the book's authorship were recorded by one gentleman reader in his annotations. Between two ruled lines on the title page, a couple of inches from the bottom, this reader carefully inscribed the name of the man whom he believed to be the author: 'By Sir H. Mackworth'. In 1711, after the attribution to Drake and Poley was made in public, he returned to the book and crossed a thin, hesitant line through the original note, replacing it with: 'By James Drake M.D. and Mr. Poley'. And so, with that simple stroke of fortune, with the flick of a pen, Mackworth was crossed out of the story and replaced by two dead men.

Harley was an inveterate hoarder. After his death in 1724, Harley's son, Edward, wrote to Jonathan Swift about the 'vast collection of letters and other papers' which his father, Swift's friend, had left behind. When Harley filed away his notes on the *Memorial* investigation, he stored them in this private collection and not among the government archives. Also among those personal papers was kept a little book from a series titled *The Political State of Great Britain*, recounting the tumultuous events of April 1711, ranging from the Guiscard incident to 'several political books and pamphlets lately publish'd'.

One of Harley's friends brought him this latest issue of the *Political State* soon after its publication, in May, while the minister was still nursing his wounds. Although it was written by one of his supporters, the journalist Abel Boyer, Harley found the book particularly irksome. Several pages were devoted to a sensational narrative of the failed attempt on his life. Harley quickly worked his way through the account with his pen, scribbling and slicing furious notes across the margins, the damp ink smudging as he turned the pages. 'Groundless', he snapped at several points, and 'Not one word true'. When the narrative claimed that Guiscard had 'stepp'd towards the table, as if he design'd to say something to Mr Harley' before stabbing him, the minister scrawled 'false', and again where it claimed the French agent also lunged at Harley's deputy, Henry St John. In the space of a single page Harley made three notes of 'not true' and another half-a-dozen underlinings and deletions. The scruffiness and pace of the annotations witness the minister's intensity of feeling as he read the book.

Much of the last six pages reported on the reappearance of the *Memorial* and on the contents of its extraordinary new preface.

> The author of this pamphlet, which, at that time, made so great a noise, had hitherto been unknown, or, at least, only guess'd at: but the editor of this new impression acquaints us in the preface, that it was written by Dr James Drake, a physician, with the assistance of Mr Poley, who are both deceas'd.

Here Harley's pen failed him. The cantankerous outbursts which had run thick and fast through the book all but dried up. He underlined the clause regarding Poley, and made an arrow in the margin, but appears not to have been interested by the new attribution to Drake. Flicking through the pages, Harley once more focused his attention. Where the book labelled David Edwards 'a papist', he underlined it. Where the book mentioned 'a promise, in writing, from Mr Secretary Harley' to the troubled printer, he underlined it. Where the book noted the allegations against Poley and Mackworth, he underlined it. And where the book quoted Poley complaining about the ministry's treatment of him and Mackworth, Harley jotted 'false' in the margin.

The very final leaf of the book turned conclusively to the 'undiscover'd' author of this 'obnoxious' pamphlet. It considered and weighed up the potential authorship of Drake and Mackworth and Poley. Here, at last, was a space for Harley to record his final thoughts on the case, his assessment of the degree to which each of those men was involved. It was a case he knew better than any man alive. Harley alone understood the twists and turns of the paper trails and where they had led. But if he did record his thoughts on Drake and his part in the *Memorial* scandal, those thoughts have not survived. For the final, revelatory leaf has been ripped from the book, and with it any notes that Harley may have made. All that remains is a stub. The rest of the leaf is gone. Was it torn out in rage? In disbelief? Was it a clumsy mistake? Or has the frail little book simply become damaged over the centuries? As so often in the hunt for the *Memorial*, what may be the final, crucial piece of evidence lurks just out of reach.

In another world, the appearance of this new *Memorial* might have prompted Harley to speak out. But he knew that he could not do so without enraging his new political rivals. Edwards, too, could have returned to the fold by issuing a response to the new edition, setting the story straight once and for all. He had much to say about those fiendish gentlemen who promised protection in an hour of need and granted none, who turned friends against him and ruined his livelihood. And yet he, like Harley, kept silent. Experience had taught him to avoid the fray.

In the letter he had written to the minister while in hiding, Edwards had spoken of his hope that 'if great trees be pull'd down, his lordship will not destroy a shrub'. The printer knew that lowly pawns were often the first casualties in elaborate games of state. His determination to survive at any cost was perhaps Edwards's greatest asset. He had his convictions and loyalties and allegiances, but only up to a point. Rather like Harley, the printer could become a chameleon when he needed. In his youth he had developed a talent for moving effortlessly between men of all parties, training under a Whig master before turning his hand to the Jacobites. As an agent for Harley, he was able to navigate both the London literary underground and the corridors of Whitehall. But it had been an exhausting and dangerous career. Edwards was ready for change, for a safer, simpler life. Though Mary's little book stall continued to do steady business, the printer had left that gruelling world behind.

One can imagine Edwards, returning home to Nevil's Alley from the customs house on a spring evening, when he spots the new edition of the *Memorial* pasted up in a city bookseller's window. His interest piqued, he steps through the door and greets the shopkeeper in his deep Welsh lilt. Asking for the book, he hands over a shilling. Carefully he folds and tucks the loosely stitched pages into his coat. For old times' sake, he stops by the Dog tavern to read a little over a drink. Opening the pamphlet, he sees the late James Drake announced as the true mastermind behind the *Memorial*. Surprised, he flicks through for some mention of his old enemy, Mackworth, but finds nothing. Perhaps he sighs, perhaps rolls his eyes, before taking a sip from his cup. It does not matter, he thinks. He has already escaped the game.

Across town, seated comfortably in the undisturbed quiet of his personal chambers, Harley scans his eyes across the same pages. When he first read the *Memorial* all those years ago, he had been more intrigued than appalled by the pamphlet. It was a puzzle waiting to be solved, a knot ready to be untangled. Back then, he had failed. And now the fruits of his failure have returned to haunt him, to back him into a corner, to force his hand. In its revamped form, the old pamphlet presents a new challenge. He lays down the papers on his desk for a moment, glancing into the fire in thought. He pours himself a drink before dipping his quill and settling into his work. For the minister, escape is not an option. The game is all there is, he thinks. And he does not play to lose.

Epilogue
Between the Lines

On the morning of Friday 6 November 1719, John Matthews awoke in his Newgate cell. He was just a boy, barely eighteen years old, convicted of printing Jacobite pamphlets in his mother's workshop. Outside it was raining, great drops that thundered against the prison walls and dripped through the windows. This morning was to be his last.

The mood on that November morning was far from sombre. Having turned his attention to the English penal system, the Dutch philosopher Bernard Mandeville was appalled by the usual atmosphere on an execution day. Where he had expected to find sorrow and sober contrition, he was instead barraged with a cacophony of howling, laughter, and quarrelling, as inmates fought over 'substantial breakfasts' and 'seas of beer'. Two other men, a highwayman and a thief who feigned blindness, would accompany Matthews to the gallows that day. They had begun drinking at dawn. Matthews was different. The previous Sunday he had enjoyed a bottle of wine in chapel with his fellow prisoners, much to the annoyance of one dour old man sitting a little further along the pew. Back then they laughed and drank and read saucy ballads, which they had sneaked into chapel beneath their hats. But this morning he alone was serious, silent, and stone-cold sober.

At noon the bells of St Sepulchre's rang out. It was the signal to move. Mr Constable, the highwayman, would travel in style, in his own personal coach. Matthews had no such comfort. He was roughly bundled into a sledge and dragged through the main gates into the street. The convoy was met with 'a torrent of mob' lining the mucky road to Tyburn. Thousands of men and women had braved the rain for the occasion. Although there were apprentices and respectable tradesmen in the crowd, most were of the lowest sort. Vast numbers proved difficult to police and, as Mandeville pointed out, supplied pickpockets and other villains with a cover for their mischief. 'All the way from Newgate to Tyburn is one continued fair', he wrote, packed equally with 'rakehells' and 'trollops'. The edges of the crowd were also where the mob was most fierce, jostling and brawling and whoring. Drunkards lurked on the periphery, hurling 'the dead carcasses of dogs and cats' like 'ill-boding meteors' into the throng, for nothing more than their own amusement. Eventually the hanging tree loomed into view. From three sturdy crossbeams of oak hung three ropes, swaying back and forth in the wind and rain. The nooses gaped open and hungry. Death awaited at Tyburn; but the route there was full of life.

In that sea of chaos, Matthews was an island of calm. Another young printer called Thomas Gent was in the throng. Years later he could still remember Matthews's journey to the gallows in vivid detail.

> I beheld him drawn on a sledge, as I stood near St Sepulchre's church; his clothes were exceeding neat, the lining of his coat a rich Persian silk, and every other thing as befitted a gentleman. I was told he talked, like a philosopher, of death, to some young ladies, who came to take their farewell, and suffered with a perfect resignation.

By the time he arrived at Tyburn, those silks were splattered with filth from the streets. The sound of balladeers singing songs of his impending doom drifted over the crowd:

> John Matthews for high treason you must die,
> First to be hang'd upon the gallows high,
> While you're alive thy body be cut down,
> Thy bowels in the burning fire thrown,
> And then thy limbs for to be cut in twain.

He remained composed, even finding time to salute Mr Constable the highwayman, shaking his hand and offering words of comfort. Beneath the scaffold he huddled and prayed 'very earnestly' with three priests, clutching his prayer book against his chest before gesturing to the presiding officer and handing it over. Inside the front cover were neatly written instructions to carry his body to an undertaker on Fleet Street. The officer nodded and explained that his sentence had been lessened. Unlike most traitors, Matthews was to receive a clean death, choking on the noose until dead. His body would be left unmutilated.

At the officer's signal, Matthews climbed the steps and placed his neck into the noose. One observer was struck that 'he appear'd very grave and compos'd and seem'd unconcern'd, and without any dread or terror at the punishment he was to undergo'. Another wrote that 'he behaved himself with an undaunted courage, shewing great magnanimity of soul, a steady and unshaken resolution, and might, had his cause been but truly meritorious, have been esteemed a more than primitive Christian martyr'. Looking out from his vantage point, Matthews saw the people of London stretched out before him, thousands of men and women who looked to be braying and cheering and weeping and screaming, though their voices were muffled by the rain. He closed his eyes and whispered his final prayers. '*Into thy hands O Lord I commend my spirit, Lord Jesus receive my soul.*' His breathing quickened while his heart thundered in his chest. His time had come.

John Matthews was the last printer to be executed on British soil. While he was the last to suffer the horrific fate of William Anderton, who went to the gallows in 1693, he was by no means the final victim of English censorship. The long-anticipated death of Queen Anne in the summer of 1714 did little to calm the nation, as she left behind no heir of her body. Her cousin, the foreign-born George I, acceded to the throne peacefully enough. But while the mischievous Tories of the October Club slunk away upon George landing in England, the Jacobite rebellion of the following year prompted a government crackdown on the opposition press. In April 1715, the ambitious political climber Robert Walpole was tasked with hunting down evidence of treason among Tories, as chairman of the new 'Committee of Secrecy'.

Bookshops were raided and presses smashed. Information was coerced from nervous printers. Among their number was Robert Tooke, who possessed seditious manuscripts in the handwriting of a young poet called Richard Savage. Fearing for his life, he handed them over to one Robert Girling, a thuggish government operative who would later assist in the capture of John Matthews. It was justice of a sort. Savage had himself escaped an earlier charge of 'having a treasonable pamphlet in his possession' only by informing on another underground printer.

The main casualty of Walpole's investigations was Harley himself. After a mental tussle and much wrangling with his conscience, the minister had answered the call of the *Memorial* in 1711. Once Bromley and the other senior Tories had expressed their support for him, and he had reciprocated by indicating his desire to enact Tory policies, the majority of the party rank and file stepped into line. On 23 May the queen elevated Harley to the House of Lords as the Earl of Oxford and, six days later, named him the new Lord High Treasurer. The ceremonial white staff of office which Godolphin had held for the better part of a decade now belonged to him.

Following his elevation to the position of Lord High Treasurer, Harley committed himself to the October Club's primary mission: the resolution of peace with France. From his Whitehall office, the minister directed a whole series of pamphlets to this end, of which the crowning glory was Jonathan Swift's *The Conduct of the Allies* in November 1711, a brutal indictment of the Whigs' bloodthirstiness and warmongering. Many months of covert negotiations ensued between diplomats from all the concerned nations, before a treaty was finally ratified in 1713. The Tories rejoiced at the news. Not least among the cheerleaders were the poets, for whom the founts of inspiration flowed free. Regarding the peace treaty's many adversaries, and the many plots and counterplots Harley managed to foil, the poet Bevil Higgons wrote:

> This Harley saw, and touch'd with gen'rous grief,
> Flew to his country's, and his queen's relief;
> This mutual good pursu'd with steady view,

And on his head the faction's vengeance drew.
Long, like a rock unmov'd the patriot stood,
And bravely stem'd the strong impetuous flood
Till threats at last and insolence prevail'd,
When black designs and subornation fail'd.

But, as Higgons's final couplet suggested, this enthusiasm was not shared by all. In the final months of Anne's reign, during the spring and summer of 1714, Harley faced a new challenge from inside his own ranks. His deputy Henry St John, now styled Viscount Bolingbroke, had formerly been a rising star of the October Club. Even while Harley appeared to be championing the policies and interests of the Tories, Bolingbroke was sowing the seeds of division afresh. When Harley's favourite daughter, Elizabeth, tragically died in November 1713, and the minister sought solace in drink, Bolingbroke exploited his absence to ingratiate himself with the queen and drive a wedge between the extreme Tories and the moderates, undoing years of patient, subtle work. Just a few days before her death on 1 August 1714, Anne was reluctantly persuaded to dismiss Harley from office, citing his riddles and cryptic manner of speech, his constant scheming, and his gradual descent into the bottle.

When George I arrived on British shores in September, the new king immediately surrounded himself with counsellors drawn from the Whigs. They agreed that the settlement of peace had been an unpardonable betrayal of England's allies, who had wished to continue hostilities against France until the bitter end. All those months of complex diplomacy and negotiations which had previously won Harley such praise would now prove his undoing. In July 1715, Walpole's committee presented sixteen articles of impeachment against the former minister and his erstwhile deputy. Mostly these articles concerned how Harley and Bolingbroke had behaved while negotiating the peace accord, but Walpole also levelled explosive claims that they had flirted with the Jacobites.

Parliament agreed to investigate. Bolingbroke fled for the Continent before he could be questioned, seeking refuge among the exiled Jacobites. Harley chose to remain in London and brave it out. Though demonstrably false, the charge of treason would hang over his neck for another two years, which time he spent shuttered away in the Tower. Although the conditions were tolerable enough, with fires and decent rations and access to books and visitors, Harley's health, mental and physical, deteriorated fast. The old wound to his chest ached and his lungs stiffened. By the time the articles of impeachment were dropped in June 1717, when Harley was acquitted without trial, he was no longer the agile political tactician of earlier years. He retired to the country and his library.

Many of Harley's former allies had either abandoned him or gone into exile. Swift was in Dublin. He had privately written a lengthy vindication of the minister's conduct in office, though never mustered the courage to publish it. In 1714 Harley's erstwhile propagandist John Toland presented an embittered work anticipating Walpole's accusations of Jacobite sympathies. Only Defoe, it seemed, would stand by his former employer. In 1714 he published *The Secret History of the White Staff*, a heartfelt exoneration of Harley from all charges of sedition, treason, and plotting. When Harley was impeached in 1715, Defoe churned out yet another defence of the old minister. But the nation was in no mood to listen.

Harley would not have approved of the execution of John Matthews. Despite his reputation as the 'president of the pillory', he always preferred more subtle means of censorship. He saw little point in silencing a potential source. Why execute a printer when one might persuade them to turn on their allies and discover further information for the government? A well-placed spy was more valuable than a corpse. Matthews took his secrets to the gallows. He surrendered nothing. When summoned by the Privy Council to offer information that could save his skin, Matthews reeled off a 'foolish story, but would not tell who was the author'. As one of his fellow inmates reported, 'in confinement neither the threats of death, the austerity of the gaoler, shackles, irons, fetters or darksome dungeon, could deter his intrepid heart'. While this is perhaps testimony to the young printer's courage in the face of certain death, it is more likely a damning indictment of his interlocutors.

David Edwards had been no such martyr. In Harley's hands he had been cajoled into surrendering all his information and persuaded to go out into the world as the minister's secret agent. His saving grace was that he knew enough to be useful. And his ultimate failure to solve the mystery of the *Memorial* is a reflection not of his ability or tenacity as an investigator, rather of the stealth of his adversaries. Even now, the woman in the vizard mask retains her disguise. If Edwards had chased up the enigmatic 'Mrs Jones in child bed' whom Nurse Gough mentioned under interrogation, or even his later suspect, Susan Garrett, a little sooner, perhaps the puzzle would have been solved. He and Mary gathered plenty of evidence in the course of their investigations, all of which points towards Drake and Mackworth and Poley being in on it together, along with the rest of their cabal. Yet without the woman in the vizard mask, it is impossible to know for sure.

History is seldom neat, and many of the secrets of the *Memorial* died with its authors. But as Harley knew, the thrill is not in the solution; it is in the chase. The paper trail led from the compositor's bench in Thomas Braddyll's workshop, where Edwards learned his trade, to the dingy upstairs corridors of the Devil tavern, where the little letter was handed to the porter; from the candlelit interrogation chamber in Whitehall, in the corner of which Harley's secretary sat taking notes, to Strahan's bookshop on Cornhill; from Mackworth's house on Snow Hill to the hanging tree of Tyburn. Only a renewed investigation into Mackworth's unconventional ideas and Drake's turns of phrase has enabled us to grasp them by the coat-tails.

Nothing survives of Edwards's workshop on Nevil's Alley. The last houses there were demolished in 1911, having fallen into disrepair. There are a couple of photos preserved by the London Topographical Society, sepia-toned and shadowy, which show the buildings in their original state: the windows which once illuminated the bustle of the pressmen and compositors, set behind a low picket fence; the narrow doorway where the mysterious woman in the vizard mask knocked one hot summer afternoon. All that remains today are the books. Against the odds, those fragile documents have survived, tucked away in libraries, safe in their manila folders and leather bindings. If the pages could speak, their mysteries might be solved in a moment. David and Mary Edwards are no longer with us. Harley and Mackworth and Drake have all returned to dust. The woman in the vizard mask has slipped into shadow. But the books remain. Between the lines, beneath the ink, the full story is there for all to see, if only we can learn to look a little closer.

Bibliographical Essay

What follows is intended to direct readers towards further reading on the topics explored in this book and to provide some sense of the body of historical scholarship on which I have drawn. For while this book is based overwhelmingly on my own grubbing in the archives, digging up fresh primary sources, it is nonetheless deeply beholden to research undertaken over the past fifty years and more. Details of primary sources can be found in my notes, but, for the sake of brevity, I have not provided references to the works of history and bibliography which govern my assumptions. Those works are listed here.

Principal Documents

The depositions and interrogation documents concerning the *Memorial* investigation are among the Portland Papers in Nottingham University Library and the British Library (formerly Loan 23: a concordance to the papers is available in the Manuscripts Reading Room, but no catalogue). The vast majority of the interrogation documents can be found in BL, Add. MS 70340. Correspondence related to the *Memorial* is scattered throughout, though the main concentration of letters is in Add. MS 70023. The manuscript of the *Memorial* used by Edwards is filed in Add. MS 70103, alongside the letter received from Nando's coffeehouse. I have also made extensive use of the State Papers in the National Archives at Kew.

Books from Edwards's workshop have been traced in a number of ways. Some forty books survive bearing the imprint of either David or Mary Edwards, or with their initials. But, as a printer whose trade was overwhelmingly clandestine and covert, most of Edwards's output bore no traceable imprint. Sometimes these books can be identified through contemporary documents. Arrest warrants, court records, and correspondence occasionally name the books for which Edwards was responsible. More often, though, these books have been traced through bibliographical means: using unique ornaments and damaged pieces of type to identify the output of Edwards's press on Nevil's Alley. On this mode of bibliographical detective work as a methodology, see Andrew Benjamin Bricker, 'Who was "A. Moore"? The Attribution of Eighteenth-Century Publications with False and Misleading Imprints', *The Papers of the Bibliographical Society of America*, 110 (2016), 1–34; and Hazel Wilkinson, 'Printers' Flowers as Evidence in the Identification of Unknown Printers: Two Examples from 1715', *The Library*, 7th ser., 14 (2013), 70–79. For bravura examples of this method in practice, see two essays by Noel Malcolm: 'The Printing of the "Bear": New Light on the Second Edition of Hobbes's *Leviathan*', in *Aspects of Hobbes* (Oxford, 2002), 336–82 and 'The Making of the Ornaments: Further Thoughts on the Printing of the Third Edition of *Leviathan*', *Hobbes Studies*, 21 (2008), 3–37. For a detailed account situating Edwards's printing career in broader historical contexts, see my article 'David Edwards and the Later Stuart Underground Press', forthcoming in *The English Historical Review*.

Historical Context

The classic study of politics in this period is Geoffrey Holmes's *British Politics in the Age of Anne* (London, 1967), of which a revised edition with an updated preface was published in 1987. Holmes's understanding of both the structure of politics and of the key issues at stake has not been surpassed. J. P. Kenyon's *Revolution Principles: The Politics of Party 1689–1720* (Cambridge, 1977) also remains an important text, although Mark Knight's two excellent books, *Representation and Misrepresentation in Later Stuart Britain: Partisanship and Political Culture* (Oxford, 2005) and *The Devil in Disguise: Delusion, Deception and Fanaticism in the Early English Enlightenment* (Oxford, 2011), provide a greater sense of the turbulence of partisan strife during the reign of Anne. Other studies include Paul Halliday, *Dismembering the Body Politic: Partisan Politics in England's Towns, 1650–1730* (Cambridge, 1998); Gary S. de Krey, *A Fractured Society: The Politics of London in the First Age of Party 1688–1715* (Oxford, 1985); James O. Richards, *Party Propaganda Under Queen Anne: The General Elections of 1702–1713* (Athens, GA, 1972); W. A. Speck, *Tory and Whig: The Struggle in the Constituencies, 1701–15* (London, 1970); and my own small intervention, *Literature and Party Politics at the Accession of Queen Anne* (Oxford, 2017).

There is no single, satisfactory biography of Robert Harley. That may be because, as Geoffrey Holmes has put it, 'One of the most subtle, oblique and complex politicians who have ever lived will always defy any interpretation of his career that is too simplistic' (xxv). However, readers familiar with scholarship on this period will immediately recognise my debt to the work of J. A. Downie, particularly his excellent book *Robert Harley and the Press: Propaganda and Public Opinion in the Age of Swift and Defoe* (Cambridge, 1979), in which the *Memorial* features as a case study. Downie's focus on Harley's exploitation of the press to advance his own political agenda remains one of the best studies of its kind. Other full-length works on Harley include Elizabeth Hamilton, *The Backstairs Dragon: A Life of Robert Harley, Earl of Oxford* (New York, 1970); Brian W. Hill, *Robert Harley: Speaker, Secretary of State, and Prime Minister* (New Haven, 1988); and Angus McInnes, *Robert Harley, Puritan Politician* (London, 1970). Important articles which have had some bearing on my approach include D. W. Hayton, 'Harley, Robert (1661–1724)', in Eveline Cruickshanks et al., eds., *The History of Parliament: The House of Commons, 1690–1715*, 5 vols. (Cambridge, 2002), IV. 244–80; Geoffrey Holmes and W. A. Speck, 'The Fall of Harley in 1708 Reconsidered', *English Historical Review*, 80 (1965), 673–98; Henry L. Snyder, 'Godolphin and Harley: A Study of Their Partnership in Politics', *Huntington Library Quarterly*, 30 (1967), 241–71; H. T. Dickinson, 'The October Club', *Huntington Library Quarterly*, 33 (1970), 155–73.

On specific elections to parliament and on individual MPs, including Mackworth and Poley, see their entries in the relevant volumes of *The History of Parliament* and the *Oxford Dictionary of National Biography*. Although the lowly hack authors and scribblers encountered in this book have not attracted a great deal of scholarly attention, there are some important studies, most notably Pat Rogers's *Grub Street: Studies in a Subculture* (London, 1972). On William Pittis, see Theodore F. M. Newton, 'William Pittis and Queen Anne Journalism', *Modern Philology*, 33 (1936), 169–86 and 279–302. On Ned Ward, see Howard William Troyer, *Ned Ward of Grub Street: A Study of Sub-Literary London in the Eighteenth Century* (Cambridge, MA, 1946). On John Tutchin, see Lee Sonsteng Horsley, 'The Trial of John Tutchin, Author of the *Observator*', *Yearbook of English Studies*, 3 (1973), 124–40; Edward Taylor, 'John Tutchin's *Observator*, Comment Serials, and the "Rage of Party" in Britain, 1678–1730', *Historical Journal*, 63 (2020), forthcoming. On Charles Leslie, see Ian Higgins, 'Jonathan Swift and Charles Leslie', in Paul Monod, Murray Pittock and Daniel Szechi, eds., *Loyalty and Identity: Jacobites at Home and Abroad* (Basingstoke, 2010), 149–66.

Mackworth is the subject of a single article dealing with his mining business: Koji Yamamoto, 'Piety, Profit and Public Service in the Financial Revolution', *English Historical Review*, 126 (2011), 806–34. The most perceptive scholar on Mackworth, Drake, and their milieu is Mark Goldie: see his 'Situating Swift's Politics in 1701', in Claude Rawson, ed., *Politics and Literature in the Age of Swift: English and Irish Perspectives* (Cambridge, 2010), 31–51 and 'Tory Political Thought, 1688–1714' (unpublished doctoral thesis, University of Cambridge, 1977); though see too J. A. W. Gunn, *Beyond Liberty and Property: The Process of Self-Recognition in Eighteenth-Century Political Thought* (Kingston, 1983), 127–33; Isaac Kramnick, *Bolingbroke and His Circle: The Politics of Nostalgia in the Age of Walpole* (Cornell, 1992), 142–3.

Two of the writers employed by Harley have received extensive scholarly treatment, though predominantly for their literary writings and not their journalistic hack work. Daniel Defoe and Jonathan Swift became titans of eighteenth-century literature, but were both for a time willing to put their pens to Harley's service. There is much good writing on both men; there is much bad writing on both men. On Defoe, the two main biographies to seek out are Paula R. Backscheider, *Daniel Defoe: His Life* (Baltimore, 1989) and Maximillian E. Novak, *Daniel Defoe: Master of Fictions* (Oxford, 2001). On Swift, see David Nokes, *Jonathan Swift: A Hypocrite Reversed* (Oxford, 1985); and John Stubbs, *Jonathan Swift: The Reluctant Rebel* (London, 2018). And on this particular phase of his career, see J. A. Downie, *Jonathan Swift: Political Writer* (London, 1984); and Ashley Marshall, *Swift and History: Politics and the English Past* (Cambridge, 2015). For both men's dealings with Harley, Downie's *Robert Harley and the Press* remains the key jump-off point.

The role of religion in political affairs during this period is complex. On the high church movement, and Sacheverell in particular, see Brian Cowan, ed., *The State Trial of Doctor Henry Sacheverell* (Malden, 2012); Geoffrey Holmes, *The Trial of Dr Sacheverell* (London, 1973); Howard Weinbrot, *Literature, Religion, and the Evolution of Culture, 1660–1780* (Baltimore, 2013); and Brent S. Sirota, *The Christian Monitors: The Church of England and the Age of Benevolence, 1680–1730* (New Haven, 2014). On varieties of dissent and their relation to politics, see the essays contained in Robert D. Cornwall and William Gibson, eds., *Religion, Politics and Dissent, 1660–1832* (Aldershot, 2010); Mark Goldie, *Roger Morrice and the Puritan Whigs* (Woodbridge, 2007); John Spurr, *The Post-Reformation: Religion, Politics and Society in Britain, 1603–1714* (Harlow, 2006); and Blair Worden, *Roundhead Reputations: The English Civil Wars and the Passions of Posterity* (London, 2001). On occasional conformity, in particular, see Ralph Stevens, *Protestant Pluralism: The Reception of the Toleration Act, 1689–1720* (Woodbridge, 2018). An interesting and important essay situating the *Memorial* and Sacheverell within the *longue durée* is Nicholas Tyacke, 'The "Rise of Puritanism" and the Legalizing of Dissent, 1571–1719', in Ole Peter Grell, Jonathan I. Israel and Nicholas Tyacke, eds., *From Persecution to Toleration: The Glorious Revolution and Religion in England* (Oxford, 1991), 17–50.

On the Jacobite movement, in which Edwards was so deeply implicated, see Paul Kléber Monod, *Jacobitism and the English People, 1688–1788* (Cambridge, 1989); Daniel Szechi, *Jacobitism and Tory Politics,*

1710–14 (Edinburgh, 1984). Our most thorough studies of conspiracy and espionage in this period are Rachel Weil, *A Plague of Informers: Conspiracy and Political Trust in William III's England* (New Haven, 2013) and Melinda S. Zook, *Radical Whigs and Conspiratorial Politics in Late Stuart England* (Pennsylvania, 1999). Whereas Zook concentrates on the radicals, Weil's focus is Jacobite plotting and counter-intelligence. On press informants, see Leona Rostenberg, 'Robert Stephens, Messenger of the Press: An Episode in Seventeenth-Century Censorship', *Papers of the Bibliographical Society of America*, 49 (1955), 131–52; Henry L. Snyder, 'The Reports of a Press Spy for Robert Harley: New Bibliographical Data for the Reign of Queen Anne', *Library*, 5th ser., 22 (1967), 326–45; and Michael Treadwell, 'A Further Report from Harley's Press Spy', *Library*, 6th ser., 2 (1980), 216–18. And on the role of women in the early clandestine services, see Nadine Akkerman, *Invisible Agents: Women and Espionage in Seventeenth-Century Britain* (Oxford, 2018).

Printing History

Information on the early modern book trade is drawn from a number of secondary sources. Chief among them are Adrian Johns's capacious study *The Nature of the Book: Print and Knowledge in the Making* (Chicago, 1998) and three books by James Raven: *The Business of Books: Booksellers and the English Book Trade 1450–1850* (New Haven, 2007), *Bookscape: Geographies of Printing and Publishing in London Before 1800* (London, 2014), and *Publishing Business in Eighteenth-Century England* (Woodbridge, 2014). Donald F. McKenzie and Maureen Bell's three-volume *A Chronology and Calendar of Documents Relating to the London Book Trade, 1641–1700* (Oxford, 2005) has been a useful starting point for research on the later part of the seventeenth century, though its coverage is by no means complete. Classic studies also include Elizabeth L. Eisenstein, *The Printing Press as an Agent of Change*, 2 vols. (Cambridge, 1980); Donald F. McKenzie's collection of seminal essays, *Making Meaning: 'Printers of the Mind' and Other Essays*, ed. Peter D. McDonald and Michael F. Suarez (Amherst, 2002); and the essays collected in Michael Harris et al., eds., *The London Book Trade: Topographies of Print in the Metropolis from the Sixteenth Century* (Oak Knoll, 2003).

On the role of the early Stationers' Company, the major work is now Peter W. M. Blayney, *The Stationers' Company and the Printers of London, 1501–1557*, 2 vols. (Cambridge, 2014). See too Cyprian Blagden, *The Stationers' Company: A History, 1403–1959* (London, 1960); and Michael Harris and Robin Myers, eds., *The Stationers' Company and the Book Trade 1550–1990* (Winchester, 1997). On the specific state of London printing in this period, see Michael Treadwell, 'London Printers and Printing Houses in 1705', *Publishing History*, 7 (1980), 5–44; and Don-John Dugas, 'The London Book Trade in 1709', *Papers of the Bibliographical Society of America*, 95 (2001), 31–58 and 157–72. On women in the book trade, see Paula McDowell's important study *The Women of Grub Street: Press, Politics, and Gender in the London Literary Marketplace 1678–1730* (Oxford, 1998).

On underground printing more generally, the classic work remains Robert Darnton's *The Literary Underground of the Old Regime* (Cambridge, MA, 1982), although his focus is strictly eighteenth-century France. On censorship, seditious libel, and the application of treason statutes to printing in England, see Paul Monod, 'The Jacobite Press and English Censorship, 1689–95', in Eveline Cruickshanks and Edward Corp, eds., *The Stuart Court in Exile and the Jacobites* (London, 1995), 125–42; Ian Higgins, 'Censorship, Libel and Self-Censorship', in Paddy Bullard and James McLaverty, eds., *Jonathan Swift and the Eighteenth-Century Book* (Cambridge, 2013), 17–98; Joseph Hone, 'Legal Constraints, Libellous Evasions', in Paddy Bullard, ed., *The Oxford Handbook of Eighteenth-Century Satire* (Oxford, 2019), 525–41; and Thomas Keymer, *Poetics of the Pillory: English Literature and Seditious Libel, 1660–1820* (Oxford, 2019). On the execution of John Matthews, see R. J. Goulden, '*Vox Populi, Vox Dei*: Charles Delafaye's Paperchase', *Book Collector*, 28 (1979), 368–90. Other books worth seeking out include Lois G. Schwoerer, *The Ingenious Mr Henry Care, Restoration Publicist* (Baltimore, 2002); and Paul Baines and Pat Rogers, *Edmund Curll, Bookseller* (Oxford, 2007).

London

For maps of London, I have worked from John Strype's of 1720 and Herman Moll's of 1736, which is the better labelled of the two, though the city had changed substantially by then. For a general history of the city in this period, see Jerry White, *London in the Eighteenth Century: A Great and Monstrous Thing* (London, 2012). On taverns and alehouses, see Peter Clark, *The English Alehouse: A Social History, 1200–1830* (London, 1983); and Mark Hailwood, *Alehouses and Good Fellowship in Early Modern England* (Woodbridge, 2014). On coffeehouses, see Brian Cowan, *The Social Life of Coffee: The Emergence of the British Coffeehouse* (New Haven, 2005); and Markman Ellis, *The Coffee-House: A Cultural History* (London, 2004). On prisons, see Tim Hitchcock, *Down and Out in Eighteenth-Century London* (London, 2004); and Tim Hitchcock and Robert Shoemaker, *London Lives: Poverty, Crime and the Making of a Modern City, 1690–1800* (Cambridge, 2015). On 'Grub Street' and the London literary scene more generally, see Pat Rogers, *Grub Street: Studies in a Subculture* (London, 1972); and Paula McDowell, *The Women of Grub Street*.

Acknowledgements

This book began life early in 2017, in the Manuscripts Reading Room of the British Library. Rummaging through the papers of Robert Harley, I encountered the sworn statements of David and Mary Edwards. I had time only for a brief look at the documents before dashing to King's Cross and the train to Cambridge. But I returned the following morning and spent the week camped upstairs in the British Library, working my way through hundreds of pages of depositions, letters, and interrogation transcripts.

That my own paper chase should have proved so much less traumatic than Harley's is testimony to the community of scholarship on which I have been able to draw. I must first thank Alan Downie, whose classic work on Harley and on the *Memorial* prompted me to dig through the papers formerly known as 'Loan 23', and whose encouragement in the latter stages of this project has been most welcome. For conversation, comments, and suggestions which have helped sustain me while researching and writing this book, I would like to thank Clare Bucknell, Justin Champion, Dennis Duncan, Martin Dzelzainis, Mark Goldie, Ashley Marshall, Jim McLaverty, Marc Mierowsky, Henry Power, James Raven, Pat Rogers, Shef Rogers, Nick Seager, Max Skjönsberg, Tim Smith-Laing, and Ashley Walsh. I have had the good fortune to begin writing this book at Magdalene College, Cambridge, and to finish writing it at Newcastle University. Colleagues at both institutions have been generous with their time and their ears, in particular Oliver Haardt, Joe Jarrett, James Woodall, and Alex Thom, for whom I reserve special thanks. Niall Allsopp has, as ever, proved himself both a good friend and a convivial sounding board. And Paulina Kewes and Tom Keymer have been more generous in their support than anyone could reasonably expect. I am grateful.

I have been equally lucky to have found so intrepid and talented an editor as Clara Farmer, who saw the spark of potential in what could otherwise have been a rather dusty project. My warmest thanks go to her, to Charlotte Humphery, and to all the team at Chatto and Windus, for their enthusiasm, creativity, and thoughtfulness. For words of wisdom and continuing guidance, I must thank Anna Webber, my agent, and Seren Adams. A quick glance at the notes to this book will show that I have spent more time than might be thought healthy in the reading rooms of the British Library and the National Archives. Thanks are also due to librarians and archivists at the Beinecke Rare Book and Manuscript Library, the Bodleian Libraries, Cambridge University Library, the Houghton Library, the National Art Library, the New York Public Library, the Pepys Library, the Royal Archives, and Senate House Library. Without their labours, and those of their predecessors, the research on which this book is based would simply not have been possible.

It is often said that writing can be a lonely business. My own experience has always been quite the opposite. To all the close friends and loose acquaintances who have been so companionable, I am thankful. My greatest debt of gratitude is and will always be to Melissa. The fact this book exists in any form whatsoever is in no small part thanks to my mother and father, who have encouraged my love of books and of history since I was a child. It is dedicated to them.

Notes

The following standard abbreviations for libraries, archives, and sources have been used.

BL	British Library
Bodl.	Bodleian Libraries
Commons	Eveline Cruickshanks, Stuart Handley, and D. W. Hayton, eds., *The History of Parliament: The House of Commons, 1690–1715*, 5 vols. (Cambridge, 2002).
HMC	Historical Manuscripts Commission
JHC	*Journal of the House of Commons*
JHL	*Journal of the House of Lords*
Memorial	*The Memorial of the Church of England* (London, 1705).
NLS	National Library of Scotland
NUL	Nottingham University Library
TNA	The National Archives
TSC	The Stationers' Company

Prologue: The Woman in the Vizard Mask

1 **'all the country . . . years'** John Evelyn, *The Diary of John Evelyn*, ed. E. S. de Beer, 6 vols. (Oxford, 1955), v. 599–604.

1 **'something . . . woman'** BL, Add. MS 70340, bundle 7.

1 **'close abodes'** John Gay, *Trivia* (1716), ii. 272, in *Walking the Streets of Eighteenth-Century London: John Gay's Trivia*, ed. Clare Brant and Susan E. Whyman (Oxford, 2011), 185.

2   **'vizard mask'** BL, Add. MS 70340, bundle 5.

2   **'copy to be printed'** BL, Add. MS 70340, bundle 7.

2   **'The Memorial . . . Constitution'** BL, Add. MS 70103, unfoliated.

3   **'By no means . . . stand by'** BL, Add. MS 70340, bundle 7.

3   **'an indented . . . delivery'** BL, Add. MS 70340, bundle 7.

4   **'I wou'd . . . drift'** BL, Add. MS 70023, fol. 79r.

4   **'done . . . Rights'** Thomas Babington Macaulay, *The History of England from the Accession of James the Second*, 8 vols. (London, 1855–62), IV. 542, 540.

5   **'fire . . . Tory'** *A Modest Attempt for Healing the Present Animosities* (London, 1690), 7.

6   **'hectick fever'** *Memorial*, 3.

1. *Land Pirates*

11   **'art or mistery'** Quoted in Peter W. M. Blayney, *The Stationers' Company and the Printers of London, 1501–1557*, 2 vols. (Cambridge, 2014), II. 1025.

11   **'lawful . . . consultations'** Edward Arber, ed., *A Transcript of the Registers of the Company of Stationers of London, 1554–1640*, 5 vols. (London, 1875–94), I. 14.

12   **last to approach** TSC, Apprentice Register 2, fol. 87r.

12   **'rather too stately'** *The Yale Edition of the Works of Samuel Johnson*, ed. Robert DeMaria Jr. et al., 23 vols. (New Haven, 1958–2019), I. 193.

12   **'surrounded . . . down into it'** National Library of Wales, MS 3290D.

12   **'dipt up to his neck'** Edward Lhuyd, *Parochialia*, ed. R. H. Morris, 3 vols. (London, 1909–11), I. 70.

13   **Lleweni Hall** Sarah Ward, '"God Almighty sanctifie thes afflictive providences to us": The Life-Writing of Robert Salusbury of Henllan', *Denbighshire Historical Society Transactions*, 65 (2017), 11–30.

13   **'columns of scandal'** [Ned Ward,] *Hudibras Redivivus* (London, 1705), I. 20.

13   **Jonathan Swift** Jonathan Swift, 'Verses on the Death of Dr Swift' (1731), lines 255–8, in *The Poems of Jonathan Swift*, ed. Harold Williams, 3 vols. (Oxford, 1937), II. 563.

13   **'stalls . . . breeze'** W. Denton, *Records of St Giles Cripplegate* (London, 1883), 104–5.

13 'chymicall . . . railes' Robert Hooke, 'The Diary of Robert Hooke, Nov. 1688–Mar. 1690 and Dec. 1692–Aug. 1693', in R. T. Gunther, *Early Science in Oxford*, 15 vols. (Oxford, 1923–67), X. 69–265 at 223.

14 'no bigger . . . people' William Leybourn, *Pleasure with Profit* (London, 1694), III. 29.

14 'should . . . amend' Joseph Moxon, *Mechanick Exercises*, 2 vols. (London, 1677–83), II. 228 and 198.

15 'when at their . . . beating' Moxon, *Mechanick Exercises*, II. 11 and 334.

15 moisture in the wood Moxon, *Mechanick Exercises*, II. 11.

15 'extreme . . . correctors' [Peter Heylyn,] *Observations on the Historie of the Reign of King Charles* (London, 1656), sig. A4.

16 'mere sots' *The Correspondence of Isaac Newton*, ed. H. W. Turnbull et al., 7 vols. (Cambridge, 1959–77), V. 7.

16 'were great . . . work' Benjamin Franklin, *Autobiography and Other Writings*, ed. Ormond Seavey (Oxford, 1993), 46–7.

16 'custom . . . accepted' Moxon, *Mechanick Exercises*, II. 356–8.

16 commandments were printed Ellic Howe, *The London Compositor: Documents Relating to Wages, Working Conditions and Customs of the London Printing Trade 1785–1900* (London, 1947), 32; T. D. Duncan Eaves and Ben D. Kimpel, 'Two Notes on Samuel Richardson', *The Library*, 5th ser., 23 (1968), 242–7.

16 'The youngest . . . house' Alan D. Boehm, 'The Bagford Chapel Rules: A Set of English Printing House Regulations, *Circa* 1686–1707', *Studies in Bibliography*, 58 (2008), 135–43.

17 'the boy . . . anthem' *Country Journal*, 725 (24 May 1740).

17 'the master . . . night' Moxon, *Mechanick Exercises*, II. 361.

17 'a base . . . pirates' John Bunyan, *The Pilgrim's Progress*, 4th edn. (London, 1680), 'Advertisement from the Bookseller'.

17 'a first-rate . . . oven' John Dunton, *The Life and Errors of John Dunton*, ed. John Nichols, 2 vols. (London, 1818), I. 251.

18 numerous run-ins *JHC*, IX. 652–6; TSC, Court Book E, fol. 112; TNA, SP 29/417, fol. 329.

18 arrested for printing TNA, SP 29/424, fols. 176r and 210r.

18 Their names were TNA, SP 29/424, fols. 176r and 230r.

19 'somewhat heav'd his body' Jack Ketch, *The Apologie of John Ketch Esq* (London, 1683).

20 'as dangerous . . . lives' TNA, SP 29/425, fol. 100r.

20 Dare's house Richard Ashcraft, *Revolutionary Politics and Locke's Two Treatises of Government* (Princeton, 1986), 378.

20   **'Catch . . . the axe'** Roger Morrice, *The Entring Book of Roger Morrice*, ed. Mark Goldie et al., 7 vols. (Woodbridge, 2007), III. 27.

21   **'the disloyal . . . men'** *A Letter of Advice to the Petitioning Apprentices* (London, 1681), 1.

21–2   **'the vanity . . . blood'** John Dunton, *The Neck Adventure* (London, 1715), vi; *The Address of Above Twenty Thousand of the Loyal Protestant Apprentices of London* (London, 1681).

22   **'printer's boy . . . invention'** *A Friendly Dialogue Between Two London-Apprentices* (London, 1681), 2–3.

22   **'gett a football . . . knockt out'** Quoted in Sir Arthur Bryant, *Samuel Pepys: The Man in the Making* (London, 1933), 65.

22   **'as the phanaticks . . . Pope'** Tim Harris, *London Crowds in the Reign of Charles II: Propaganda and Politics from the Restoration Until the Exclusion Crisis* (Cambridge, 1987), 166.

23   **'wild huzzas and acclamations'** *The Ellis Correspondence*, ed. George Agar Ellis, 2 vols. (London, 1829), II. 11.

23   **'in other . . . proportion?'** *An Account of the Pretended Prince of Wales* (London, 1688).

24   **'sneaking . . . apprentice'** John Oldmixon, *The History of England During the Reigns of the Royal House of Stuart* (London, 1730), 757.

24   **'they would . . . Portsmouth'** *Ellis Correspondence*, II. 350.

24   **'served . . . candlesticks'** *Ellis Correspondence*, II. 350.

24   **'boys . . . others'** *The Autobiography of Sir John Bramston* (London, 1845), 332; cf. BL, Add. MS 34487.

24   **'This house is to be lett'** *London Mercury*, 1 (15 December 1688).

24   **'some shouting . . . huzzas'** Oldmixon, *History*, 762; Edmund Bohun, *The History of the Desertion* (London, 1689), 100.

24   **'in a caball . . . Mary'** TNA, SP 32/1, fol. 206r.

24–5   **'the brave . . . nation'** *A Copy of a Trayteros Libell* (London, 1689).

25   **'sworne . . . Company'** TSC, Register of Freemen, fol. 158v.

2. *Messengers After Supper*

27   **torrential rain** Evelyn, *Diary*, V. 147.

27   **'well set . . . suit'** This detailed description of Newbolt is borrowed from an advertisement in the *London Gazette*, 1961 (4 September 1684), when he ran away from his master.

27   **difficult harvest** Anthony à Wood, *The Life and Times of Anthony à Wood*, ed. Andrew Clark, 5 vols. (Oxford, 1891–v1900), III. 431; Evelyn, *Diary*, v. 145.

27   **Duke of Norfolk's butler** J. P., *A New Guide for Constables* (London, 1692), 7.

28   **'contemptible . . . oglio'** Thomas Brown, *The Reasons of Mr Bays Changing His Religion* (London, 1688), 19.

28   **'drew fornication . . . child'** John Wilmot, Earl of Rochester, *Familiar Letters* (London, 1699), 149.

28   **'words were heard'** *Proceedings of the Old Bailey, 28 August 1695* (London, 1695), 3.

28   **woman had been imprisoned** TNA, SP 44/341, 441–2.

28   **'at the expence . . . money'** TNA, Mint 19/1, fol. 501r.

29   **'make swift . . . treason'** TNA, SP 44/343, 316.

29   **'Instead of grace . . . musqueteers'** *Guzman Redivivus: A Short View of the Life of Will. Chaloner* (London, 1699), 6.

29   **'make diligent . . . books'** *JHL*, XIV. 490; TNA, SP 44/343, 61. On Gellibrand's earlier career, see TSC, Court Book F, fol. 47v; TNA, SP 44/340, 78.

30   **'toare . . . beast'** BL, Add. MS 70039, fol. 39r.

30   **'a carrelesse drunken sotte'** BL, Add. MS 72570, fol. 64r.

30   **byword for corruption** *Calendar of Treasury Books*, xv. 11.

30   **'the negligence of others'** TNA, SP 44/99, 138.

31   **bribe of £20** BL, Add. MS 72570, fol. 64r.

31   **Thomas Farr . . . apprenticeship** D. F. McKenzie, *Stationers' Company Apprentices 1641–1700* (Oxford, 1974), 120.

31   **'a great . . . them'** Narcissus Luttrell, *A Brief Historical Relation of State Affairs*, 6 vols. (Oxford, 1857), III. 164.

32   **'He that will . . . it self'** *Animadversions upon that Proclamation of September 13. 1692. Entitled, For the Better Discovery of Seditious Libellers* (London, 1692), 4.

32   **'at least . . . sedition'** BL, Add. MS 72568, fol. 47r.

32   **Chaloner walked away** TNA, Mint 19/1, fol. 501r.

32   **'between . . . house'** HMC, *Report on the Manuscripts of Allan George Finch*, 5 vols. (London, 1913–2004), IV. 515–16.

33   **led her interrogation** TNA, SP 44/341, 442.

33   **'all your . . . surprized'** HMC, *Finch*, IV. 515.

33   **'the fire . . . sentence'** *A Warning for Bad Wives* (London, 1678), 7.

33   **'discover . . . pardon'** Luttrell, *Brief Relation*, III. 21.

33   **stay of execution** TNA, SP 44/341, 491.

34   **evaded capture** TSC, Court Book F, fol. 171v.

34   **'a private . . . in paper'** *An Account of the Conversation, Behaviour, and Execution of William Anderton* (London, 1693).

34   **'Wild Boar . . . London** *Observator*, 32 (28 July 1703).

34   **'in a great . . . obey'** *State Trials*, VII. 956.

34–5   **'reflected . . . crew** TNA, SP 29/417, fol. 329.

35   **'printed . . . not see it'** Dunton, *Life and Errors*, 253.

35   **'cowardice . . . throwne'** BL, Add. MS 72570, fol. 64r.

35–6   **'I am assured . . . hang** Samuel Grascome, *An Appeal of Murther from Certain Unjust Judges* (London, 1693), 29 and 13–14.

36   **Chaloner's later record** BL, Add. MS 72568, fol. 49r.

36   **'for printing . . . government'** Luttrell records that 'the queen remitted the quartering of his body, and it was delivered to his friends' (*Brief Relation*, III. 111).

36   **'that calm . . . themselves?'** Grascome, *Appeal of Murther*, 35–7.

36–7   **printer had named colleagues** Luttrell, *Brief Relation*, III. 113.

37   **'orders . . . libells'** Luttrell, *Brief Relation*, III. 115.

37   **great crowds . . . funeral** Wood, *Life and Times*, III. 425.

37   **diverted their request** TNA, SP 44/236, 348.

37   **'accused . . . declarations'** Luttrell, *Brief Relation*, III. 192.

37   **stayed their execution** TNA, SP 44/236, 367.

37   **'hellish . . . into it'** Daniel Defoe, *Moll Flanders*, ed. Linda Bree (Oxford, 2011), 97.

38   **'a popish . . . sword'** HMC, *Finch*, III. 364–5.

38   **'a great many guineas'** *Proceedings of the Old Bailey, 6 September 1693* (London, 1693), 4–5.

39   **'she . . . sustenance'** HMC, *Lords*, I. 54.

40   **Mary's little stall** *A True Copy of the Paper Delivered by Margaert* [sic] *Martels Own Hand, Before She Went to the Place of Execution* (London, 1697); *The True Confession of Mr George Norton, Concerning the Murther of Mr Harris the Dancing-Master* (London, 1699).

3. A Printer's Progress

41   **'appears . . . can do?'** *Reasons Humbly Offered for the Liberty of Unlicensed Printing* (London, 1693), 5.

42	**Bohun's protestation** *JHC*, x. 786.
42	**their first apprentice** McKenzie, *Stationers' Company Apprentices 1641–1700*, 51.
42	**jobbing work** An instance of this jobbing work is *An Adventure for a Sale of Jewels &c. the Value of 3000l by John Relfe Jeweller* (London, 1694).
43	**'more like . . . furiously'** William Fuller, *The Whole Life of Mr. William Fuller* (London, 1703), 34.
43	**'J. C.'** One well-informed Catholic reader scrawled Corker's name across the title page: Ushaw College, Ushaw IV.B.10.14.
44	**decorated capital 'O'** The decorated capital 'O' appears in both *A Manuel of Devout Prayers and Other Christian Devotions, Fitted for all Persons and Occasions* ([London,] 1696), 1 (sig. A1r); *A True Copy of the Paper Delivered by Margaert Martels Own Hand, Before She Went to the Place of Execution* (1697).
44	**'apprehend and secure'** TNA, SP 44/343, 638.
44	**'Stephens . . . government'** Luttrell, *Brief Relation*, III. 384.
44	**'accused . . . government'** TNA, SP 44/346, 99.
44	**'a private . . . pamphlets'** Luttrell, *Brief Relation*, III. 510.
45	**'receives . . . Westminster'** BL, Add. MS 72570, fol. 64r.
45	**'with the rest of his brethren'** *Heraclitus Ridens*, 4 (14 August 1703).
45	**'as the same . . . law'** TNA, PC 2/76, fol. 122v.
45–6	**'in soe clandestine . . . thereof'** TNA, C/8/378/41.
46	**'for some . . . against'** TSC, 1/E English Stock E/11/01/06, 8–9.
46	**'I must certainly perish'** HMC, *Portland*, VIII. 127; cf. NUL, Pw2 Hy 575.
46	**'one of . . . religion'** *A True History of the Horrid Conspiracy to Assassinate His Sacred Majesty, King William* (London, 1696), sig. A2r.
47	**'damn'd . . . depose'** NLS, Ry.III.a.19(48).
47	**'most . . . print'** *Proceedings of the Old Bailey*, 8 July 1696 (London, 1696), 5.
47	**'severely pelted by the mob'** *Post Man*, 332 (17 June 1697); *Post Man*, 706 (25 January 1700); *Flying Post*, 735 (25 January 1700).
47	**'favourably used by the mob'** Luttrell, *Brief Relation*, III. 140.
47–8	**'hallow'd . . . against'** *Heraclitus Ridens*, 2 (7 August 1703).
48	**'to see . . . devil did'** *Heraclitus Ridens*, 45 (8 January 1704).
48	**'I was stifled . . . pounds'** Fuller, *Life*, 107.
48	**hidden presses** TNA, SP 44/349, 29; SP 44/275, 134–5; SP 44/345, 510.
49	**'great quantity . . . the Strand'** *Calendar of Treasury Books*, XIV. 155–6.

49   'great numbers . . . idolatry' *JHC*, XII. 517.

49   'received . . . imported' TNA, SP 44/349, 123.

49   'popish . . . full of them' HMC, *Portland*, VIII. 68.

49   **minor brush with the law** TNA, SP 44/349, 108; Luttrell, *Brief Relation*, IV. 558.

49   'with very little alteration' *An Ode on the Death of the Late King James* (London, 1701).

49–50   'so solemnly . . . publick' *The Memoirs of King James II* (London, 1702), sigs. A2v–A4r.

50   **trouble with the law** TNA, SP 44/352, 118.

50   'there is not . . . produc'd' *The Late King James His Advice to His Son* (London, 1703), sigs. A3v–A4v.

50   'overwhelmed with grief' *The Diary of Ralph Thoresby*, ed. Joseph Hunter, 2 vols. (London, 1830), I. 353.

51   'well customed . . . upon it' John Strype, *A Survey of the Cities of London and Westminster*, 2 vols. (London, 1720), II. 117; Thomas Fairchild, *The City Gardener* (London, 1722), 55.

51   'where wine . . . claret' Ned Ward, *The London-Spy Compleat* (London, 1703), 88.

52   'I'll say . . . claret' John Dunton, *Dunton's Whipping-Post* (London, 1706), 28.

52   'promis'd . . . reckoning' *Tom Brown Arrested by the Devil* (London, 1698).

52   'lads . . . Temple Bar' *Wit and Mirth*, 5 vols. (London, 1719), IV. 284.

52   'a great . . . himself' Dunton, *Whipping-Post*, 27–8.

52   **Dog tavern** *Heraclitus Ridens*, 4 (14 August 1703).

52   'never fights . . . off again' *Observator*, 96 (8 March 1704).

52   'old friend Davy' *Heraclitus Ridens*, 2 (11 March 1704).

53   'Martyrs . . . bum' Dryden, *Mac Flecknoe* (1682), line 101, in *The Poems of John Dryden*, ed. Paul Hammond and David Hopkins, 5 vols. (London, 1995–2005), II. 323.

53   'may last . . . contrary' *Heraclitus Ridens*, 58 (26 February 1704).

53   'destructive . . . stands upon' *Heraclitus Ridens*, 43 (1 January 1704).

4. Inamicable Collisions

55   'Was there ever . . . England' *Observator*, 34 (28 July 1705).

55   'He that comes . . . read them' *The Character of a Coffee-House* (London, 1673), sig. A2r.

55   **'when a newspaper . . . them'** *The Case of the Coffee-Men of London and Westminster* (London, 1728), 13–15.

55   **John Shank** *Post Boy*, 663 (8 July 1699) and 905 (8 March 1701).

56   **'brought . . . coffeehouses'** *Spectator*, 10 (12 March 1711).

56   **vexatious party rags** *The Case of the Coffee-Men*, 15; John Macky, *A Journey Through England* (London, 1714), 111.

56–7   **'All politeness . . . understandings'** Antony Ashley-Cooper, third Earl of Shaftesbury, *Characteristicks of Men, Manners, Opinions, Times*, ed. Douglas Den Uyl, 3 vols. (Indianapolis, 2001), 42.

57   **'A sweet . . . salvation'** John Locke, *A Letter Concerning Toleration and Other Writings*, ed. Mark Goldie (Indianapolis, 2010), 44.

58   **'pompous nonsense'** Soame Jenyns, *A Free Inquiry into the Nature and Origin of Evil* (London, 1757), 84.

58   **riding in the whirlwind** Joseph Addison, *Miscellaneous Works*, ed. A. C. Guthkelch, 3 vols. (London, 1914), I. 165.

59   **'be very careful . . . support it'** *History and Proceedings of the House of Commons*, III. 202–3.

60   **'too wild to succeed'** Cited in Clyve Jones, '"Too Wild to Succeed": The Occasional Conformity Bills and the Attempts by the House of Lords to Outlaw the Tack in the Reign of Anne', *Parliamentary History*, 30 (2011), 414–27.

61   **'a mystery . . . man'** Clyve Jones, 'A Scottish Whig View of the Character of Robert Harley, Earl of Oxford, in 1713', *The Electronic British Library Journal*, 34 (2010), 1–5.

61   **'sagacious . . . fly before him'** *Examiner*, 27 (1 February 1711).

61   **'that humour . . . cunning'** *The Private Diary of William, First Earl Cowper*, ed. E. C. Hawtrey (Eton, 1833), 30.

61   **'Parties draw . . . limbs'** *Review*, 29 (10 May 1705).

62   **'it is absurd . . . arrive at it'** [James Drake,] *Some Necessary Consideration Relating to All Future Elections of Members to Serve in Parliament* (London, 1702), 20.

62   **'the government . . . crown'** *Mercurius Politicus*, 2 (16 June 1705).

62–3   **'Be these . . . diff'rent air'** William Shippen, *Moderation Display'd* (1705), lines 153–64, in *Poems on Affairs of State: Augustan Satirical Verse, 1660–1714*, ed. George de Forest Lord et al., 7 vols. (New Haven, 1963–75), VII. 30.

63   **'religion . . . design'** [Sackville Tufton], *The History of Faction, Alias Hypocrisy, Alias Moderation* (London, 1705), sig. A3r.

63   **'[They] are . . . trade again'** S[amuel] G[rascome], *Moderation in Fashion* (London, 1705), 143.

64   **'so eminently'** [Henry Sacheverell et al.], *The Rights of the Church of England Asserted and Prov'd* ([Oxford], 1705), 41.

64   **instructing his students** Philopatrius[?], *Reflexions upon Sach—l's Thanksgiving-Day* (London, 1713), 20.

64   **'at his private . . . Oxford'** Beinecke Library, Mhc9 P235 R4 (copy 2).

64   **public letter** [Sir Humphrey Mackworth,] *A Letter from a Member of Parliament to His Friend in the Country* (London, 1705), 1–2, 8. The first edition is very rare, which is suggestive of its ephemeral status as polling-day propaganda; the second and third editions were printed from standing type.

64   **'a hamper of wine'** Beinecke Library, Mhc9 P235 R4 (copy 2).

65   **'under . . . land'** *An Essay upon Government. Wherein the Republican Schemes Reviv'd by Mr. Lock, Dr. Blackal, &c. are Fairly Consider'd and Refuted* (London, 1705), 1.

65   **'which was . . . churchmen'** BL, Add. MS 70340, bundle 7.

65   **'a kind . . . gunshot of us'** *A Word of Advice to the Citizens of London* (London, 1705), 4. The layout of this pamphlet is almost identical to the layout of the *Memorial*; moreover, the final page mentions the pamphlet *Pro Aris et Focis*, which Edwards certainly printed.

65   **'who were . . . schism'** *The Countryman's Remembrancer* (London, 1705), title page.

65   **'favour and protection'** Sir Humphrey Mackworth, *A Vindication of the Rights of the Commons of England* (London, 1701), sig. A4r.

66   **'Mackworth . . . succeed'** Cornwall Records Office, X1277, 283.

5. Break All

69–70   **'Those that look . . . being of it'** All quotations from the *Memorial* manuscript are from BL, Add. MS 70103.

71–2   **'particular friend . . . otherwise'** NUL, MS Pw2 Hy 570.

73   **'see her . . . break all'** BL, Add. MS 70340, bundles 7 and 8.

73   **'so great a fright . . . the book'** BL, Add. MS 70340, bundle 7.

74   **Fox's base** Walter M. Stern, *The Porters of London* (London, 1960).

74   **'great badge . . . nine a clock'** BL, Add. MS 70340, bundles 7 and 8.

74   **'apprehended . . . indemnify him'** BL, Add. MS 70340, bundle 8.

75   **'Sir . . . Yours'** BL, Add. MS 70103, unfoliated.

75   **'refreshing showers'** Evelyn, *Diary*, v. 601.

75   'a pott . . . Fetter Lane' BL, Add. MS 70340, bundle 7.

76   'cryed' on the streets Thomas Hearne, *Remarks and Collections*, ed.
      Charles Edward Doble et al., 11 vols. (Oxford, 1885–1921), I. 180. John
      Dyer records this date, 7 July, in his newsletter for that week.

76   'very pretty title' BL, Add. MS 70340, bundle 7.

76   'when a customer . . . vogue' Jonathan Swift, *A Tale of a Tub* (1704),
      in *The Cambridge Edition of the Works of Jonathan Swift*, ed. Claude
      Rawson et al., 18 vols. (Cambridge, 2008–), I. 134.

76   hopped onto a waterman's boat BL, Add. MS 70340, bundle 7.

77   'To where Fleet-ditch . . . silver flood' Alexander Pope, *The Dunciad*
      (1728), II. 263–70, in *The Twickenham Edition of the Poems of Alexander
      Pope*, ed. John Butt et al., 11 vols. (London, 1939–69), V. 133.

77   'dung, guts, and blood' Jonathan Swift, 'A Description of a City
      Shower' (1710), line 61, in *The Poems of Jonathan Swift*, ed. Harold
      Williams, 3 vols., 2nd edn. (Oxford, 1958), I. 139.

77   'would insinuate . . . more sense' Dunton, *Life and Errors*, I. 252;
      TNA, SP 44/343, 348.

77   Anne Croome Cf. Dunton, *Life and Errors*, I. 236.

78   'Sir the book . . . does not live' BL, Add. MS 70022, fol. 214v.

78   'for printing . . . libels' TNA, SP 44/77, 19; cf. BL, Add. MS 70335,
      bundle 18.

78–9 'That wretch . . . his patronage' *The Letters of Daniel Defoe*, ed.
      George Harris Healey (Oxford, 1955), 90–91.

79   'the discovery . . . presse' BL, Add. MS 70022, fol. 214v.

6. General Detestation

83   'very giddy-headed . . . worth mentioning' John Macky, *Memoirs
      of the Secret Services of John Macky*, 2nd edn. (London, 1733), 154.

83   'strong box' BL, Add. MS 4291, fol. 41r.

84   'In this camp . . . stand long' *The Marlborough–Godolphin
      Correspondence*, ed. Henry L. Snyder, 3 vols. (Oxford, 1975), I. 475.

84   'I can't forbear . . . world' *Marlborough–Godolphin Correspondence*,
      I. 475–6.

84   'would be glad . . . litle head' *Marlborough–Godolphin Correspondence*,
      I. 475–6.

85   'was mighty . . . took?' Bodl., MS Ballard 35, fol. 59r.

85   'The book . . . indifferency' BL, Add. MS 70022, fol. 214v.

85   **'I never saw . . . the book'** HMC, *Portland*, IV. 211–12.

85   **reported by . . . Tutchin** *Observator*, 47 (12 September 1705). There
        is some evidence to suggest that Harley thought Fitzgerald, the
        author of *The Exorbitant Grants of William III*, another Edwards
        production, was also responsible for the *Memorial*. As a known
        associate of the printer, he was seized on 26 July 1705 'concerning
        some matters relating to affairs of state' (TNA, SP 44/77, 21).

86   **'Not one . . . *Rehearsal*'** *Observator*, 35 (1 August 1705).

86   **'Lesley, and his brood'** *Some Considerations on the Present Danger of
        the Religion of the Church of England* (London, 1706), 29.

86   **''Tis said . . . other subjects'** Hearne, *Remarks*, I. 40 and 43.

86   **Leslie had not . . . been arrested** *Rehearsal*, 102 (8 May 1706).

86   **'he made . . . *belles lettres*'** [James Drake et al.?,] *The Memorial of
        the Church of England* (London, 1711), iv.

87   **'false . . . instructed'** Drake, *History*, sigs. A6v–A7r.

87   **'he came . . . evil design'** BL, Add. MS 70020, fol. 176r.

87   **'a studied . . . faction'** *Mercurius Politicus*, 1 (12 June 1705).

88   **'a person . . . atheist'** *Commons*, IV. 244.

88   **'I am fully . . . club with them'** Defoe, *Letters*, 92–4.

89   **'great patrons . . . turn'd out'** *Memorial*, 25.

89   **'I don't know . . . too much'** HMC, *Bath*, I. 64.

89   **'style . . . assertions'** HMC, *Portland*, IV. 212.

89   **a manuscript treatise** Arthur Maynwaring, *The Life and Posthumous
        Works of Arthur Maynwaring, Esq.* (London, 1715), 27–8.

89   **''tis said . . . said in it'** Hearne, *Remarks*, I. 6.

89   **'was alwais . . . himself'** BL, Add. MS 4291, fol. 40v.

89–90   **'brass knobs . . . chairs'** Senate House Library, MS 533, fol. 10r.

90   **'staying in town . . . underneath it'** John Sheffield, *The Works of
        John Sheffield, Earl of Mulgrave, Marquis of Normanby, and Duke of
        Buckingham*, ed. Alexander Pope, 2 vols. (London, 1723), II. 275–6.

90   **cost above £34,000** Senate House Library, MS 533, fol. 10r.

91   **'state of nature . . . short'** Thomas Hobbes, *Leviathan*, ed. Noel
        Malcolm, 3 vols. (Oxford, 2012), I. 192.

91   **'state of nature . . . resist'** *Memorial*, 45.

92   **'the kingdome . . . doctrines'** Hobbes, *Leviathan*, III. 956.

92   **debts to Hobbes** See Hearne, *Remarks*, I. 235.

92–3   **'unity . . . state'** Sir Humphrey Mackworth, *Peace at Home* (London,
        1703), I, 10–11.

93   **the Huguenots** Mackworth, *Peace at Home*, sig. B1r.

94   'field of blood' Rennell, *Nature, Causes, and Consequences of Divisions*, 2.
94   'Religion seems ... this world' *Mercurius Politicus*, 5 (26 June 1705).
94   'men of fix'd ... religion' Sir Humphrey Mackworth, *The Principles of a Member of the Black List* (London, 1702), xi.

7. A Most Just Doom

95–6   'secretly ... her people' Quoted in Nicholas Tindal, *The History of England by Mr. Rapin de Thoyras Continued*, 2 vols. (London, 1744–7), IV [i.e. II]. 717.

96   'false ... common hangman' Luttrell, *Brief Relation*, V. 588; Hearne, *Remarks*, I. 41.

96   'made twice ... prosecution' Philip Skelton, *Ophiomaches*, 2 vols. (London, 1749), II. 374.

96   'a great number ... other places' *JHL*, XXI. 235.

96   'most just doom' *Review*, 84 (15 September 1705); Hearne, *Remarks*, I. 45.

96   'only two ... presentment' John Dyer, *A Collection From Dyer's Letters* (London, 1706 [i.e. 1705]), 19.

96   'impotent slander!' *Review*, 84 (15 September 1705).

96   'not at al ... presenters' Hearne, *Remarks*, I. 40.

97   'But we can ... be dead' Luttrell, *Brief Relation*, V. 600; Hearne, *Remarks*, I. 44; *An Elegy on the Burning of the Church Memorial* ([London], 1705).

97   'Some would have ... Mammon' *Poems on Affairs of State* (London, 1707), 37.

97–8   'Books have souls ... encircle them' Jean Claude, *An Historical Defence of the Reformation* (London, 1683), sig. B2r–v.

98   'manifesto ... oracle' Hearne, *Remarks*, I. 12; Clyve Jones, 'Debates in the House of Lords on "The Church in Danger," 1705, and on Dr Sacheverell's Impeachment, 1710', *Historical Journal*, 19 (1976), 759–771 at 767.

98   'now againe ... the author' Hearne, *Remarks*, I. 12.

98   'done purely ... prevent' Defoe, *Letters*, 93.

98   'answers ... triffles' Defoe, *Letters*, 93.

98   'search for the author' TNA, SP 44/77, 20.

99   'that such ... to him' Quoted in Theodore F. M. Newton, 'William Pittis and Queen Anne Journalism', *Modern Philology*, 33 (1935), 169–86.

99   **sentenced to . . . the pillory** TNA, KB 28/16/43.

100   **'I find . . . service'** HMC, *Eighth Report*, I. 43.

100   **'read most . . . porters** Ned Ward, *Vulgus Britannicus: or the British Hudibras in Fifteen Canto's* (London, 1710), 120.

100   **'cannot read . . . into them'** Charles Leslie, *The Rehearsal* (London, 1704–7), I. iv.

101   **'any hint . . . possible'** Defoe, *Letters*, 91.

101   **'virulent . . . fellow to it'** *Review*, 56 (12 July 1705).

101   **'no small . . . me'** John Toland, *A Collection of Several Pieces*, 2 vols. (London, 1726), II. 354.

102   **'the high . . . Commons'** Private manuscript quoted in W. A. Speck, 'The Choice of a Speaker in 1705', *Bulletin of the Institute of Historical Research*, 37 (1964), 20–35.

102–3   **'I find . . . lose it'** Private manuscript quoted in Speck, 'Choice of a Speaker'.

103   **'a great . . . Speaker'** Hearne, *Remarks*, I. 58.

103   **'interest . . . aside'** *Mercurius Politicus*, 29 (18 September 1705).

103   **'Court places . . . place'** *Mercurius Politicus*, 30 (22 September 1705).

104   **'Have . . . *Travels*?'** John Oldmixon, *The History of England* (London, 1735), 345.

104   **'This . . . several places'** Henry George Bohn, *Bibliotheca Parriana* (London, 1827), 702.

8. *In From the Cold*

Unless otherwise stated, all quotations from Clare's reports to Harley are from BL, Add. MS 70217, unfoliated.

105   **informing government agents** TNA, SP 44/349, 170.

107   **'a nobleman's . . . lookd for'** BL, Add. MS 72570, fol. 100. The house was at Lynsted in Kent.

108   **'The ignorant . . . paid for'** Defoe, *Letters*, 97.

108   **'spreading . . . kingdom'** Defoe, *Letters*, 98.

108–9   **'here was . . . caution'** Defoe, *Letters*, 100.

109   **'I think . . . danger'** Defoe, *Letters*, 99–100.

111   **'the authors . . . us'd accordingly'** *Review*, 91 (2 October 1705).

111   **'amongst us . . . this time'** *JHL*, XVIII. 8.

III	'in a most . . . kingdom' *JHC*, xv. 58.
III	'charms and spells' BL, Lansdowne MS 1024, fol. 168.
III–12	'open . . . danger' W. A. Speck, 'An Anonymous Parliamentary Diary, 1705–6', *Camden Miscellany*, 4th ser., 7 (1969), 29–84 at 45–6.
112	'We do . . . law' *London Gazette*, 4186 (24 December 1705).
112	'commanded . . . danger' Luttrell, *Brief Relation*, v. 627.
112	£500 *The Private Diary of William, First Earl Cowper*, ed. E. C. Hawtrey (Eton, 1833), 29.
112–13	'with this Edwards . . . business' BL, Add. MS 70023, fol. 1r.
113	'if I have . . . know' BL, Add. MS 70023, fol. 1r.
113	'gentlemen . . . Memorialists' BL, Add. MS 70023, fol. 1r.
113	'offer . . . may be' BL, Add. MS 70023, fol. 1r.
113	January papers *London Gazette*, 4191 (10 January 1706) and 4194 to 4198 (21 January 1706).
114	'The frowns . . . blind' Dunton, *Life and Errors*, 248.
114	'finding work scarce' BL, Add. MS 70023, fol. 1r.
114–15	'I understand . . . away' BL, Add. MS 70023, fol. 102r.
115	'people . . . government' BL, Add. MS 70023, fol. 102r.
115	'which . . . to you' NUL, Pw2 Hy 565.
115–16	'I beg . . . in it' NUL, Pw2 Hy 565.
116	'[I] desire . . . anybody' NUL, Pw2 Hy 565.
116	'heavy charge' NUL, Pw2 Hy 565.
116	'I am willing . . . shrub' NUL, Pw2 Hy 565.
117	'This letter . . . proper' HMC, *Portland*, iv. 278.
117	'I have . . . 'em' BL, Add. MS 70023, fol. 6r.
117	'be mark'd . . . against me' NUL, Pw2 Hy 565.
117–18	'shall within . . . same' BL, Add. MS 70340, bundle 5.

9. Recollect Yourself

The bulk of this account, including all quoted speech, is drawn from the interrogation notes and transcripts contained in BL, Add. MS 70340, bundles 6 to 8. The bundles are unbound and unfoliated. Other sources are noted below.

119	'deepe snow' Evelyn, *Diary*, v. 622.
122	raising £125,000 Luttrell, *Brief Remarks*, iv. 434 and 489.
122	'little Poley the lawyer' *Commons*, v. 168.

122–3	'a man . . . England' Hearne, *Remarks*, I. 203.
124	The prisoners BL, Add. MS 70023, fols. 19r, 22r and 53r.
127	late into the night Luttrell, *Brief Relation*, VI. 10.
128	'messengers . . . truth of things' BL, Add. MS 70023, sig. 37r.
128	'Davis . . . freely' NUL, Pw2 Hy 568.
128–9	'I know . . . kick't him' NUL, Pw2 Hy 568.
129	'extream . . . examinations' Cowper, *Diary*, 37.
130	'the opinion . . . guilty' Cowper, *Diary*, 37.
131	'believe[d] . . . or not' *State Trials*, XII. 295–6.
132	'cold damp room' Hearne, *Remarks*, I. 180.
132	'increas'd . . . *Memorial*' Hearne, *Remarks*, I. 180.
132	'evidently . . . libells' Cowper, *Diary*, 39.
132	'if I . . . calculation' BL, Add. MS 70023, fol. 79r.

10. *Mercury and Venom*

135	'no money . . . spirits' BL, Add. MS 70023, fol. 126r.
135	'I must . . . found it' BL, Add. MS 70023, fol. 126r.
135	galley proofs BL, Add. MS 70023, fols. 127–8.
136	'were both . . . letters' BL, Add. MS 70340, bundle 5.
136	'found . . . *Property*' BL, Add. MS 70340, bundle 7.
136	'we are . . . justice' Swift, *Works*, VIII. 229.
137	'T—m Br—wn . . . danger' *Spectator*, 567 (14 July 1714).
137	'It is the . . . hand' BL, Add. MS 70023, fol. 20r.
137	'precarious . . . Lords' [Sir Humphrey Mackworth,] *Pro Aris et Focis* (London, 1705), 1.
138	'absurd . . . estates' *Memorial*, 46.
138	'I know . . . country' *State Trials*, XIV. 762–5.
138	'farther satisfaction' [William Pittis,] *The Memorial of the Church of England, Consider'd Paragraph by Paragraph*, 2nd edn. (London, 1706), 50.
139	'more invective . . . smoother' BL, Add. MS 70023, fol. 20r.
139	'I told . . . alterations' BL, Add. MS 70023, fol. 126r.
140	'came . . . mind' Unless otherwise stated, the following quotations are all from BL, Add. MS 70340, bundle 7.
142	'the health . . . *Memorial*' Hearne, *Remarks*, I. 71.
143	'the chief . . . street' Hearne, *Remarks*, I. 10.

143   **Charlett . . . Tory propaganda . . . Strahan** Bodl., MS Ballard 35, fols. 90 and 93; MS Ballard 39, fol. 77r.

143   **John Hutton** Bodl., MS Ballard 35, fol. 59r.

143   **'for not burning . . . hangman'** Hearne, *Remarks*, I. 135.

143–4   **'Sir . . . A. B.'** BL, Add. MS 70023, fol. 30r.

144   **'John White . . . already done'** Bodl., MS Ballard 34, fol. 85r.

144–5   **'The *Memorial* . . . leave'** BL, Add. MS 70340, bundle 7.

11. *The Club At the Devil*

148   **'that tipling . . . brew'** Ward, *Hudibras Redivivus*, IV. 7.

148   **memorable lunch** Swift, *Works*, IX. 35.

148   **Jonson . . . Devil** Percy Simpson, 'Ben Jonson and the Devil Tavern', *Modern Language Review*, 34 (1939), 367–73.

148   **club suppers** Sir John Hawkins, *The Life of Samuel Johnson* (London, 1787), 286–7.

149   **'a little snug room'** *The Tavern Hunter* (London, 1702), 115.

149   **'racy'** *The Honest London Spy* (London, 1706), 33–4.

149   **'seven . . . smoke** BL, Add. MS 70340, bundle 6.

149   **'bid . . . give him'** BL, Add. MS 70340, bundle 8.

150   **'I do not know . . . Salop'** BL, Add. MS 70340, bundle 8.

150   **'so vain . . . emulation'** Ned Ward, *The Secret History of Clubs* (London, 1709), 48.

150   **'loose . . . assemblies'** Ward, *Secret History of Clubs*, 2–3.

151   **'are often . . . societies'** Ward, *Secret History of Clubs*, 7–8.

151   **'interfer[ing] . . . them'** *A Kit-Kat C[lu]b Describ'd*, 6.

151   **'calves-skull . . . Whigg'** [Ned Ward,] *The Secret History of the Calves-Head Club* (London, 1703), 8–9.

152   **Green Ribbon men** Melinda S. Zook, *Radical Whigs and Conspiratorial Politics in Late Stuart England* (Pennsylvania, 1999), 7–8.

152   **''twas . . . devils'** Cambridge, Pepys Library, MS 2875, 488.

152   **'a certain . . . Tavern'** Tufton, *History of Faction*, 74.

153   **'several . . . convicted'** TNA, T1/45/6 and T1/45/85.

153   **according to informants** TNA, SP 44/338, 255.

153   **French spies** Luttrell, *Brief Relation*, II. 189.

153   **'Bowe[d] . . . Taverne'** TNA, SP 32/15, fol. 111v.

153   **'several . . . damage'** Luttrell, *Brief Relation*, III. 484.

153 **'Not a word . . . Succession'** *A Full and True Relation of a Horrid and Detestable Conspiracy Against the Lives, Estates and Reputations of Three Worthy Members of This Present Parliament* ([London, 1701]).

153 **Vine tavern** *A List of One Unanimous Club of Members of the Late Parliament* (London, 1701); Mackworth denied its existence in *The Principles of a Member of the Black List* (London, 1702), sig. A2v.

154 **senior Anglican clergymen** William Laick [i.e. George Ridpath], *A Continuation of the Answer to the Scots Presbyterian Eloquence* (London, 1693), 12.

154 **'We may . . . vizors'** P. M., *The Vanity, Mischief and Danger of Continuing Ceremonies in the Worship of God* (London, 1690), 4.

154 **Jacobite traitors** *A Midnight Touch at an Unlicens'd Pamphlet* (London, 1690).

154 **'scores . . . Parliament'** Morrice, *Entring Book*, v. 53–4, 86, 98, 390.

154 **'agreed . . . thanks'** Morrice, *Entring Book*, v. 391.

155 **'secret designs'** *Memorial*, 50.

155 **'there was a club of them'** [John Toland,] *The Memorial of the State of England* (London, 1705), 2; Defoe, *Letters*, 94.

155 **'Don't you . . . kingdom'** *Observator*, 88 (2 February 1706).

155 **'there were more concerned'** BL, Add. MS 70340, bundle 7.

12. Study My Ruine

159 **'pray . . . debtors'** Moses Pitt, *The Cry of the Oppressed* (London, 1691), t.p.

159 **'divers . . . unknown'** Moses Pitt, *Proposals for Printing a New Atlas* (London, 1678), 1.

160 **'starving . . . misfortunes'** Pitt, *Cry*, sig. A2r.

160 **'dangerous fellows'** Fuller, 90.

160 **'of a poor . . . life'** Pitt, *Cry*, sig. A2v.

160 **'han't I often . . . earnest)'** John Dunton, *Mordecai's Dying Groans from the Fleet-Prison* (London, 1717), 10–11.

161 **'into an indigent . . . carry it on'** BL, Add. MS 70023, fol. 79r; cf. NUL, Pw2 Hy 568.

161 **'dare[d] . . . another'** NUL, Pw2 Hy 571.

161 **'swife'** BL, Add. MS 70023, fol. 89r.

161 **'They have . . . powerful'** BL, Add. MS 70023, fol. 207r.

161 **'I am mark'd out'** NUL, Pw2 Hy 571.

161	'you see . . . enough' NUL, Pw2 Hy 571.

161   'you see . . . enough' NUL, Pw2 Hy 571.

161   'I have . . . wine' NUL, Pw2 Hy 568.

161–2 'If I . . . time' NUL, Pw2 Hy 571.

162   'I am perswaded . . . family' BL, Add. MS 70023, fol. 79r.

162   'I beseech . . . addition' BL, Add. MS 70023, fol. 89r.

162   'I hope . . . enemies' NUL, Pw2 Hy 567.

162   'She is . . . can BL, Add. MS 70023, fol. 20r.

163   'like a tyger . . . loose' BL, Add. MS 70023, fol. 20r.

163   'as if . . . tails' BL, Add. MS 70023, fol. 79r.

163   'an old . . . army' *Mercurius Pragmaticus*, 45 (20 February 1649).

163   'a plaguy . . . sides' NUL, Pw2 Hy 568.

163–4 'ready . . . ladies' NUL, Pw2 Hy 566.

164   'a crooked . . . wigg' NUL, Pw2 Hy 566.

164   'suitable . . . consider me' NUL, Pw2 Hy 566.

164   £6 arrived Henry L. Snyder, 'The Reports of a Press Spy for Robert Harley: New Bibliographical Data for the Reign of Queen Anne', *The Library*, 5th ser., 22 (1967), 326–45 at 330.

165   'Rt Honble . . . purpose' NUL, Pw2 Hy 567.

165–6 'I told him . . . direction' The report is in BL, Add. MS 70197, unfoliated.

167   'enemies . . . England' Walter Garrett, *Theorems* (London, [1699]).

169   'a very . . . word' *An Account of the Life and Conversation, Birth, Parentage, and Education of William Greg* (London, [1708]), 6.

169   'customary . . . open' Oldmixon, *History*, 397.

170   'the blackest . . . into' TNA, SP 34/9, fol. 136r.

170   'a true . . . crime' *An Account of the Life*, 8.

170   'whereby . . . crime' *JHL*, XVIII. 516.

170   'no arts . . . treason' Abel Boyer, *The History of the Life and Reign of Queen Anne* (London, 1722), 332.

170   'solace . . . bottle' Oldmixon, *History*, 397.

171   'I am . . . you!' HMC, *Bath*, I. 190.

171   'he could not . . . fellow' *The Correspondence of Jonathan Swift, D.D.*, ed. David Woolley, 5 vols. (Oxford, 1999–2014), I. 175.

13. *The Flourishing Year*

175   'according . . . England' *Post Boy*, 2467 (6 March 1711).

175   'a great . . . church' *Post Boy*, 2467 (6 March 1711).

240 NOTES

176 **'without . . . accent'** [White Kennett,] *A Visit to St. Saviour's Southwark* (London, 1710), 16.

176 **'the most . . . heard'** Beinecke Library, MS Osborn S 13043, fol. 16r.

176 **'to make . . . noise'** BL, Lansdowne MS 1024, fol. 278v.

176 **initially preached at Oxford** Hearne, *Remarks*, I. 138–9.

176 **'professed enemies . . . religion'** Henry Sacheverell, *The Perils of False Brethren, Both in Church and State* (London, 1709), 25.

177 **'will be . . . produc'd'** BL, Add. MS 61364, fol. 88v.

177 **'from the ashes . . . kingdom'** *The Tryal of Henry Sacheverell Before the House of Peers* (London, 1710), 142.

178 **'so large . . . hallooing'** *State Trials*, XV. 561.

178 **5,000 angry hooligans** Geoffrey Holmes, 'The Sacheverell Riots: The Crowd and the Church in Early Eighteenth-Century London', *Past and Present*, 72 (1976), 55–85 at 72.

178 **'headed . . . burnt'** *A Vindication of the Last Parliament* (London, 1711), 298–9.

178–9 **'very unwillingly . . . with him'** TNA, SP 34/12, fol. 59r.

179 **'the like . . . den of devils'** John England, *Pray for the Peace of Jerusalem* (London, 1710), 25–7.

179 **'professed . . . stabbing'** *Commons*, II. 46.

180 **pictures . . . swords** *Commons*, II. 63.

180 **'graft . . . party'** BL, Add. MS 70333, bundle 19.

181 **'They are most . . . old'** *The Wentworth Papers, 1705–1739*, ed. James J. Cartwright (London, 1883), 180.

181 **'give . . . necessary'** Quoted in H. T. Dickinson, 'The October Club', *Huntington Library Quarterly*, 33 (1970), 155–73 at 158.

181–2 **'that scandalous . . . opinions'** *The Character and Declaration of the October Club* ([London], 1711), 5–6.

182 **'growing . . . Whigs do'** Swift, *Correspondence*, I. 335.

182 **'in the hands . . . Tory'** [Daniel Defoe,] *The Secret History of the October Club*, 2 vols. (London, 1711), I. 26.

183 **rumours** Swift, *Correspondence*, I. 347.

183 **'my heart . . . him'** Swift, *Works*, IX. 158–9.

183 **advertised in the newspapers** *Post Boy*, 2478 (31 March 1711).

183 **'As to faction . . . reprinted it'** *Medley*, 28 (9 April 1711).

184 **'was always . . . trade'** BL, Add. MS 70024, fol. 147r.

184 **Ilive . . . apprenticeship** McKenzie, *Stationers' Company Apprentices 1641–1700*, 156.

184   'an expeditious . . . touch' Edward Rowe Mores, *A Dissertation upon Typographical Founders* (London, 1778), 64–5.

185   'The pamphlet . . . escaped' *The Memorial of the Church of England* (London, 1711), i.

185   'insolently reprinted' *Medley*, 29 (16 April 1711).

185–6   'This indefatigable . . . Guiscard' *Memorial* (1711), x–xi.

186   'was of great . . . person' Gilbert Burnet, *Bishop Burnet's History of His Own Time*, 2 vols. (London, 1724–34), II. 567.

187   **Mackworth's mining company** *JHC*, XVI. 391.

187   **Their solution was** Koji Yamamoto, 'Piety, Profit and Public Service in the Financial Revolution', *English Historical Review*, 126 (2011), 806–34.

188   'it may . . . violence' *Examiner*, 32 (15 March 1711).

188   'has wonderfully . . . attempts' *The Congratulatory Speech of William Bromley, Esq* (London, 1711).

188   **observed the dangling plural** See, for instance, BL, Add. MS 61422, fol. 163r.

188   'absolutely refused' *Commons*, III. 354.

188   'unwearied . . . reputation' *The Congratulatory Speech of William Bromley, Esq.*

14. *To This Day Unknown*

191   'As to . . . published' BL, Lansdowne MS 1024, fol. 164v.

191   'where there . . . Drake' BL, Lansdowne MS 1024, fol. 164v.

192   'the *Memorial* . . . Drake's' Oldmixon, *History*, 367; Oldmixon, *The Life and Posthumous Works of Arthur Maynwaring* (London, 1715), 104–5.

192   'By Counsillor . . . Drake' BL, 4107aaa9.

192   'This is . . . England' Beinecke Library, Ik D362 C701 2.

192   'By Dr . . . Whigs' Wren Library, Cambridge, I.2.14. There is another copy in this library (PW.68.2) with the bookplate of Henry Poley's brother, Edmund, dated 1707. Edmund did not note his brother's involvement with the pamphlet.

192   'Doctor . . . with him' *Observator*, 39 (15 August 1705).

192–3   'great . . . writing' *Post Boy*, 1841 (4 March 1707).

193   'declared . . . snare' [James Drake,] *The History of the Last Parliament* (London, 1702), sig. A4r–v.

193   'the treachey . . . negligence' *Memorial*, 4.

193   'The sudden . . . Whiggs' *Mercurius Politicus*, 2 (19 June 1705);
        Memorial, 4.

193   'for the better . . . man' *Mercurius Politicus*, 5 (26 June 1705).

193   'civil . . . another' *Memorial*, 45.

193–4   '*Data* . . . resist' *Memorial*, 45.

194   'That the House . . . burthen' Drake, *History*, 94–5.

195   'principles . . . churchman' *Rehearsal*, 99 (27 April 1706).

195   'plain . . . air' *Rehearsal*, 99 (27 April 1706).

195   'from the Whiggish . . . nation' Hearne, *Remarks*, I. 169–70.

195–6   'it plainly . . . worse' Hearne, *Remarks*, I. 235.

196   'in concert' *Memorial* (1711), v.

197   **commissioned a portrait** The portrait was sold at Bonham's on 21
        May 2014. On its likely provenance, see C. F. Bell and Rachel Poole,
        'English Seventeenth-Century Portrait Drawings in Oxford
        Collections', *Volume of the Walpole Society*, 14 (1926), 43–80 at 76.

197   **error in the indictment** 88 Eng. Rep. 905; 90 Eng. Rep. 1092.

198   'a gentleman . . . in it' *The Roll of the Royal College of Physicians*, 3
        vols. (London, 1861), II. 17.

198   'the severe . . . died' TNA, KB 15/54, 144.

199   'By James . . . Poley' Beinecke Library, Brit Tracts 1705 M519.

199   'vast . . . papers' Swift, *Correspondence*, II. 527.

199   'several . . . publish'd' *The Political State of Great Britain for the
        Month of April 1711* (London, 1711), t.p. Harley's copy is BL, Add. MS
        70274.

201   'if great . . . shrub' NUL, Pw2 Hy 565.

Epilogue: Between the Lines

203   'substantial . . . beer' Bernard Mandeville, *An Enquiry into the Causes
        of the Frequent Executions at Tyburn* (London, 1725), 18–19.

203   **wine in chapel** TNA, SP 35/18, fol. 97r.

204   'a torrent . . . meteors' Mandeville, *Enquiry*, 20–22.

204   'I beheld . . . resignation' Thomas Gent, *The Life of Mr Thomas
        Gent, Printer of York* (London, 1832), 91.

204   'John. . . twain' TNA, SP 35/19, fol. 113r.

205   **words of comfort** TNA, SP 35/19, fol. 108r.

205   **carry his body** *Weekly Journal* (7 November 1719).

205   '**he appear'd . . . undergo**' *Weekly Packet*, 384 (14 November).

205   '**he behaved . . . martyr**' TNA, SP 35/19, fol. 108r.

205   '*Into thy hands . . . soul*' TNA, SP 35/19, fol. 108r.

206   **Robert Girling** TNA, SP 35/7, fol. 147r; SP 35/16, fol. 247r.

206   '**having . . . possession**' *Weekly Packet*, 175 (12 November 1715).

206–7 '**This Harley . . . fail'd**' Bevil Higgons, *A Poem on the Peace* (London, [1713]), 3.

208   '**foolish . . . author**' *State Trials*, xv. 1391.

208   '**in confinement . . . heart**' TNA, SP 35/19, fol. 108r.

Index